Education, Crisis, and the Discipline of the Conjuncture

Education, Crisis, and the Discipline of the Conjuncture

Scholarship and Pedagogy in a Time of Emergent Crisis

Scott Ellison

LEXINGTON BOOKS
Lanham • Boulder • New York • London

Published by Lexington Books
An imprint of The Rowman & Littlefield Publishing Group, Inc.
4501 Forbes Boulevard, Suite 200, Lanham, Maryland 20706
www.rowman.com

6 Tinworth Street, London SE11 5AL, United Kingdom

British Library Cataloguing in Publication Information Available

Library of Congress Cataloging-in-Publication Data

Names: Ellison, Scott, 1971- author.
Title: Education, crisis, and the discipline of the conjuncture : scholarship and pedagogy
    in a time of emergent crisis / Scott Ellison.
Description: Lanham : Lexington Books, 2021. | Includes bibliographical references
    and index.
Identifiers: LCCN 2021026330 (print) | LCCN 2021026331 (ebook) |
    ISBN 9781793645883 (cloth) | ISBN 9781793645890 (epub) |
    ISBN 9781793645906 (pbk)
Subjects: LCSH: Conservatism. | Right-wing extremists. | Populism. | Education—
    Political aspects.
Classification: LCC JC573 .E55 2021 (print) | LCC JC573 (ebook) | DDC 320.5—dc23
LC record available at https://lccn.loc.gov/2021026330
LC ebook record available at https://lccn.loc.gov/2021026331

Thank you to RJ, SJ, and JR for all the help along the way and to Kate for being everything.

Contents

List of Figures

Chapter 1

Introduction

The radical right is having a moment. A wave of right-wing populist movements predicated on nationalism, xenophobia, racism, and the delegitimization of leftist impulses (both actual and perceived) are making political gains across the globe. In the United States, the emergence of the so-called alt-right and the election of Donald Trump as president in 2016 destabilized what was already a polarized and dysfunctional political culture. In Europe, growing nativism and xenophobia have fueled the rise and increasing normalization of radical right parties, such as Alternative for Germany, Fidesz, Law and Justice, Lega, National Rally, and Sweden Democrats, and was the driving force behind the UK's vote to exit the European Union. In Brazil, Jair Bolsonaro won the presidency in 2018 on a nationalist agenda built around nostalgia for the era of military dictatorship. And, in India, the Hindu nationalism of Narendra Modi and the Bharatiya Janata Party is working to rewrite Indian history in pursuit of a new national identity that can solidify its political power.

The rise to prominence and growing normalization of a radical right politics has generated countless headlines and think pieces in popular discourse, but the way in which political actors talk about these movements is all too frequently deeply reductive and simplistic. Popular political media across the global North frequently frame the rise to prominence of the radical right as a populist response to the global financial crisis of 2008 or (relatedly) to economic changes associated with neoliberal globalization. The first frame describes the rise of the radical right as an expression of populist rage against the impunity of economic elites who caused the crash of 2008 (Funke et al., 2018). The second frame describes the radical right as a populist political force inhabiting the space abandoned by the center-left in an era of neoliberal consensus around the inevitability of globalization and financialization

(Mouffe, 2018). This frame asserts that populists have captured the rage of working classes which should gravitate toward left-leaning politics and have channeled this rage into political power.

The problem with these economic frames, however, is that they fail to capture the complexity of the phenomenon they seek to describe. They cannot explain why these political energies are gravitating toward the radical right nor do they offer insight into the societal processes and mechanisms by which this right-wing populism is socially constructed and propagated. How is it that political rage toward economic elites is so easily channeled toward racism, xenophobia, and sexism? Wouldn't leftist impulses toward redistribution and democratization speak to the rage of working- and increasingly precarious middle classes? How is it that the anti-elite rage of right-wing populism has found voice in elite political actors?

It is not that these economic frames are necessarily false. In fact, I would argue that there is a kernel of truth to these perspectives. The problem is that these economic frames convey only a partial or one-sided explanation of what is a complex social phenomenon and are, therefore, a distortion; "[n]ot in the sense that [they are] a lie about the system, but in the sense that a 'half-truth' cannot be the whole truth about anything" (Hall, 1986, p. 37). The problem is that they tell an incomplete and distorted story about this political moment.

This book is an attempt to tell a better story about right-wing populism. I want to analyze right-wing populism as a social phenomenon bound up with the ensemble of social forces and structures that define this historical moment. Put another way, I want to contextualize right-wing populism within the ensemble of forces that constitute and are constituted by it. My hope is to contribute to the development of analytic tools to understand the resurgence of a radical right politics in the global world system and to help find a better path out of this historical moment than the one we are currently traveling, a task that I want to argue is especially important for education scholars.

Right-wing populism did not emerge overnight as a global political movement, and the challenges it poses will not be easily or quickly resolved. It has a history, and its resolution will be achieved through political struggle. What is clear is that right-wing populism is an emergent political force in the early twenty-first century that should make students of twentieth-century history wary. I will spare the reader trite statements about history repeating or rhyming. What I will say is that the emergence and increasing normalization of a radical right politics reflect dangerous trends in the global world system, and how left-leaning (or even liberal) political actors come to both understand and challenge these trends will ultimately be what defines this historical moment.

In other words, the stories that political actors tell about the emergence of right-wing populism matter. How political actors conceptualize the rise to prominence of right-wing populism will inform the political strategies they employ. This is to say that the making of contemporary history will be defined by both intellectual and political work.

As an education scholar, I also want to tell a better story about right-wing populism that can conceptualize this radical right politics as a pedagogical problem. What educational questions are posed by right-wing populism? How can educational research and pedagogy respond to the questions it poses? Or, more fundamentally, what does it mean to do educational work in this historical moment? The field of education is, by definition, oriented toward both the present concerns facing society and the undiscovered country of an imagined future. This book is my attempt to answer these questions through an analysis of right-wing populism and to think through the implications of this analysis for pedagogical practice and educational inquiry oriented toward a more just and democratic future.

I want to think about this historical moment as being a period of crisis, but I do so with no small amount of trepidation. Crisis discourse is a peculiarly modern phenomenon that has given rise to a crisis industry of journalistic and academic texts seeking to diagnose the various pathologies afflicting human societies (Roitman, 2014; Walby, 2015; Gilbert, 2019). An internet search of popular and scholarly texts will quickly reveal that the United States, for example, faces an ever-expanding array of crises ranging from the timely, such as the economic crisis brought on by the COVID-19 pandemic, to the absurd, such as a crisis of masculinity.

The problem is that the concept of crisis employed in these texts is not so much defined as diagnosed. Crisis is often conceptualized as a singular event of short duration. "The" crisis is a failure or breakdown of a system, an immediate shock in which heretofore unforeseen forces congeal into a sudden break in which the past offers no guide for the future. It is societal pathology in need of a technical fix. This is not how I want to think about crisis.

Crisis is defined here as a *rupture* or *historical break in which the viability of a social formation is brought into question*, thereby opening up new potentialities for societal transformation with no guarantee as to the nature of the settlement that follows (Ellison, 2019). A crisis is a historical moment of varying duration in which the relations of force stabilizing a social formation are threatened by the *various antagonisms and contradictions they both produce and work to contain*. I will, therefore, think about crisis at two levels of analysis. First, I will attempt to map the movement of forces and relations of force at work in specific domains constituting the contemporary social formation, that is, economic, political, and cultural domains. I will attempt to demonstrate that the dominant forces within these individual social fields have set loose forces that now threaten the hegemonic order structuring each domain. That is, I will attempt to marshal evidence that there are emerging economic, political, and cultural crises. Second, I will map the relations of force working across these various domains to demonstrate that these crises are conjoining in this historical moment as a period of emergent crisis. Crisis, then, will be conceptualized as a period of time often lasting years or even decades in duration in which various crises in a social formation conjoin into a period of potential rupture.

I speak here of a crisis of hegemony in which the dominant ideologies of a historical bloc structuring a social formation begin to fracture and fragment across multiple social domains. A crisis of hegemony is, therefore, conjunctural. It marks the conjoining of crises across multiple social fields into a period of crisis. Importantly, while a crisis of hegemony is a period of potentiality that might be welcomed by progressive political actors, it is also, as Gramsci (2000) correctly notes, a period of great danger in which "charismatic men of destiny" can rise to power with catastrophic results (pp. 217–221).

Thus, in contrast to the way crisis is frequently employed in journalistic and academic texts, I am interested in crises in the plural, and I seek to extend the time horizon of analysis beyond the immediate to think about a period of crisis. What follows is a structural analysis that traces the historical development of the contemporary conjuncture. I do not conceptualize crisis as being the product of failure as much as success. I will seek to demonstrate that the means by which the dominant forces within each domain achieved hegemonic dominance constructed the conditions of possibility for the emergent crises threatening both the hegemonic order structuring each domain and, ultimately, the larger social formation in which they are embedded. Further, while I will end the analysis that follows with a discussion on how educators, scholars, and activists can contribute to a liberatory path out of this period of emergent crisis, I do not presume to offer a precise road map to travel nor do I prescribe a treatment for what ails society.

I will argue in this book that right-wing populism is bound up with a series of crises at work in the contemporary social formation that are converging in this historical moment as a potential rupture, a moment of conjunctural crisis. Right-wing populism is, therefore, not a unitary object of analysis to be taken at face value but must be understood as the confluence of an array of social forces at work across the contemporary formation. It must be understood as a social phenomenon. I will argue that a radical, re-contextualizing analysis of this historical moment is one way to answer the questions posed by the emergence of right-wing populism.

In this introductory chapter, I will work to outline a method of inquiry for analyzing the emergence and increasing normalization of right-wing populism as a social phenomenon. I will begin with a discussion on the role of crises in understanding societal change. I will then draw upon the cultural studies tradition to develop a method of inquiry that will be used to rigorously contextualize right-wing populism. I will then work to connect the practice of cultural studies to educational work. And, I will conclude by briefly outlining the inquiry that will unfold in subsequent chapters.

CRISES AND CONJUNCTURES

The role of crises as the engine of historical change has long been central to the critical tradition in social theory. Karl Marx understood crisis as a progressive and ultimately destructive force within modern capitalist society. For Marx, the capitalist mode of production goes through predictable cycles of competition, innovation, overproduction, and crisis that drive societal progress (Marx, 1973, pp. 745–758).

During periods of economic growth, producers seek out ways to increase productivity and lower the cost of labor which is in high demand. The producers who most effectively introduce new technologies into the production process can lower production costs, under-cut competitors, and drive them from the market, but this movement of innovation and consolidation also puts downward pressure on the cost of labor and fuels growing precarity among the working classes. The continual growth in productive capacity and efficiency coupled with a reduction in the cost of labor inevitably produces an economy in which productive capacity outstrips consumer demand, what Marx called a crisis of overproduction and has since been re-framed in modern economics as a problem of under-consumption.

This contradictory cycle of growth and crisis leads to contradictory outcomes. Each crisis creates an opening for new producers to take up previous technologies or introduce new innovations and, thus, establish the conditions for a new period of economic growth. However, at the same time, the continuous push to increase productivity and lower the cost of labor not only ensures the recurrence of new crises but also fuels growing political antagonisms between the capitalist class and the working classes. These antagonisms become manifest in periods of crisis as political demands for societal transformation.

Therefore, in Marx's model, crises are paradoxically the realization of the inherent contradictions between the forces of production and the social relations of production, the well-spring of capitalist expansion, and ultimately the force driving modern capitalist society toward collapse and socialist transformation. Modern capitalist society advances by lurching from one crisis to the next toward its historical mission of self-transformation, a process that Joseph Schumpeter (1976) would later term creative destruction (Elliott, 1980). Like Schumpeter and the world-system analysts that would follow, Marx argued that it was this propensity to crisis that would ultimately be the undoing of

capitalist relations. The continual advancement of technological and productive forces and the recurrent crises this advancement produces will establish
the necessary preconditions for epochal historical crisis and the socialist
transformation of capitalist societies, a process that Marx envisioned taking
place first in the most economically advanced nations of Western Europe and
North America.

Antonio Gramsci came of age in an era in which the epochal crisis of
capitalism seemed at hand only to witness the reversal of the revolutionary
project into fascism (Hall, 1988c). The eclipse of this "proletarian moment"
led Gramsci to ask important questions about crisis, political struggle, and the
politics of intellectual work. For Gramsci, crises are moments of potentiality, but the settlements that follow are a product of political strategies and
the critical analyses that inform them. Gramsci's project shifted the focus of
critical work away from mechanistic analyses of the iron laws of economics
that characterized the classical Marxism of his era toward analyses of the
relations of force at work in specific moments of crisis as a means of informing political strategy.

According to Gramsci, the eclipse of the proletarian moment in the economically advanced nations of Western Europe and North America could be
explained by the resiliency of the "complex, contradictory and discordant
ensemble of the superstructures" to structural (economic) crises (Gramsci,
2000, p. 192), or (put another way) that the highly developed "civil societies"
of "advanced nations . . . [were] resistant to the catastrophic 'incursions' of
the immediate economic element (crises, depressions, etc.)" (Gramsci, 2000,
p. 227). Gramsci argued that dominant classes in advanced nations were
able to eclipse the proletarian moment by mobilizing political, cultural, and
ideological forces during periods of economic crisis to (re)construct a new
synthesis, that is, a new social formation. The liberal democratic societies
that Gramsci classified as the "West" were, therefore, not simple constructs
defined by an economic structure (base) mechanically determining an epiphe-
nomenal superstructure, the vulgar Marxist model, but dynamic systems in
which the political, cultural, and ideological possess the "energy" of a "material force" (Gramsci, 2000, p. 200).

Gramsci's response to the eclipse of the proletarian moment was to
develop a dynamic political theory grounded in a Marxian critique of political
science (Coutinho, 2012). What Gramsci contributed to Marxian analysis is
a robust political theory grounded in the concept of "historical bloc," conceptualized as the articulation of structure and superstructure, in dialectical
relation to the concept of "social bloc," understood as an alliance of social
classes organized around the dominant ideologies, or hegemony, of a leading
class. For Gramsci, it was on the ideological, cultural, and political fields that
various social classes confront one another over the preservation or potential

transformation of a social formation, and it was on these fields that power relations are actively produced, reproduced, and challenged.

Gramsci went to great lengths to make clear that there is a dialectical relationship between structure and superstructure. His goal was to demonstrate the importance of the cultural, ideological, and political fields; not to stand Marx on his head, so to speak, but to identify the political terrain upon which the ongoing processes of constructing and re-constructing a social formation play out. This insight was not a purely academic exercise for Gramsci but had political implications. The realization of capitalism's "historical mission" would not emerge from the mechanical laws of economics but from political work on the ideological and cultural fields. The thrust of Gramsci's intervention in Marxian theory is that political actors must attend to the dynamic forces, the relations of force, at work on these fields to inform political strategies oriented toward liberatory goals.

Gramsci argued that an analysis of the relations of force at work in a moment of crisis must make a distinction between what is organic, the "relatively permanent" economic structure, and what is conjunctural, the "immediate" political and ideological concerns of a specific historical moment.

> When a historical period comes to be studied, the great importance of this distinction becomes clear. A crisis occurs, sometimes lasting for decades. This exceptional duration means that incurable structural contradictions have revealed themselves (reached maturity), and that, despite this, the political forces which are struggling to conserve and defend the existing structure itself are making every effort to cure them, within certain limits, and to overcome them. These incessant and persistent efforts (since no social formation will ever admit that it has been superseded) form the terrain of the "conjunctural," and it is upon this terrain that the forces of opposition organize. These forces seek to demonstrate that the necessary and sufficient conditions already exist to make possible, and hence imperative, the accomplishment of certain historical tasks (imperative, because any falling short before a historical duty increases the necessary disorder, and prepares more serious catastrophes). (Gramsci, 2000, p. 201)

Gramsci argued that critical scholars and political actors must attend to the conjunctural as a site of political struggle over the preservation or transformation of a social formation that has entered a period of crisis. In Gramsci's model, an "organic crisis" is a crisis of a social formation in which an economic crisis has repercussions across the ensemble of superstructures, and the conjunctural forms the political, cultural, and ideological terrain upon which hegemonic struggle over an organic crisis will be resolved in a new historical settlement. Social formations do not emerge from the aether but are constructed. "Political and ideological work is required to disarticulate formations, and to rework their elements into a new configuration" (Hall, 2017a, p. 175).

Gramsci's intervention in Marxian theory shifted analytic focus toward the political, ideological, and cultural domains. Gramsci developed a conjunctural mode of analysis that would have a significant impact on critical intellectual projects in the second half of the twentieth century, none more so than the cultural studies project that would emerge from the Centre for Contemporary Cultural Studies at the University of Birmingham in the UK. Early cultural studies scholars, such as Stuart Hall, Raymond Williams, and Richard Hoggart, took up Gramsci's conjunctural perspective as the condensation of crises at work across multiple social domains, and it is this perspective that will inform my analysis of right-wing populism.

A conjunctural crisis forms the terrain upon which structural and superstructural contradictions condense into a moment of crisis and upon which a hegemonic social bloc and oppositional forces struggle over the historic settlement that will emerge from the crisis. Specifically, a conjunctural crisis is a historical moment in which multiple crises produced by the internal contradictions and accumulated antagonisms at work in a social formation manifest themselves as a site of political struggle. A conjunctural crisis is never simply economic. It is a moment in which crises at work across multiple domains of a social formation (cultural, political, ideological, etc.) conjoin in a moment of crisis and political struggle. Stuart Hall notes:

> Gramsci, who struggled all his life against "economism," was very clear about this. What he says is that no crisis is only economic. It is always "over-determined" from different directions. . . . Different levels of society, the economy, politics, ideology, common sense, etc, come together or "fuse." Otherwise, you could get an unresolved ideological crisis which doesn't have immediate political connotations, or which you can't see as being directly related to a change in the economy. The definition of a conjunctural crisis is when these "relatively autonomous" sites—which have different origins, are driven by different contradictions, and develop according to their own temporalities—are nevertheless "convened" or condensed in the same moment. Then there is crisis, a break, a "ruptural fusion." (Hall & Massey, 2010, pp. 59–60)

A conjunctural crisis is, therefore, both over-determined and under-determined. It is over-determined in that it is a product of multiple crises condensing in one historical moment. It is under-determined in that it is a historical moment of political potentiality in which political actors struggle over the preservation or transformation of a social formation.

A conjunctural perspective rejects the reductive search for singularity and instead seeks out the multiplicity of social forces, contradictions, and crises converging in one historical moment in a potential break or rupture. Analyses of conjunctural crises seek out antagonisms and contradictions at work in the relatively autonomous economic, political, and cultural domains that "conjoin" in the production of a crisis. "[I]t enables us to ask: how many crises are there? how are they connected/articulated?" (Clarke, 2010, p. 343).

Gramsci reworked the classical Marxist model of societal change and development as a movement from economic crisis to economic crisis, itself a reductive simplification of Marx's thought, to a movement from conjunctural crisis to conjunctural crisis. Conjunctural analysis speaks to an ontological perspective on the fundamental fragility of a social formation as a "complex, contradictory, and over-determined unity" (Grossberg, 2010a, p. 21). It seeks to understand how social forces congeal into a relatively stable social order of power relations and how the structures that constitute a formation actively produce/contain underlying antagonisms that threaten its stability.

A social formation is neither fixed nor static. It is characterized by the dynamic movement of social forces that can temporarily congeal into a period of relative stability but is always already contested and subject to centrifugal forces that work to destabilize it. "[Conjunctural] analysis . . . focuses on crises and breaks, and the distinctive character of the 'historic settlements' that follow" (Hall, 2011, p. 9). The concept of conjuncture is therefore "not a Theory, but an orientation—a way of focusing analytic attention on the multiplicity of forces, accumulated antagonisms, and possible lines of emergence from the conjuncture (rather than assuming a singular crisis and one line of development)" (Clarke, 2014, p. 115).

CONJUNCTURAL ANALYSIS: TELLING BETTER STORIES

It was Gramsci who first articulated a sophisticated program for critical analyses of the relations of force at work in specific conjunctural crises, but it was Stuart Hall and the collective work of the University of Birmingham's Centre for Contemporary Cultural Studies that most creatively employed this method of analysis (Clarke, 2010, 2014; Grossberg, 1986a). For example, in the now-canonical text *Policing the Crisis*, Hall and coauthors sought to understand the moral panic around "mugging" and street violence in 1970s Great Britain as a social phenomenon (Hall et al., 1978). The focus of their analysis was not specifically the moral panic but its context. *Policing the Crisis* traced the racial, economic, ideological, and political configurations surrounding this phenomenon to demonstrate that it was symptomatic of conjunctural crisis and political struggles with both immediate and structural implications. The immediate concern in *Policing the Crisis* was the permanent criminalization of black youth in the UK, a prescient warning of an emerging carceral state that would reach its apotheosis in the United States, but the analysis also sought to contextualize this immediate political struggle within larger systemic struggles, such as the erosion of social welfare systems and the emergence of Thatcherism. The focus of *Policing the Crisis* was not the racist "law and order" policing in 1970s Great Britain but the racialized structures in which this phenomenon was embedded; the focus was the context that constituted and was constituted by the moral panic.

Lawrence Grossberg argues that context defines both the object and practice of cultural studies. The object of analysis in cultural studies is not specific phenomena but the context that shape and is shaped by them.

> [T]he identity, significance, and effects of any practice or event are defined only by the complex set of relations that surround, interpenetrate, and shape it, and make it what it is. No element can be isolated from its relations, although those relationships can be changed, and are constantly changing. Any event can only be understood relationally, as a condensation of multiple determinations and effects. Cultural studies thus embodies the commitment to the openness and contingency of social reality, where change is the given or norm. This radical contextualism is the heart of cultural studies. (Grossberg, 2010a, p. 20)

Cultural studies is defined by its concern with the contexts and power relations, "multiple determinations and effects," that constitute and are constituted by an object of analysis. The analytic focus of cultural studies is the power relations, or in Gramscian terms the relations of force, surrounding a specific phenomenon, and it is this analytic focus that defines the intellectual practice of cultural studies. It is an intellectual practice that seeks to understand specific articulations of contexts and power relations as a mode of politically engaged scholarship.

The projects that cultural studies scholars take up are defined by the "intellectual and political concerns of the present" (Wood, 2019, p. 23); they are defined by the "discipline of the conjuncture" (Hall, 1988c, p. 162). Following Gramsci, cultural studies inquiry is never a purely intellectual exercise but "acquire[s] significance only if [it] serve[s] to justify a particularly practical activity, an initiative of will" (Gramsci, 2000, p. 209). Grossberg observes:

> [T]he project of cultural studies is to tell better stories about what's going on, and to begin to enable imagining new possibilities for a future that can be reached from the present—one more humane and just than that promised by the trajectories we find ourselves on. Cultural studies then is a form of conjunctural analysis, which re-describes a context, often viewed with some sense of pessimism and even despair, into one of possibilities, by rejecting all forms of

simplification and reduction, and embracing the complexity, contradiction and contingency of the world. (Grossberg, 2010b, p. 241)

Cultural studies inquiry is defined by a commitment to radical contextualism via conjunctural analysis. Put simply, it is defined by a commitment to telling "better stories" about the contemporary social formation as an intellectual practice oriented toward the imaginative opening of possibilities and political strategies. "Telling better stories is an intention (and not an end) that wholly affects one's practice. (. . .) Politically speaking then, 'better' is a measure of the *means by which* the intellectual work of storytelling opens up possibilities, real or imagined, for changing the present" (Wood, 2019, p. 23).

Cultural studies inquiry may begin with an immediate political concern (such as right-wing populism), but it is defined by its commitment to the radical contextualization of immediate political concerns into problem spaces or problematics constructed through conjunctural analysis. Social formations and conjunctural crises pose their own questions and political demands. A problem space can be conceptualized as the questions and political demands surrounding an immediate political concern that establish the boundaries around as well as the various forces, elements, and contexts relevant to conjunctural analysis. Cultural studies inquiry does not begin with a ready-made, predefined object of analysis assumed by one's political and theoretical commitments. It is a mode of inquiry that seeks to construct a problem space through conjunctural, re-contextualizing analysis.

Grossberg argues that analysts tell bad stories when their own political assumptions displace empirical and theoretical work or when they substitute "theory for social analysis" (Grossberg, 2010a, p. 54). The imposition of an analyst's political assumptions or theoretical commitments onto an object of analysis is, in Marxian terms, a form of mystification that blinds the analyst to the specificity of the conjuncture. Put simply, bad stories make for bad politics. This is not to say that there is any guarantee that telling better stories will inform better politics. "There is no necessary relations between knowledge and politics, only the possibilities of their articulation" (Grossberg, 2010a, p. 55). The goal of cultural studies inquiry is to construct new knowledge through rigorous analysis informed by a political commitment to creating a more just world but always with a healthy dose of intellectual humility.

Telling better stories is, therefore, an intellectual commitment to radical contextualism via conjunctural analysis. It defines an intellectual practice that seeks to contextualize immediate concerns within problem spaces that pose their own questions and political demands. The questions that cultural studies asks, its problematics, are defined in the work of analysis. Cultural studies inquiry seeks to construct problem spaces through sustained conjunctural analysis of a social formation or crisis to open up the future to new possibilities, new political strategies, and new lines of inquiry.

My goal here is to expand the horizon of political analysis in this historical moment beyond election cycles or the electoral fortunes of specific actors, such as Donald Trump or Jair Bolsonaro. I want to argue that the right-wing populism rising to power in this historical moment is symptomatic of an emergent conjunctural crisis that will play out in the coming years. Right-wing populism is bound up with a series of crises in the economic, political, and cultural domains operating according to their own logics and time lines that are converging in this historical moment of potential rupture. I speak here of a crisis of hegemony not in the sense of a singular, unifying ideology and structural crisis but of ideologies and hegemonies articulated into a hegemonic order or social formation that has entered into a period of emergent crisis.

Telling a better story about this period of emergent crisis will require a conjunctural perspective that traces the movement of forces and ideological discourses at work in the various domains of an articulated social formation, that teases out the contradictions and antagonisms threatening the stability of this hegemonic order, and that maps the terrain of struggle upon which hegemonic and counter-hegemonic forces will organize and confront one another in ideological struggle. This is the task for the project presented in these pages. I want to tell a better story about this moment of conjunctural crisis that can contribute to collective political struggle and that can contribute to the construction of a more democratic and just social formation. What I offer here is not solutions or easy answers but a mapping of the terrain that must be traversed to make progressive societal change possible.

CONJUNCTURALISM AND EDUCATION

I come to this project as a scholar and educator in the field of social and cultural foundations of education with a background in cultural studies. The social and cultural foundations of education, or simply educational foundations, emerged from the Progressive Era and is closely associated with historical figures such as John Dewey and William James. Educational foundations are grounded in the interdisciplinary study of education and schooling that draws upon theories and tools from anthropology, history, philosophy, political economy, and sociology. The goal of educational foundations is to move beyond the instrumental study of education focused on curriculum development, instructional techniques, and assessment strategies to the study of education as a social institution that is foundational to the possibility of democracy and the realization of a socially just society. Over its history, the fortunes of this academic discipline rose with Progressive era reforms in the early- to mid-twentieth century and has waned over the past forty years as educational policies associated with human capital development, standardized assessment, school accountability, and "school choice" have risen to prominence.

One disciplinary field that is missing from the list offered above is cultural studies. Cultural studies developed as a scholarly practice at the Centre for Contemporary Cultural Studies at the University of Birmingham in the 1960s, although its roots as a political practice are more diverse and global (Wright, 1998). Early scholars, such as Richard Hoggart, Paul Willis and Stuart Hall, sought to develop an interdisciplinary, even anti-disciplinary, approach to the serious study of mass media and popular culture. Early work at the Centre sought to break out of the conventions of traditional, elitist practices in literary analysis and sociology in British universities and quickly developed into a scholarly and political project drawing upon the fields of anthropology, communication and media studies, history, linguistics, philosophy, and sociology. Cultural studies developed at the Centre into an intellectual intervention into the humanities and social sciences with an explicit left-liberatory politics drawing upon Marxian critiques of capitalist relations; the interrogation of racial, ethnic, gender, and sexual inequalities; and the postcolonial challenge to systems of domination constructed by the nations of the global North.

Cultural studies gained a foothold in American universities and expanded rapidly in the 1990s, and it quickly found a home in colleges of education within educational foundations programs. The connection between the two scholarly practices is obvious. Both cultural studies and educational foundations are interdisciplinary scholarly practices and both have an explicit political orientation, although it must be said that the politics of cultural studies is, with a few exceptions, more radical than the more progressive-liberal politics traditionally associated with educational foundations. The 1990s and early 2000s were a time in which cultural studies became an integral part of educational foundations, and it looked as though it would continue to flourish within colleges of education. However, that potential remains unfulfilled. Today, cultural studies of education is even more marginalized in colleges of education than is educational foundations, and its influence within the field of educational foundations is similarly waning, as its disappearance from educational foundations conference programs testifies.

One of my goals for the present project is to contribute to the reinvigoration of cultural studies of education, but I must acknowledge that the challenges this project entails are formidable and extend well beyond the marginalized status of educational foundations programs. Kathy Hytten (2011, p. 217) notes that despite the obvious connections between cultural studies and "critical race and identity-based theories and critiques of neoliberal globalization . . .

the marginalized scholars who are offering much of the compelling, radical, identity-based social justice scholarship in education today are not locating it within the tradition of cultural studies." She correctly notes that the cultural studies project has been most frequently taken up in educational foundations by white (mostly male) critical pedagogues, an observation that hits close to home. I am a white male foundations scholar whose work is informed by Marxian and critical theory, although I would not classify it as critical pedagogy. Hytten's concern that cultural studies is (or at least perceived as being) a "particularly white, or at least dominant way of cultural thinking, theorizing and writing" gives me pause and forces me to consider my own work through that lens.

I also share, however, Hytten's qualified optimism that the conjuncturalism of cultural studies can open up new spaces for Marxian and critical race and identity-based scholarship to enter into productive dialogue and collaboration to reimagine schooling and education in this time of emergent crisis. I believe that such spaces of intellectual exchange and political activism can contribute to the reinvigoration of both cultural studies of education and educational foundations as a scholarly practice. More importantly, I argue that such a reinvigorated educational practice can contribute to the necessary political work that will be required to chart a transformative path out of the contemporary conjuncture.

I take my inspiration for this project from Stuart Hall's foundational work interrogating the social construction of a radical right social formation in the UK, the United States, and the global North from the 1970s forward, what I term here the post-1970s social formation. Hall drew upon and applied Marxian, postcolonial, and post-structuralist theories to the study of political struggle in the conjunctural crisis of the 1970s and the articulation of a new social formation from 1980 forward. Hall developed a robust set of analytic tools to understand the crisis of the 1970s as a condensation of multiple crises into a moment of conjunctural rupture and to understand how a new hegemonic bloc was constructed around a set of ideological discourses that offered a compelling explanation for the crisis, one that spoke to the commonsense beliefs of strategic groups and that informed a relatively stable political program for societal change.

I want to take up the tools that Hall developed to study this historical moment of emergent conjunctural crisis. Specifically, I want to trace how the post–World War II formation in the United States entered into a period of crisis in the 1970s, how a new social formation was constructed from the wreckage of the 1970s through ideological and political struggle, and how the contradictions and antagonisms at work in this formation are pushing it into a period of emergent conjunctural crisis. Right-wing populism is the immediate political concern informing this analysis. However, following

Hall, I want to argue that the rise to prominence of this radical right politics is bound up with larger political struggles and the relations of force structuring the contemporary formation. I want to think about right-wing populism not as a point of departure for analysis but a point of arrival (Hall, 1973). I will attempt to contextualize this immediate political concern within the ensemble of forces that constitute and are constituted by it through a materialist analysis of the agents, political movements, and ideological discourses at work in the post-1970s formation.

This project is, at its most basic level, methodological. I will attempt to construct an approach to doing conjunctural analysis informed by Marxian theory that seeks to map the terrain of political struggle in the contemporary conjuncture. The translation of the cultural studies project into the American academy largely erased the complicated and contentious engagement between British cultural studies and Marxian theory (Nelson, 1991). I will draw upon Hall's life-long engagement with the Marxian problematic to develop a methodology for politically engaged inquiry that can, in turn, inform scholarly and pedagogical practice. To be clear, I am not trying to equate cultural studies and Marxian theory nor am I attempting to lay claim to *the* way to do cultural studies inquiry. One of the defining characteristics of cultural studies research is its methodological openness (Saukko, 2003). My goal is to build on a mode of societal inquiry developed at Birmingham that begins with a simple problem or phenomenon and seeks to construct a context of dynamic relations and social forces that surround it (Frow & Morris, 2000). I want to think about critical inquiry as a form of storytelling that situates the everyday and taken-for-granted into the dynamic relations of force at work in a social formation.

The primary goal for this project is to map the terrain of political struggle in this historical moment. I will attempt to construct a context around right-wing populism to understand the movement of forces surrounding and being influenced by this immediate problem. Meeting the political challenges posed by right-wing populism requires that scholars, educators, activists, and cultural workers tell better stories about the post-1970s social formation and the period of emergent conjunctural crisis into which it is entering.

I also want to explore the implications of this conjunctural analysis for scholars in educational foundations, specifically, and education, more generally. I want to think about what it means to do educational inquiry at this moment of potential rupture. What does it mean to do politically engaged educational research? How can educational inquiry contribute to the telling of better stories about the contemporary conjuncture? And, how does this approach to educational inquiry position the researcher? I hope to demonstrate that the conjunctural analysis I develop in this project can be applied to educational problems and to demonstrate how the issues, problems, and topics of debate in the field are bound up with the movement of forces and ideological discourses at work in the contemporary conjuncture.

And, I want to think about the implications of this conjunctural analysis for pedagogical practice. I will explore what a pedagogical response to the problem space I construct around right-wing populism might look like. What does a pedagogy of telling better stories entail? How can the method of inquiry I develop in this project inform a classroom practice that can contribute to the necessary political work of this historical moment?

My task here is to construct a pedagogical problem space around right-wing populism and to think through its implications for educational inquiry and pedagogical practice. Or, more simply, the goal is to think through the emergent crisis of this historical moment as an educational problem. My hope is that this project will reintroduce cultural studies to researchers, practitioners, and activists in educational foundations and education and that it can open up a space for intersectional dialogue and collaboration. What I offer is not the final word on the topic; it is an invitation to dialogue, collaboration, and imaginative practices working toward a progressive, democratic, and just future.

THIS BOOK

There is a standard format to academic writing. In a typical academic book, the first chapter defines its object of analysis and outlines the argument to be made in broad strokes. Subsequent chapters provide the reader with the granular detail and analysis behind the central argument being made, and the conclusion reiterates the broad outline of the argument and its implications. This is not that kind of book.

My goal for this project is to conduct a conjunctural analysis of this historical moment as a mode of radical contextualization and politically engaged scholarship. The analytic focus of the inquiry will be the movement of forces and ideological discourses at work within the economic, political, and cultural domains of the United States; however, I believe that the problem space developed from this conjunctural analysis will hold relevance for scholars, practitioners, activists, and cultural workers beyond the United States. The immediate political concern for this inquiry is the rise to prominence and increasing normalization of right-wing populism in the United States, but this immediate political concern is not in itself a ready-made or self-evident object of analysis. The conjunctural analysis that I take up in this project will seek to construct the problem space of right-wing populism via sustained inquiry into the relations of force, structures, and ideological discourses that constitute the post-1970s American social formation. The basic thesis that will be argued in this book is that right-wing populism is bound up with an emergent conjunctural crisis, what I will term the *emergent crisis of the present*.

I also intend to think through the implications of this conjunctural analysis for educational foundations and education studies, my areas of study. My goal for this project is to construct a pedagogical problem space around right-wing populism via conjunctural analysis of the contemporary social formation. I ask: What are the educational questions and demands posed by the contemporary conjuncture? What does it mean to do politically engaged educational scholarship in this time and this place? To be clear, this is not yet another liberal call for technocratic educational fixes to some perceived social ill. The goal is to conduct a conjunctural analysis of this historical moment that acknowledges the constitutive role of education in the continuous renewal and potential transformation of human societies, a task that is very much in line with the future orientation of cultural studies as an intellectual practice.

I will begin the analysis in the next chapter by exploring economic trends in the United States. Taking a historical long-wave perspective, this analysis will explore how the post–World War II economic boom entered into a period of crisis in the 1970s, how a new synthesis emerged from the crisis, how that new synthesis has fundamentally restructured the American economy, and how this synthesis produced a set of economic antagonisms that are working to destabilize the post-1970s formation. In chapter 3, I will conduct a political analysis of the modern conservative movement in the United States. This analysis will explore the ideological discourses, institutional infrastructure, political strategies, and propaganda apparatuses constructed by the conservative movement to achieve political dominance and will explore the forces it has unleashed into the political culture. In chapter 4, I will explore the technological transformation of popular political culture. This analysis will examine the ways in which technological changes associated with social media, user-interface design, and machine learning are fragmenting shared reality and how these changes have impacted the political culture.

Chapter 5 will begin to synthesize the preceding analyses through a recovery of the neoliberal political project. This analysis will trace the development of a political project at work within and across the economic, political, and cultural domains, and it will synthesize the economic, political, and cultural contradictions and antagonisms conjoining in this historical moment. Chapter 6 will take a necessary detour through theory to continue this movement toward synthesis. It is at this point in the conjunctural analysis that I will construct the problem space of right-wing populism and begin to think through what it means to do critical scholarship in this problem space. In chapters 7 and 8, I will tease out the educational questions and demands of this historical moment and then think through what it means to do critical educational work in this problem space. And, I will conclude with a reflection on how this project might contribute to the field of educational foundations and the reinvigoration of cultural studies of education.

The overall structure of the book involves three analytic moves. Chapters 2 through 5 are relatively self-contained analyses informed by different theoretical frameworks that trace and retrace the movement of political forces within and across the economic, political, and cultural domains. Chapter 6 will synthesize the movement of forces identified in the preceding four chapters and will construct a problem space around the simple problem of right-wing populism. Chapters 7 and 8 will build upon that synthesis to think about the problem space surrounding right-wing populism as a pedagogical problem space and to think through its implications for doing scholarly and pedagogical work in the field of education. Accordingly, these analytic moves will involve shifts in writing style and authorial voice.

In broad strokes, the conjunctural analysis that follows takes up two problematics from the cultural studies tradition, hegemonic state politics and historical periodization (Grossberg, 2010a, p. 51), and works across four social domains: economic, political, cultural, and ideological. It is, of course, impossible to tell a total and complete story of this historical moment. But, it is possible to tell a better story about this time and this place that can open up new possibilities and opportunities for societal change. I hope to tell a better story about this historical moment to think through what it means to be an educator and education scholar in this time and place, in this problem space.

The audience for this project is primarily scholars and students in educational foundations, education studies, and cultural studies. However, I believe that this project can contribute to the work of scholars in teacher education and education policy studies with an interest in politically engaged scholarship and pedagogical practice. Students and scholars in social scientific fields, such as cultural anthropology, media studies, sociology, and so on, may also find the conjunctural analysis developed here to be relevant to their disciplinary fields.

That said, scholars with strong disciplinary or theoretical commitments may bristle at the conjunctural analysis employed in this project. One of the defining characteristics of cultural studies is its commitment to interdisciplinary or transdisciplinary inquiry. The conjunctural analysis in the following chapters will draw upon a wide array of resources from different disciplinary fields, discipline-specific theories, and social theories to construct a problem space around an immediate political concern, but the scope of the inquiry requires that the analysis not get bogged down in ongoing debates within those disciplinary and theoretical traditions.

Scholars committed to a positivist, "value-free" view of social scientific inquiry will also likely take issue with the analysis that follows. This project is informed by a Left politics, and I will at times direct my focus to scholars, practitioners, activists, and cultural workers doing politically engaged, left-liberatory work. One of my goals for this project is to contribute to political projects that can chart a transformative path out of the emergent crisis. If the reader expects a dispassionate analysis in pursuit of objective truth then s/he will surely be disappointed.

Likewise, the unorthodox presentation of the conjunctural analysis I have chosen may give pause to readers accustomed to traditional academic approaches to writing. I would think that, by this point, it is clear to the reader that I have carried out the conjunctural analysis, constructed the problem space around right-wing populism, and thought through to some extent the implications of this inquiry prior to sitting down to write this book. Yet, I have intentionally used this introductory chapter only to set up an immediate political concern, develop a method inquiry from cultural studies, and offer a basic map of the chapters that follow. I have done so because it follows the method of analysis employed in this project. My intention is to not only "tell a better story" about this historical moment but to also demonstrate "how to tell a better story."

THINGS TO CONSIDER

I would ask the reader to consider the enormity of the task I have set for this project. One of the challenges involved in a project such as this involves delineating the time horizon of inquiry and establishing what phenomena, social forces, ideological discourses, structures, and so on that are relevant to the analysis. Some readers will undoubtedly expect that an analysis of the contemporary social formation will include a discussion on specific political actors and political parties, or perhaps they may well expect an exploration of the ecological and climate crisis looming just over the horizon. I have chosen to use a conjunctural perspective to establish the time horizon for this project so as to extend analysis beyond the day-to-day, in the case of electoral politics, while excluding the epochal, in the case of ecological crisis and global climate change. This framing does not mean that these topics are unimportant or that they are not relevant to the overall goals for this project. In fact, one of my goals here is to situate the day-to-day political concerns of public debate in the United States within a longer time horizon of analysis to enrich collective political struggle. Likewise, while the crisis of global climate change looms just beyond the time scale of the present analysis, I invite the reader to situate the inquiry I offer here within the longer-term analytical frame of a potentially epochal ecological crisis. One of the most important criteria for rigorous inquiry is feasibility, and the conjunctural framing that I use here should be understood in that vein.

Even within this framing, I will not claim that the analysis of any one social domain is comprehensive or complete. A comprehensive analysis of any one of the domains I examine in this inquiry (economic, political, or cultural) is more of a research agenda or life's work than an object of analysis that can be easily taken up in one project. Yet, I am attempting here to move across all three domains so as to map the terrain of political struggle in this period of conjunctural crisis. What I offer here is not a precise cartographic mapping of the post-1970s formation that captures every agent, political movement, ideological discourse, phenomenon, and so on, at work in the present conjuncture. I am attempting to tell a better story. What I offer here is not the only story to be told nor the only story that needs to be told.

There is a certain conceit in writing a book of this scope. To take up a project such as this one is to adopt the authorial voice of the expert, of someone who has it all "figured out." I do not see myself as someone who has all the answers. In fact, as will become clear, I will offer no answers at all! Nor do I see myself as being an influential figure within my areas of study. I have had the privilege to meet many scholars in the fields of social and cultural foundations of education and cultural studies who are far more talented than I am. I see this book as an invitation to scholars, practitioners, activists, and cultural workers to situate their work within a conjunctural framework. It is an invitation to critical dialogue. I want to start a conversation that others more talented than myself can move forward and employ in this historical moment of political struggle.

My motivation for taking up this project is the increasingly dangerous politics of this historical moment and the short time horizon of popular political discourse. American politics took a radical turn toward the right in the twenty-first century. The Bush administration's global war on terror and Iraq War flouted international law and turned the United States into a torture state. The Obama administration that followed not only failed to prosecute the illegality of Bush's policies but expanded its use of extrajudicial killings and military intervention. The inadequate economic and health care reforms pursued during the Obama years were met with total obstruction from the Right and the astro-turf politics of the so-called Tea Party that presaged what was to come. The election of Trump on an agenda of aggressive nationalism and white supremacy unleashed neo-nazi marches in places like Charlottesville, fueled increasingly fantastical and dangerous conspiracies, and spawned a new wave of militia movements dreaming of race wars and a second American civil war.

What is perhaps most concerning is the way in which the presidency of Donald Trump is treated in popular political discourse as an aberration. Public intellectuals appear to be constitutionally unable or unwilling to, at the very least, connect the Trump administration to political trends over the past twenty years let alone contextualizing it within a longer historical framework.

The Trump administration was not an aberration. It was, as will become clear, a manifestation of the movement of forces and ideological discourses that rose to hegemonic dominance over the past five decades.

My motivation here is not purely academic. The rise of Trump and the radical right around the globe is driving the collapse of the American-led global hegemonic order and is fueling the rise of a multipolar world. Many may well celebrate the dismantling of Pax Americana, but they would do well to remember that multipolar worlds have, historically, produced global conflagrations of increasing violence and intensity. However, the collapse of this hegemonic order has more immediate effects than the potential for global conflict. As I worked to complete the first draft of this manuscript, the COVID-19 pandemic swept the globe. The lack of coordination at the global level and the deadly policies pursued by nations led by so-called right-wing populists (United States, India, Brazil, etc.) has ensured that this disease will continue to spread until a global vaccination program can bring the pandemic to an end. Millions will surely die and many more will suffer disabilities as a result. We live in a time of dangerous politics with no guarantees as to what the future may hold, and this is why I am taking up this project.

There are, of course, tentative glimmers of hope amid the gloom. Anti-systemic movements are thriving in Chile, Lebanon, and (until recently) Hong Kong. The Extinction Rebellion movement continues to militate for a global Green New Deal to control carbon emissions. And, the Kurdish people of Rojava are conducting an experiment in what they term post-national socialism amid the bloody politics of the Syrian civil war and the machinations of global and regional powers.

The United States has witnessed a revival in Left politics in recent years. Youthful enthusiasm around political figures, such as Bernie Sanders and Alexandria Ocasio-Cortez, has demonstrated that there is a growing appetite for social democratic policies among younger generations. More hopeful still is the explosion of activism that erupted in the wake of the murders of George Floyd, Breonna Taylor, and countless others at the hands of law enforcement. A decentralized Black Lives Matter (BLM) movement has mobilized mass protests around the nation and the globe; toppled Jim Crow statues and monuments to slavery; changed the national conversation about race, policing, and the carceral state; and crafted a set of concrete policies to defund police departments, shift those resources to social services, and distribute additional resources to communities of color to make up for a long history of systemic inequality and racist policies. There is good reason to look on at these developments with some sense of optimism and hope, but it is important to not lose track of the enormity of the task that lay ahead.

Translating this enthusiasm into a counter-hegemonic movement capable of not only stemming the advance of the radical right but constructing a new hegemonic order will require sustained political work over the coming years, and the barriers to be overcome are significant. The right-wing populists have made significant political gains and, as we shall see, are well-positioned to recuperate the post-1970s formation or construct an even more dangerous hegemonic order from the wreckage of the contemporary conjuncture. The Left, meanwhile, remains divided and disorganized. The Democratic presidential primaries that took place between 2019 and 2020 demonstrated that social democratic candidates were able to make inroads with young voters and Latino/a and Hispanic voters but have limited support among the African American base and older white voters (Bacon, 2020). Polling data indicate that BLM protests have shifted the views of white liberals on issues related to systemic racism and policing, but what remains to be seen is how committed they are to redressing structural inequality through wealth redistribution and educational change, policies that have historically had limited support among this group of voters (Conroy & Bacon, 2020). It is one thing to voice support for a protest movement but quite another to support rezoning schools to increase the racial, ethnic, and economic diversity of the schools attended by the children of white liberals. Barbara Ransby (2020) argues, in a similar vein, that whites in the Democratic Socialist movement and on the Left flank of the Democratic Party who supported the candidacy of Bernie Sanders are not the allies they would appear to be. She argues that the rejection of "identitarian" politics by white leftists demonstrates a lack of awareness on their part of the centrality of black and intersectional struggle for the realization of a more democratic and just society.

My point is that these day-to-day political processes are playing out in and are a reflection of a conjunctural crisis, a period of time when the contemporary social formation is destabilizing and in which hegemonic and counter-hegemonic forces are mobilizing forces in political struggle over the potential recuperation of the existing hegemonic order or the construction of a new social formation. The outcome of this period of collective struggle will determine what kind of society will be constructed from the crisis and will determine how well we collectively respond to the epochal challenges looming just over the horizon, if we respond at all. My goal is to map the terrain of collective political struggle and to invite other scholars, practitioners, activists, and cultural workers to take up this work as well. I want to use right-wing populism as a heuristic device to construct a problem space around present struggles and to think through how educational scholarship and pedagogical practice can contribute to the task of constructing a more democratic and socially just formation. I want to tell a better story about this historical moment to inform educational scholarship and practice. And, with those considerations in mind, I will now turn to the tasks at hand.

Chapter 2

Economic Crisis

Telling a better story about this historical moment requires that I begin with an economic analysis. I noted in the introduction that contemporary trends in the economic sphere provide a necessary, if inadequate, explanation for the rise to prominence of right-wing populism in the United States and the global North. One need not fall prey to crude economism to argue that structural changes in the American economy over the past forty years have contributed to the rise of right-wing populism nor does it require adopting the reductive shorthand often employed in popular political discourse to explain these structural changes.

The structural transformation of the American economy is too often presented in popular political discourse as being the product of the objective forces of globalization and automation, concepts frequently discussed as though they are forces of nature beyond human control. There is, of course, a grain of truth to this explanation (especially with regard to automation), but the problem with this reductive shorthand is that it obscures the politics and policies driving changes in the economic domain. Globalization and financialization are not the organic product of objective economic forces; it was planned.

The structural transformation of the American economy was not natural but was the necessary outcome of policies informed by neoclassical economics. The term "neoclassical" was first applied to economic science by Thorston Veblen (1900), but the neoclassical economic model we know today arose as an intellectual and political reactionary movement to the Keynesian political economy of the post–World War II era. Neoclassical economists argued for the loosening of trade barriers to encourage global free trade, the reduction of taxes to encourage private investment, and the dismantling of the administrative state apparatus that was, they argued, "crowding out" the private sector. The rise of neoclassical economic theory to hegemonic dominance in the economic sphere from the 1980s forward advanced the globalization of production and finance, the upward distribution of wealth, the dismantling of social safety net protections, and the growing precarity of the working and middle classes.

Telling a better story about this historical moment requires an analysis of this transition from Keynesian political economy to the rise of neoclassical political economy and the structural transformation of the economic sphere it has engendered. The goal here is not to lament the passing of a golden era but to understand the contemporary social formation and the emergent economic crisis into which it is entering. I will begin this chapter with a discussion on the economic theory informing the analysis presented here. I will then begin the analysis by discussing the Keynesian political economy of the postwar era and its collapse in the economic crisis of the 1970s. I will continue the analysis by tracing the rise to dominance of neoclassical economics from the 1980s forward, the structural transformations it has produced, and the emergent crisis it has engendered. I will argue that neoclassical political economy successfully restored capital accumulation in a period of secular economic stagnation, but, in so doing, it has produced economic polarization, precarity, and growing economic antagonisms that now threaten this hegemonic order. I will argue that, in Gramscian terms, the intellectual and political champions of neoclassical economics are no longer in a position of leadership but are working instead to shore up the crumbling edifice of neoclassical political economy in the face of an emergent economic crisis.

CYCLES AND WAVES

Marx's analysis of the cyclical movements of capitalist development was perhaps one of his most lasting and well-recognized contributions to economic thought. Marx's critique of classical political economy challenged the assumption that unfettered markets will naturally achieve a steady-state equilibrium by demonstrating that crisis is endemic to capitalist markets. However, one of his most important contributions to economic theory was to a subfield that has largely disappeared from modern economics. Marx's political economy is defined by its historicity. His work sought to demystify the concepts of classical political economy by, in part, demonstrating that markets and capitalist social relations are historically constructed.

One of the more important examples of economic history inspired by Marx's political economy can be found in Karl Polanyi's *The Great Transformation* (Polanyi, 1944). Polanyi sought to trace the development of modern capitalism through a historical analysis of the long nineteenth century

(1789–1917). His historiography traces the political struggles to dis-embed markets and market relations from the social sphere and attempts by those dislocated by the free market to re-embed market relations within cultural and societal norms. The free market of nineteenth-century society was not the natural outcome of organic economic forces but was, in his telling, planned. More importantly, Polanyi described a double movement in which the move toward economic liberalism and the ideology of the self-regulating market in the nineteenth century collapsed in the twentieth century into economic and political crisis that fueled political moves toward regulation and the amelioration of economic dislocation.

> [The double movement] can be personified as the action of two organizing principles in society, each of them setting itself specific institutional aims, having the support of definite social forces and using its own distinctive methods. The one was the principle of economic liberalism, aiming at the establishment of a self-regulating market, relying on the support of the trading classes, and using largely laissez-faire and free trade as its methods; the other was the principle of social protection aiming at the conservation of man and nature as well as productive organization, relying on the varying support of those most immediately affected by the deleterious action of the market—primarily, but not exclusively, the working and the landed classes—and using protective legislation restrictive associations, and other instruments of intervention as its methods. (Polanyi, 1944, p. 132)

Polanyi argued that the collapse of nineteenth-century civilization "was not the outcome of some alleged laws of economics" but by "the measures which society adopted in order not to be, in its turn, annihilated by the action of the self-regulating market" (Polanyi, 1944, p. 249).

Like Marx and Schumpeter, Polanyi argued that capitalist markets experience cyclical crises that fuel oligopoly and polarization, but the primary focus of his analysis was the social costs the free market exacts from society (polarization, environmental degradation, etc.) and the political moves during the twentieth century to re-embed markets and market relations within cultural and social norms to ameliorate those costs. Polanyi clearly favored socialist policies that sought to "transcend the self-regulating market by consciously subordinating it to a democratic society," but his primary concern in *The Great Transformation* was the global emergence of fascism which he understood as being a diverse set of movements to re-embed markets and market relations within social and cultural norms defined by nationalism, xenophobia, traditionalism, and antidemocratic politics (Polanyi, 1944, p. 234).

My read of *The Great Transformation* is that Polanyi's double movement is not so much a teleological argument for progressive change as much as a warning about the dangers of a political economy oriented around free-market policies. The socially destructive cycles of market capitalism produce recurrent crises that exact a heavy toll on society, but there are no guarantees that cyclical crises produced by the free market will lead to positive progressive change. The fascist solution is an equally likely outcome. What Polanyi offers is a conceptual model to understand the cyclical movement of capitalist markets and the political dynamics surrounding those movements.

An important critical theory tradition that draws upon the historical approaches of Marx, Polanyi, and (to a lesser degree) Schumpeter is world-systems analysis. World-systems analysis is an ambitious theoretical project within critical sociology with roots in the Latin American dependency theory model. There is significant diversity of thought among the most notable founding names in the field, such as Immanuel Wallerstein (2011), Andr'e Gunder Frank (1983), and Ernest Mandel (1980), and the growing body of work in contemporary world-system analysis is a site of robust debate and intellectual diversity. However, within this diversity, there are a shared set of concepts that provide theoretically rich tools of inquiry to understand contemporary economic trends.

One of the defining characteristics of world-systems analysis is, following Marx and Polanyi, its historicity. World-systems analysis takes up Fernand Braudel's and the French Annales School's longue dur'ee approach to history and sociological analysis (Braudel, 1960). Put simply, a longue dur'ee perspective understands present circumstances as being the product of long-term processes of sufficient duration to defy recognition by historical agents. Longue dur'ee is a methodological tool "for the analysis of particular problems" by situating phenomena within "temporal rhythms so slow and stable that they approximate physical geography," forming a "stabilizing ground against which cyclical variations of other temporal structures are established" (Tomich, 2012, pp. 10–11).

The unit of analysis in this theoretical framework is the world system. Wallerstein (2004) positions this expansive unit of analysis as being an explicit rejection of traditional forms of social scientific research. He argues that in the traditional social sciences of the twentieth century, "historians had been ana-lyzing national histories, economists national economies, political scientists national political structures, and sociologists national societies" (Wallerstein, 2004, p. 16). World-systems analysis calls for modes of inquiry that situate the study of individual states, political struggles and conflicts, anti-systemic move-ments, and so on, within the ebbs and flows, or the movement, of the capitalist world system. Wallerstein states that world-systems analysis is:

[N]ot about systems, economies, empires *of the* (whole) world, but about systems, economies, empires *that are* a world (but quite possibly, and indeed usually, not encompassing the entire globe). This is a key initial concept to grasp. It says that in "world-systems" we are dealing with a spatial/temporal zone which cuts across many political and cultural units, one that represents an integrated zone of activity and institutions which obey certain systemic rules. (Wallerstein, 2004, pp. 16–17)

Thus, an analysis of a national economy, such as the United States, should not be taken up as a self-evident unit of analysis that is projected back through time but can only be understood as a process of historical development taking place within a larger framework of the capitalist world system.

World-systems analysis situates individual states within a tripartite framework of core, semi-periphery, and periphery. Core nations possess quasi-monopolies over high-technology, high-value production requiring highly skilled labor and are primarily concentrated in the global North. Peripheral nations are characterized by a reliance on low-value, labor-intensive production, resource extraction, and agricultural production and are concentrated in the global South. Semi-peripheral nations specialize in high-cost, industrial production but also possess sectors that resemble both core and peripheral nations, the so-called BRICS nations (Brazil, Russia, India, China, and South Africa) being a commonly used example. The classification of the world system into core, semi-periphery, and periphery reflects an international division of labor and uneven economic development that is historically constructed. However, this tripartite framework and the positionality of individual nation-states within it is not fixed.

Core nations do possess a historical advantage over semi-peripheral and peripheral nations that speaks to the primitive accumulation of the colonial period and the uneven movement of capitalist development from the global North to the global South. Core nations possess the industrial and technological infrastructure to both revolutionize and create new high-value industries, markets, and educational infrastructure to ensure the continuation of a highly skilled workforce for these industries and to further drive innovation. More importantly, core nations are able to leverage their economic and political capital to structure the world system in their favor. The international institutions associated with the Washington Consensus (which will be discussed later in this chapter) are commonly used as an example of this form of neocolonial politics.

Semi-peripheral and peripheral nations compete with core nations and each other in this asymmetrical structure. Semi-peripheral nations work to compete with the core nations by seeking entry to high-value markets. These nations seek to leverage their lower labor costs, generally lax environmental and labor regulations, and public-private partnerships to take up new innovations, gain access to high-value markets, and compete on price. Further, these nations work to challenge the political dominance of core nations over international institutions and trade networks, China's gaining membership in the World Trade Organization (WTO) in 2001 and Xi Jinping's Belt and Road Initiative being excellent examples. Likewise, peripheral nations work to leverage their resources, low labor costs, and lax regulations to develop their economies and compete in high-value markets, and they often work through international institutions to advance their own positions. Nevertheless, it is clear that they inhabit a clearly disadvantaged position within the asymmetries of the world system.

The tripartite division of the world system is not static but is defined by economic and political competition over the structure of the world system and the rules of the game that regulate it. Core nations can be understood as entrenched regulators with the leverage to ensure their dominance, but their primacy is not uncontested. Core nations compete with one another as well as semi-peripheral and peripheral nations over the structure of the world system. Thus, while world-systems analysis is primarily an economic model, the politics of what Wallerstein terms the interstate system are a key component of this theoretical model.

One of the ways in which world-systems analysis seeks to explain the historical development of capitalist modernity is through the oscillation between unipolarity and multipolarity in the world system. Polarity in the world system refers to the distribution of political power within the interstate system. In a bipolar or multipolar world system, two or more nations are actively competing to establish cultural, economic, military, and political dominance. When one nation emerges triumphant from this competition, the world system enters into a unipolar phase. A commonly used example of this dynamic is the eighteenth-century conflict between the UK and France. The UK emerged victoriously and established a unipolar world in the nineteenth century under the banner of Pax Britannica. However, it would be a mistake to think about unipolarity as being strictly about military power, that is, the British victory at Waterloo.

An important aspect of unipolarity is ideological. A unipolar world system is led by a hegemonic state that is not simply the greatest military power, although that is usually the case, but is also the dominant ideological power. The hegemonic state of a unipolar world system achieves political dominance through the propagation of common sense understandings on the organization and structure of political and economic institutions and the doxa which structure the rules of the game in the world system. Thus, ideology is a means of achieving and maintaining power within the interstate system and to counter anti-systemic movements across both domains.

Thus, to sum up the preceding discussion, the world system is composed of, in Wallerstein's terminology, a *world economy* defined by a tripartite structure of core, semi-peripheral, and peripheral nation-states; an *interstate*

system of loosely organized nation-states in economic and political competition, and a *geoculture* of hegemonic struggle. This constitutes the conceptual
framework of world-systems analysis, but it is the way in which this theoretical model is operationalized that is of interest to the present inquiry. World-
systems analysis is first and foremost a theoretical model to understand
macro-level societal change and transformation within capitalist modernity.

World-systems analysis seeks to explain the uneven development of
capitalist modernity. The world system goes through knowable cycles of
economic expansion and stagnation. World-systems analysts have identified
and debated the validity of cycles and waves of various amplitudes, but the
most commonly employed cycle in this theoretical model is the Kondratieff
cycle (or K-wave), named after Nikolai Kondratieff, the Russian political
economist who first hypothesized this identifiable pattern in the early twentieth century. A K-wave is made up of an A-phase of economic expansion and
a B-phase of economic stagnation lasting approximately fifty to sixty years
in length.

An A-phase is marked by the confluence of the emergence of new high-
value leading industries made possible by technological development and
the emergence of a hegemonic state regulating the world system. The quasi-
monopoly over leading industries held by core nations and the relative peace
of a unipolar interstate system under the aegis of a hegemonic state sets the
stage for a period of rapid economic growth, but it is often short-lived. The
relative peace, stability, and prosperity of a unipolar world create opportunities
for semi-peripheral and peripheral nations to adopt new technologies and to
challenge the quasi-monopolies of core nations over leading industries, a
process that leads to a falling rate of profit (what Marx termed a crisis of
overproduction) and entry to a B-phase of stagnation. Wallerstein describes
the cyclical movement of a K-wave this way:

> A [new] major leading industry will be a major stimulus to the expansion of
> the world-economy and will result in considerable accumulation of capital. But
> it also normally leads to more extensive employment in the world-economy,
> higher wage-levels, and a general sense of relative prosperity. As more and
> more firms enter the market of the erstwhile quasi-monopoly, there will be
> "overproduction" (that is, too much production for the real effective demand
> at a given time) and consequently increased price competition (because of the
> demand squeeze), thus lowering the rates of profit. . . . When this happens,
> we tend to see a reversal of the cyclical curve of the world-economy. . . . The
> process we have been describing . . . can be drawn as an up-and-down curve
> of so-called A-(expansion) and B-(stagnation) phases. A cycle consisting of an
> A-phase followed by a B-phase is sometimes referred to as a Kondratieff cycle.
> (Wallerstein, 2004, pp. 30–31)

Thus, an A-phase is marked by a rapid expansion of the world economy that ends in a period of stagnation, but the entry into a B-phase does not mean that there is no economic growth nor that some nations will not experience growth and rapid development. The B-phase denotes a period of slowing growth in the world economy and a tendency toward crisis in the world system. The endpoint of a Kondratieff cycle is a crisis, the resolution of which is defined by the ways in which the global hegemon attempts to stave off and resolve the crisis, the emergence of new innovations and leading industries, the outcome of political and (often) military conflict among states competing for hegemonic status, or (more often than not) some combination of the three.

World-systems analysts have constructed a compelling model to under-stand macro-level societal change that pushes us to extend the time horizon of societal inquiry. However, there are a number of issues with world-systems analysis that bear consideration. First, world-systems analysis is unapologeti-cally structuralist and does tend toward a mechanistic economism. Despite recognizing the importance of ideology (geoculture) and the political (inter-state system), world-systems analysis positions economic changes in the world economy as the primary force and engine of change in the world system. Second, and relatedly, world-systems analysis constructs a teleo-logical model of societal change similar to the crude, classical Marxism of the early twentieth century. This is perhaps best captured in the title of one of the most influential pieces in this field of thought: "The Rise and Future Demise of the World Capitalist System" (Wallerstein, 1974). And, third, I would argue that world-systems analysis, and Wallerstein in particular, are guilty of scientism and intellectual conservatism. Wallerstein conceptualizes world-systems analysis as providing a scientific explanation of capitalist development and is, accordingly, somewhat dismissive of historical works focused on the industrial revolution and the long nineteenth century, such as Polanyi's. Wallerstein has been especially vocal about what he terms a "crisis in the sciences" brought about, in part, by a turn toward postmodern theory, feminist theory, cultural studies, and so on. I admire Wallerstein's project and the expansive theoretical model that he has helped construct, but his conser-vatism on this topic resurrects debates among social theorists from the 1990s that produced far more heat than light and are, in my reading, indefensible at this late date.

Nevertheless, if we take seriously Terry Gilliam's wise observation that "it's only a model" (Gilliam & Jones, 1975), it is clear that world-systems analysis is a powerful theoretical tool for economic analysis. el Ojeili (2015, p. 694) reminds us that the "function of social theory" is to provide a "set of tools that enables us to organize our inquiries, rather than as an aspiration to create to-scale maps of the territory we seek to cover." The longue dur'ee lens of world-systems analysis offers an important corrective to the erasure of economic history from contemporary economics (Mirowski, 2011). World-systems analysis provides tools to understand the historical development of contemporary trends in the economic domain as cycles of growth and stagnation and links these cycles to global, ideological, and hegemonic politics. An important strength of world-systems analysis is that it situates economic cycles within political struggles between nations in the world system for hegemonic dominance and within national struggles over the embeddedness or disembeddedness of markets and market relations.

The economic analysis that follows will employ world-systems analysis as its theoretical framework. Specifically, I will draw upon Wallerstein's observation that the post–World War II economic boom constituted the "biggest A-phase expansion in history" that entered into a period of crisis in the 1970s marking entry into a B-phase period of stagnation from the early 1980s forward (Wallerstein, 2010, p. 137). This theoretical framework will inform both the structure of the analysis and the evidence that I will employ. I will begin with an analysis of the global infrastructure and economic theory that, in Polanyi's terminology, sought to embed market relations in the social and cultural domains and the economic trends that defined the post–World War II era. I will then trace the unraveling of this social formation in the 1970s and the emergence of a movement to dis-embed market relations. This will be followed by an analysis of the global structures constructed in the aftermath of the 1970s and the economic trends that define this historical moment. The focus of the analysis will be the United States, but I will attempt to situate national trends within a global framework. For example, when discussing economic growth trends, I will use both gross domestic product (GDP) and gross national product (GNP), because GNP captures net income from abroad and situates American economic growth in a global context.

The task for this chapter is to tell a better story about the economic trends of the contemporary formation. My goal is to situate this historical moment in economic cycles of expansion and stagnation in the world system and the hegemonic struggle over economic theory informing policy at the global and national levels. I hope to denaturalize the contemporary social formation by contextualizing the economic antagonisms that, in part, animate the emergence and normalization of right-wing populism.

A-PHASE

The foundation for the post–World War II economic boom (A-phase) was laid in July of 1944 at the Mount Washington Hotel in Bretton Woods, New Hampshire. The Bretton Woods conference brought together delegates from forty-four nations led by senior American Treasury Department official Harry Dexter White and the famous British economist John Maynard Keynes. The goal for the conference was as ambitious as the deliberations were contentious. White and Keynes sought to construct a new economic infrastructure to regulate the global economy. Specifically, the aim of the Bretton Woods conference was to create an international monetary system that would reduce the risk of dramatic economic crises, such as the Great Depression of the 1930s, and the risk of repeating the competitive race to the bottom of the interwar period in which nations devalued their currencies and erected trade barriers to protect their national economies, policies that only slowed a global economy already in free fall. The attendees at Bretton Woods were, for the most part, bureaucrats and functionaries with little political power. It would seem an unlikely place for revolutionary change, but that is exactly what happened (Conway, 2015).

What emerged from the Bretton Woods conference was a global monetary system built around four institutions. First, a gold system was constructed by pegging the value of national currencies to the U.S. dollar which was pegged to gold at thirty-five dollars per ounce. Second, the International Monetary Fund (IMF) was created as a lender of last resort for nations facing economic and currency crises. Third, the International Bank for Reconstruction and Development, or simply the World Bank (WB), was created to fund postwar reconstruction efforts and to promote economic development in semi-peripheral and peripheral nations through development loans. And, fourth, the outline for a General Agreement on Tariffs and Trade (GATT) to encourage international trade was developed at Bretton Woods and was later ratified in 1948. What emerged from the Bretton Woods conference was a new global infrastructure that reflected a larger transformation in economic theory away from nineteenth-century liberalism.

The economic thought of the postwar era was dominated by the work of John Maynard Keynes (1936). Keynesian economics sought to regulate the excesses of the capitalist economy through state intervention and public spending designed to maintain full employment. The Keynesian economics of the postwar period envisioned activist states regulating the financial and industrial sectors and using relatively high taxation, public spending, and welfare policies to ensure a basic level of economic security for individuals and to ensure widely shared economic growth. Keynesian political economy was by no means a rejection of liberal economic thought but was seen by its advocates as a means of ensuring the continuance of market capitalism. Keynesian economists and policymakers saw their intervention as being founded on the recognition that mid-twentieth-century capitalism was no longer the domain of individual capitalists but was defined by the dominance of large-scale, publicly traded industries operating under technocratic management. They argued that technocratic governance could foster an affluent society through a sophisticated planning system and technostructure in which the private and public sectors cooperate in the regulation of national economies (Galbraith, 1958, 1968).

A key area of private-public cooperation involved labor relations. In the United States, the regulations implemented in the 1930s in response to the Great Depression and the industrial mobilization of World War II forced a tenuous peace in labor-capital relations that carried over into the postwar period. This era of relative peace, often termed the era of Fordism after Henry Ford's reported observation that industry must pay its workers enough money so that they could purchase the commodities they produce, was marked by a large unionized industrial labor force that was well-positioned in terms of both organizational size and governmental policy to command high salaries and benefit packages. The unionized industrial labor force was able to benefit from growing profitability and productivity gains to turn what was once dangerous, low-wage work into a path to the middle class. More importantly, the ability of the unionized labor force to command high wages drove wage growth for the labor market as a whole. Coupled with federal subsidies to encourage homeownership and large-scale public works projects, the United States was transformed in the postwar period into a middle-class society of suburbs, consumerism, and broadly shared prosperity.

The dominance of Keynesian policies in the postwar era constituted Polanyi's double movement in which markets and market relations were re-embedded into the social and cultural domains through the economic policy of an activist state. Core nations led by the United States constructed a global system that laid the foundation for a period of rapid economic growth in the world system, growth that was not limited to Western market economies but included the planned economies in the Soviet sphere. Bretton Woods built a global monetary system that would serve as a model for future moves toward global economic cooperation and multilateral trade agreements. Keynesian theory advocated for a new economic system of public-private cooperation at the national level and cooperation among nations at the global level, and the wide-spread adoption of Keynesian policies in the global North was considered an overwhelming success by the political leaders of the postwar era. From 1948 onward, the world system entered into an expansionary A-phase that was unrivaled in the long history of capitalist development.

The United States emerged from World War II as the global hegemon with its industrial infrastructure intact, the military superiority to enforce its will across the globe, and the ideological leadership to shape the rules of the game regulating the world system. Public works projects expanded the nation's economic infrastructure, and public investment in higher education encouraged scientific innovations that led to the creation of new high-value markets. American industry quickly shifted from military mobilization to the production of consumer goods for both American consumers as well as other core nations devastated by the war.

The excesses of Wall Street speculation that had brought economic devastation in 1907 and 1929 were curbed, and banking regulations ensured that the financial sector efficiently recycled surpluses to productive areas that fostered economic growth. A unionized labor force ensured that workers were able to benefit from the growing prosperity of the era and had the spending power to purchase the growing array of consumer goods produced by a thriving industrial sector.

The postwar era is generally considered to be the golden age of American capitalism defined by rapid economic growth, an increasingly activist state, and widely shared prosperity (figure 2.1). Between 1948 and 1968 median annual real GDP growth was 4.4% with an average annual growth rate of 4.1% (Federal Reserve Bank of St. Louis, 2019a). The U.S. government made public investments that helped fuel economic growth and constructed a welfare state of government transfers, all of which was funded by progressive taxation (figure 2.2). The average top marginal income tax rate for individuals between 1948 and 1968 was 85.5% with a peak in 1952 and 1953 of 92%. The top corporate tax rate between 1948 and 1968 averaged 47.65% with only two tax brackets for every year except 1948 in which there were five brackets (U.S. Internal Revenue Service, 2018). Importantly, during this time period, the American labor

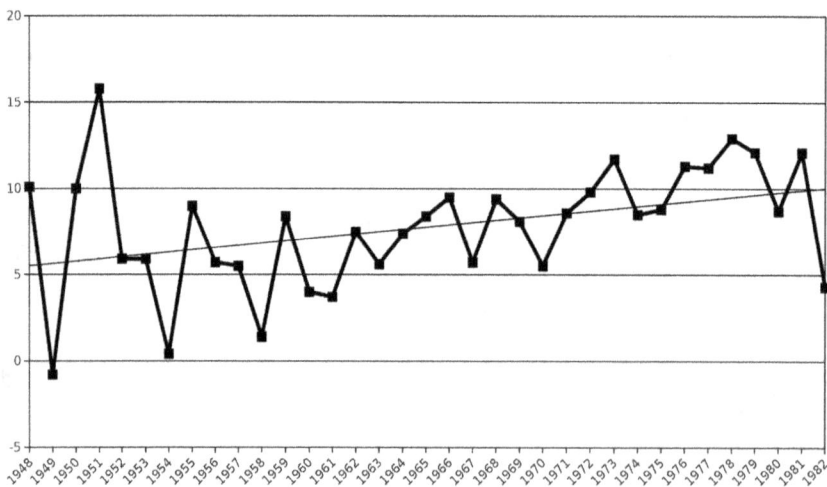

Figure 2.1 Gross National Product, Percent Change from Preceding Period, Annual, 1948–1982. *Source*: Federal Reserve Bank of St. Louis.

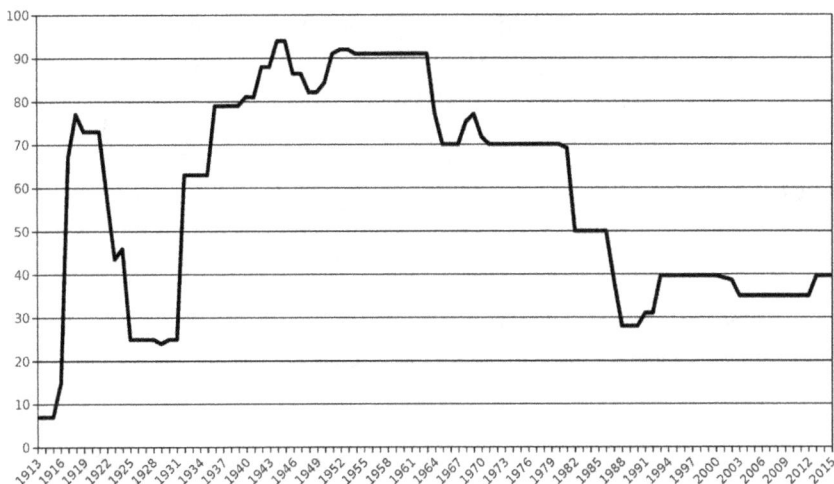

Figure 2.2   U.S. Individual Income Tax: Tax Rates for Regular Tax: Highest Bracket, Percent, Annual, Not Seasonally Adjusted, 1913–2015. *Source*: Federal Reserve Bank of St. Louis.

force was able to benefit from public investment and economic growth through collective bargaining. Roughly 50% of annual gross domestic income between 1948 and 1970 was captured by labor through compensation (Federal Reserve Bank of St. Louis, 2019b). The American economy was thriving in the postwar era, and its hegemonic leadership constructed a global infrastructure that provided a foundation for rapid growth in the world system and widely shared prosperity among the populations of core nations. However, it was an era of economic expansion that would quickly become a victim of its own success.

Cracks began to appear in the postwar system in the late 1960s. The stability provided by the Bretton Woods system, the GATT agreement, and the direct American aid of the Marshall Plan created opportunities for Japan and West Germany to quickly re-industrialize and compete with U.S. industry. The emergence of the Newly Industrialized Countries of Hong Kong, Singapore, South Korea, and Taiwan in the late 1960s intensified competition and eroded the profitability of leading industries in the United States. As the U.S. share of global production began to shrink, global demand for dollars began to fall at the same time that the massive spending associated with the American war in Viet Nam and international development aid increased the global supply of dollars. Faced with a deteriorating balance of payments and a loss of confidence among global investors in the ability of the United States to honor gold convertibility of the dollar, President Richard Nixon ended the gold system in 1971 and, with the stroke of a pen, effectively destroyed the Keynesian system of political economy established at Bretton Woods. The collapse of the Bretton Woods system set off a period of economic instability that was amplified in 1973 when the Organization of Arab Petroleum Exporting Countries (OAPEC) cut oil exports to the United States and other core nations to protest Western support for Israel in the Arab-Israeli war. The confluence of these economic shocks pushed the United States into a period of economic crisis marked by slowing economic growth and rapid inflation, what became known in the 1970s as stagflation.

The U.S. economy entered recession four times between 1968 and 1982 (1969–1970, 1973–1975, 1980, and 1981–1982). Median annual real GDP growth fell from 4.4% of the 1948–1968 period to 3.2% with an average of 2.7% between 1968 to 1982 (Federal Reserve Bank of St. Louis, 2019a). Repeated recessions and slowing economic growth inflicted pain on middle-class households that was amplified by rapid inflation. Inflation between 1948 and 1968 averaged 2% but averaged 7.4% between 1968 and 1982 with a peak of 11.3, 13.5, and 10.3% in 1979, 1980, and 1981, respectively (Minneapolis Reserve Bank, 2019).

The economic crisis of the 1970s marked the end of the postwar economic boom in the United States and the transition of the world system from expansionary A-phase to a B-phase of stagnation (figure 2.3). Global GDP growth that was averaging 5.5% in the 1960s slowed to an average of 2.9% annual growth from 1970 to 2017 (figure 2.4). Despite spirited

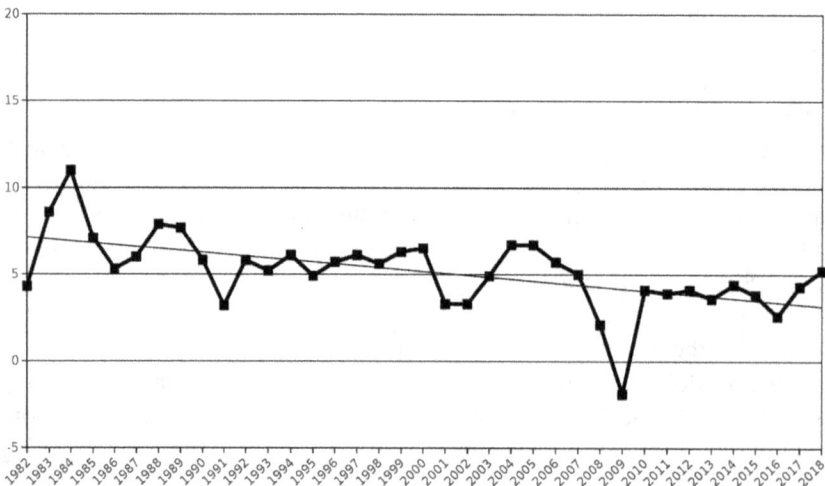

Figure 2.3 Gross National Product, Percent Change from Preceding Period, Annual, 1982–2018. *Source*: Federal Reserve Bank of St. Louis.

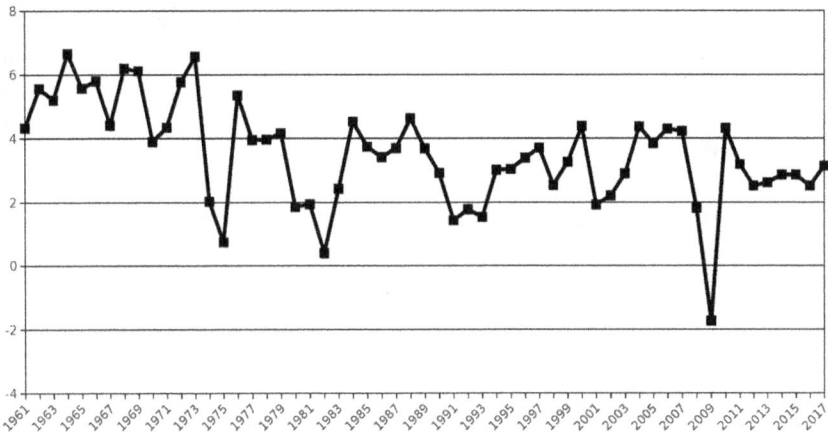

Figure 2.4   Global GDP Growth, Annual Percent Change, 1961–2017. *Source*: World Bank National Accounts Data.

defenses of Keynesian economics (Minsky, 1975), the collapse of the Bretton Woods system and the economic turmoil of the 1970s was seen as largely discrediting the technocratic management of Keynesian political economy and opened the door to the neoclassical school of economic thought, a theoretical orientation toward economic policy that advocated for the dis-embedding of markets and market relations from the social and cultural domains.

B-PHASE

The Keynesian political economy of the mid-twentieth century was a move to re-embed markets and market relations within cultural and societal norms. The Keynesianism of the postwar era used public investment paid for through high taxation to encourage full employment and drive economic growth through consumption and demand. It was an economic policy regime oriented around stability and widely shared prosperity. However, by the 1970s, Keynesian political economy was intellectually exhausted, and the economic turmoil of the decade created an opening for a new economic model to rise to hegemonic dominance.

The neoclassical theory of Milton Friedman, Eugene Fama, and Robert Lucas and most closely associated with the University of Chicago School of Economics posed a direct challenge to the Keynesian model (Appelbaum, 2019). They argued that it is impossible to technocratically manage a complex economy and argued that the economic crises of the 1970s were the inevitable product of attempting to do so. The Chicago school resurrected the nineteenth-century idea that unfettered markets tend toward a stable equilibrium that efficiently recycles surpluses toward productive growth and encourages technological innovation without the need for heavy-handed regulation or public investment. Neoclassical economic theorists advocated for the radical deregulation of the business sector (especially labor markets) (M. Friedman, 1962) arguing that the primary role of governmental oversight should be to ensure stable growth in the money supply (M. Friedman, 1963). Neoclassical economists argued for the lowering of individual and corporate taxes to put money into the pockets of consumers to fuel economic growth and to encourage corporate investment in new technology and product development.

The economic logic of the neoclassical school is grounded in the Ricardian assumption that the mostly rational, self-interested decisions of individual actors in a marketplace will ensure the development of a rational, spontaneous order (Hayek, 1956). More importantly, the political economy of the neoclassical school took a dark view on the possibility of public servants working in the public interest, countering that governmental bureaucrats serve their own rational interests and not those of the public at large (Buchanan, 1972). They argued instead that genuine human liberty can only be realized by liberating economic actors from regulation and the tyranny of state services (M. Friedman & Friedman, 1990).

The neoclassical theory of the Chicago school constituted an intellectual counter-revolution against the Keynesian revolution of the mid-twentieth century. It was an explicit rejection of public-private cooperation instead asserting the primacy of private interests over those of the public. Neoclassical theory was not simply an economic theory that occupied the minds and debates of intellectuals in far removed ivory towers but was a theoretical counter-revolution that informed a radical reorientation of global institutions and national governmental policy toward the goal of dis-embedding markets and market relations from the social and cultural norms of the postwar era. Neoclassical economics was informed by a reactionary politics. It was a counter-revolution against Keynesian political economy.

The United States emerged from the 1970s economically bruised but still the reigning global hegemon, both economic and political, and it was the shift toward the neoclassical model of political economy in the United States that would drive the structural transformation of the world system after the 1970s. The "Washington Consensus" among the U.S. Treasury Department, the IMF, and the WB enforced "structural adjustment" policies on developing nations in the semi-periphery and periphery in exchange for economic assistance. Structural adjustment policies required developing nations to open up their national economies to foreign trade and investment with the goal of integrating their economies into a new era of global trade that was billed as an engine of growth and economic development. These policies were couched in the language of economic development, but, in reality, they served the interests of core nations that possessed both a comparative advantage in high-value industries and the ability to shield strategic industries from the global competition they championed (Stiglitz, 2002).

The "Washington Consensus" reoriented the mission of the global institutions of the Bretton Woods era away from a focus on stabilization and cooperation (always tenuous at best) toward introducing dynamism into the world system, a transformation that was completed with the transition of GATT to the WTO during the Uruguay round in 1994. Public intellectuals proclaimed a new era of globalization conceptualized almost as a force of nature that levels the playing field of economic competition among nations (T. L. Friedman, 2005) and that held out the promise of putting an end to poverty across the globe (Sachs, 2005). However, it was anything but the result of objective "economic forces." The new era of globalization that emerged from the crisis of the 1970s was the product of a coherent set of policies informed by neoclassical economic theory.

The counter-revolution away from Keynesianism toward neoclassical policies in the United States is generally marked by the election of Ronald Reagan as President in 1980 (although as we will see in chapter 3, the transformation began long before then) and was cemented into the policymaking apparatus with the adoption of third-way policies by the opposition Democratic Party in the 1990s (Mudge, 2018). While differences remained between the two parties (and recent moves in the Democratic Party could potentially lead to more substantiative differences), policy elites in the United States reached a broad consensus around economic policy that would fundamentally transform the American economy.

Five broad economic policies are important here. First, policymakers sought to dramatically reduce barriers to trade. This involved both opening new foreign markets to U.S. goods and financial investment and opening specific sectors and markets of the American economy to inexpensive goods produced in semi- and peripheral nations. Second, policymakers dismantled financial regulations put into place in the aftermath of the crash of 1929 and the Great Depression to spur both investment and innovation in the financial sector. Third, labor policies shifted from the relatively union-friendly orientation of the postwar era to one of hostility. Reagan's breaking of the PATCO strike in 1981 marked the beginning of an assault on labor rights that culminated in the Supreme Court's decision in *Janus v. AFSCME* (Curry, 2019). Fourth, policymakers sought to spur consumption and investment by dramatically lowering individual and corporate taxes (figure 2.2). Statutory corporate tax rates reached a high point of 52% in the 1950s but fell to 35%

in the 2000s and to 21% in 2019, and it should be noted that the wide array of deductions introduced from the 1980s forward means that the effective tax rate for large, profitable corporations is far lower than the statutory rate (U.S. Government Accountability Office, 2016). Fifth, in the name of liberating citizens (now re-branded as "taxpayers") from stultifying bureaucracy, policymakers implemented a two-fold strategy of privatizing state services and scaling back the social safety net, the "Welfare-to-Work" legislation of the 1990s being a prominent example.

Put simply, the post-1970s policy regime fundamentally restructured the American economy with dramatic results. The lowering of trade barriers encouraged producers to abandon the industrial heartland (now termed the Rust Belt) and exploit low-wage labor and lax environmental regulations in the global South, a structural change that significantly eroded the labor power of unions in the United States (Loomis, 2015). The promise of policymakers since the publication of *A Nation at Risk* in 1983 (National Commission on Excellence in Education, 1983) has been that education and re-training (now termed human capital development) would provide displaced workers and the younger generations following them entry into high-paying jobs in the technology sector. In reality, industrial jobs were replaced with low-wage jobs in the service sector, and this trend looks to continue into the near future (U.S. Bureau of Labor Statistics, 2020). More recently, the introduction of new piece-work industries enabled by mobile technology has fueled the casualization of work across various sectors and the growing precarity of the working and middle classes (Standing, 2011).

The deregulation of the financial sector unleashed a wave of innovation that has served as one of the primary engines for economic growth in an era of de-industrialization and a growing service sector. Wall Street banks and investment houses created waves of new investment vehicles and engaged in increasingly complex speculative trading schemes to generate profits and handsome compensation packages. This growing reliance on the financial sector to generate economic growth (termed the financialization of the economy) led to perverse outcomes (Long, 2019). Mariana Mazzucato (2018) argues that the financialization of the economy provided an engine for growth, but it came with the cost of increasing systemic fragility, transferring wealth to the top of the economic ladder, incentivizing short-termism oriented toward maximizing shareholder value, transferring risk to the public sector, and enabling the privatization of public investment. Financialization of the real economy has not led to value creation but value extraction.

Anti-union policies and de-industrialization have led to the erosion of labor power and union membership. The percentage of wage and salary workers who are members of a union declined from 20.1% in 1983 to 10.5% in 2019

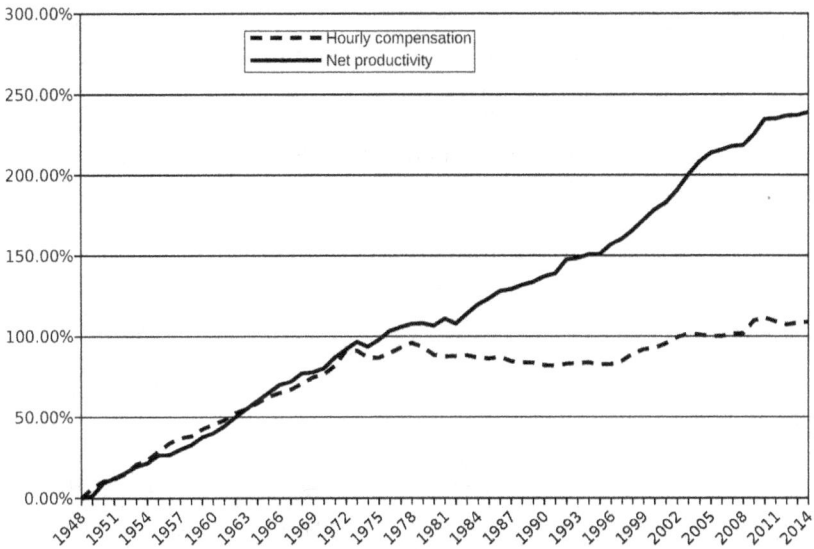

Figure 2.5 Disconnect Between Productivity and a Typical Workers Compensation, 1948–2014. *Source*: Economic Policy Institute.

(U.S. Bureau of Labor Statistics, 2019). The erosion of collective bargaining rights (coupled with a labor market increasingly dominated by precarious work in the service sector) has led to wage stagnation. During the postwar A-phase, American labor had the leverage to claim the benefits of productivity and profitability growth through compensation, but that linkage was broken in the 1970s and the divergence accelerated from the 1980s onward (figure 2.5).

Changes in tax policy have led to a significant drop in progressivity from the postwar era to today, primarily driven by the lowering of corporate taxes as well as estate and gift taxes affecting individuals at the top of the income distribution (Piketty & Saez, 2007). The percent of total tax receipts collected from individual income taxation has remained relatively stable since the 1970s rising from 47.2% in 1980 to 50.1% in 2018; however, the percent of total receipts collected from corporate taxes fell from 12.5% in 1980 to 6.1% in 2018 (U.S. Office of Management and Budget, 2019). Neoclassical economists argued for the lowering of the tax burden on corporations and wealthy individuals to spur private investment and economic growth, but the effective outcome of these changes in tax policy has been a significant upward distribution of wealth that has fueled growing federal budget deficits (Federal Reserve Bank of St. Louis, 2019b) and debt (Federal Reserve Bank of St. Louis, 2019a).

As wealthier households take in a greater share of economic and pro-ductivity growth, the increasingly precarious middle and working classes found themselves with little support. Roughly fourteen million Americans (4.6 million adults and 9.6 million children) received public assistance when welfare-to-work legislation was introduced in the mid-1990s but fell to just over two million (474,000 adults and 1.7 million children) by 2018 (U.S. Office of Family Assistance, 2004, 2019). The growing precarity of the work-ing and middle classes is amplified by an eroding social safety net leading to significant growth in the number of people living in absolute poverty (Edin & Shaefer, 2016).

In short, the structural transformation of the American economy driven by the neoclassical counter-revolution against Keynesian political economy from the 1970s onward has led to a dramatic rise in inequality and an equally dramatic fall in absolute mobility (Chetty et al., 2017). The mythos of the American Dream that was cemented in the mid-twentieth century has been replaced by polarization and inequality, precarity and anxiety, and an increas-ingly rigid class structure. Financialization and tax changes have transferred wealth up the economic ladder to such a degree that distribution patterns now resemble those of the 1920s (World Inequality Database, 2019). Income has stagnated in real dollars for the working and middle classes but has grown rapidly for the top 20% and (especially) the top 5% of households (figure 2.6).

Four in ten American adults report that they would be unable to cover an unexpected four hundred dollar expense while 20% report that they

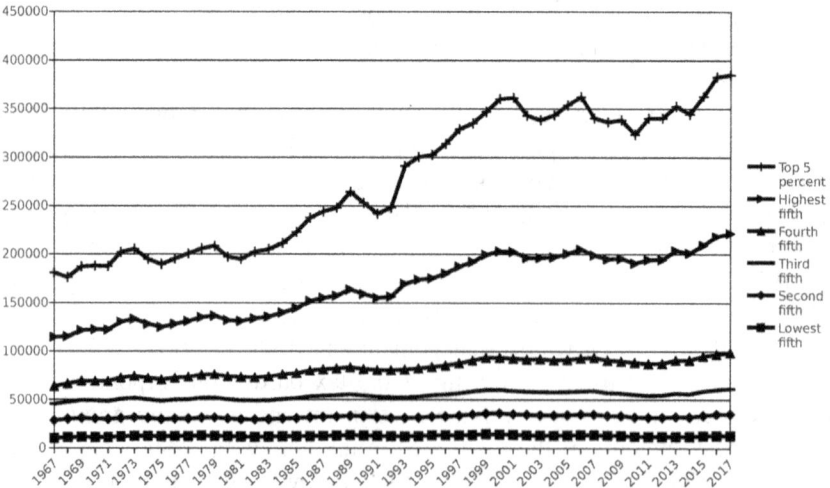

Figure 2.6 Mean Household Income Received by Each Fifth and Top 5%, 1967–2017. *Source:* U.S. Census Bureau Current Population Survey.

are not able to pay all of their monthly bills in full (U.S. Federal Reserve Bank, 2018). Prospects for the future remain dim as advances in automation (McKinsey Global Institute, 2017) and growth in precarious service sector jobs (L. F. Katz & Krueger, 2019) will continue to put downward pressure on wages for working- and middle-class families.

The American economy increasingly resembles a "dual economy" characterized by "two separate economic sectors . . . divided by different levels of development, technology, and patterns of demand" that is traditionally associated with developing economies in the global South (Temin, 2018, p. xiii). One economic sector is characterized by high-value industries, such as finance and technology, in large urban areas that are concentrated, although not exclusively so, along the Eastern and Western coasts. The other economic sector is characterized by low-value, service industries in de-industrializing cities and rural areas and a workforce trapped by stagnating incomes and declining mobility. In this way, the United States increasingly resembles a semi-peripheral nation and is evidence of its loss of global hegemonic leadership.

ECONOMIC CRISIS

The postwar era marked the emergence of Pax Americana. The United States emerged from World War II as the global hegemon dominating the world system economically, ideologically, militarily, and politically. The United States played a dominant role in constructing new global institutions to rebuild a war-torn world system (i.e., the United Nations and the Bretton Woods system). The United States inhabited a position of leadership in the world system, and it was the American model of political economy that informed the institutions and policies that would come to regulate and structure the world system. The postwar era was a unipolar world dominated by the United States, and it was the New Deal liberalism of mid-twentieth-century America that informed the structuring of the global economy, the global institutions mediating interstate relations, and the global political culture of the world system.

The New Deal liberalism of mid-twentieth-century America was informed by Keynesian theory. Keynesianism was organized around a technocratic model of political economy committed to stable economic growth, full employment, and widely shared prosperity. The focus of Keynesian political economy was to ensure social stability by curbing the excesses of the free market and to ensure that the economic collapse of the Great Depression and the rise of fascist politics were not repeated. In Polanyi's terminology, the Keynesianism of the mid-twentieth century worked to re-embed markets and market relations within cultural and social norms to ensure social stability. And, for all intents and purposes, it was successful. The two decades following the war were a time of rapid economic growth marking entry into an A-phase in the world system.

The economic crisis of the 1970s marked the collapse of Keynesian political economy and the postwar formation, and it marked the beginning of a dramatic shift toward the neoclassical model of political economy developed at the Chicago school. The United States remained the global hegemon, and it used its position of leadership in the world system to encourage the dis-embedding of markets and market relations through free trade policies, financial deregulation, and so on. Neoclassical economic theory achieved hegemonic dominance in the wake of the economic crisis of the 1970s, and the economic policies informed by neoclassical theory successfully restored capital accumulation and stability in a period of secular stagnation.

The economic crisis of the 1970s marked the transition of the world system from an expansionary A-phase to a contractionary B-phase. The slow growth and polarization of this B-phase was temporarily masked by a flood of cheap consumer goods from semi- and peripheral nations and increasing access to credit made possible by financial innovation, but the financial crises of 2001 and 2008 have laid bare ongoing trends toward slow growth, systemic fragility, widening disparity, and the erosion of opportunity. Wallerstein notes:

> What has sustained the accumulation of capital since the 1970's has been a turn from seeking profits through productive efficiency to seeking them through financial manipulations, more correctly called speculation. The key mechanism has been the fostering of consumption via indebtedness. This has happened in every Kondratieff B-phase; the difference this time has been the scale. After the biggest A-phase expansion in history, there has followed the biggest speculative mania. Bubbles moved through the whole world-system—from the national debts of the Third World and socialist bloc in the 1970's to the junk bonds of large corporations in the 1980's, the consumer indebtedness of the 1990's and the US government indebtedness of the Bush era. The system has gone from bubble to bubble, and is currently trying to inflate yet another. . . . The downturn into which the world has fallen will continue now for some time, and will be quite deep. . . . As this happens, the main concern of every government in the world will be to avert uprisings of unemployed workers and the middle strata whose savings and pensions are disappearing. (Wallerstein, 2010, p. 137)

The world system is entering a period of economic crisis the length and ultimate outcome of which can only be speculated. The emergent economic crisis of this historical moment constitutes a moment of possibility in which the dominant economic ideology of the contemporary formation (neoclassical economics) is showing signs of intellectual exhaustion and the doxa regulating the world system are becoming increasingly contested.

Core nations caught in a low growth trap have yet to fully recover from the financial crisis that began in 2008, and the economic collapse associated with the COVID-19 pandemic marked the official end of this period of uneven and unequal recovery. The erosion of American hegemony has opened up space for other nations in the core and semi-periphery to challenge the doxa regulating the world system, and the weakness of the U.S. dollar as a reserve currency in the aftermath of the novel coronavirus foreshadows a coming fragmentation of the international monetary system (El-Erian, 2020). The world system is entering a period of global instability in which a weakened hegemon is competing with other core nations in the European Union (EU) and semi-peripheral nations, such as China and Russia, to construct a new framework to regulate the global economy, interstate system, and geoculture. We are collectively entering a period of instability and potentiality the outcome of which will be decided by political movements operating at global and national scales.

It would be a mistake, however, for those with left-leaning politics to assume this moment of political potentiality will inevitably lead to progressive change and just outcomes. If we apply Polanyi's model of dis-embedding and re-embedding to understand this historical moment then there would appear to be three probable trajectories out of the emergent crisis. The first path is that ongoing attempts by the global hegemon to rehabilitate the existing formation and maintain the supremacy of the free market could prove successful. For example, trade war policies introduced by Trump could prove to be successful in rehabilitating the post-1970s formation by forcing core nations in the EU and China to further embrace free-market policies and (potentially) open up new ways to restore growth and capital accumulation. The second path out of the emergent crisis is that political moves to re-embed the free market within cultural and social norms could be achieved either through policies analogous to the Keynesianism of the mid-twentieth century or through more radical articulations that are necessarily indeterminate. The growing prominence of neo-Keynesian, heterodox economics in core nations is evidence of intellectual and political moves in that direction, and ongoing debates within the Left is evidence of the weakening of the neoclassical hegemonic order. Indeed, center-left political parties across the global North are now torn by a conflict between party elites seeking to protect the free-market policies of the 1990s and early 2000s from the social democratic and socialist policies being championed by their left flank. A third (and more troubling) path out of the emergent crisis involves moves to re-embed the free market within cultural and social norms through what Polanyi termed the fascist solution. The fascist solution "can be described as a reform of market economy achieved at the price of the extirpation of all democratic institutions, both in the industrial and in the political realm" (Polanyi, 1944, p. 237). Fascists of the twentieth century sought to embed markets and market relations into the social and cultural norms of nationalism and a state religion. The proliferation of far-right populist parties across the global North and South provides ample evidence that the fascist solution is a politics already at work in the world system and that it is gaining ground.

Focusing now specifically on the United States, the neoclassical political economy of the post-1970s social formation fundamentally restructured the American economy. Neoclassicals implemented policies that successfully restored capital accumulation and relative stability in a period of low growth and accelerating global competition. However, like the Keynesian economic model that proceeded it, the neoclassical economic model has become a victim of its own success. The Bretton Woods system and Fordist policies of the postwar period embedded markets and market relations within the normative regulation of the social and cultural spheres and established an infrastructure for rapid economic growth and broadly shared prosperity. The neoclassical counter-revolution of the 1970s and 1980s worked to dis-embed markets and market relations from the social and cultural spheres and has fostered the emergence of a New Gilded Age of growing inequality, precarity, economic antagonism, and plutocratic politics (Bartels, 2016). This transition was not the product of iron laws of economics but policies informed by the neoclassical orthodoxy that rose to hegemonic dominance in the wake of the economic crisis of the 1970s. The free-market policies of the post-1970s era and the upward distribution of wealth it has engendered was, in Polanyian terms, *planned*, and the social costs of those policies have become clearly visible in the aftermath of the financial crisis of 2008 and the economic collapse associated with the COVID-19 pandemic.

The American economic recovery from the 2008 global recession was the longest on record, but the damage inflicted on the American economy by the crash remains clearly visible. The recovery was marked by uneven growth and persistently low inflation befuddling the Federal Reserve Bank as well as central banks around the world (Vollgraaff et al., 2019). While the wealthiest households in the United States were able to recoup the wealth they lost in the crash, households in the middle and the bottom of the distribution have yet to fully recover (Dettling et al., 2018). The unemployment rate reached its lowest point in decades in 2019, yet wage inflation remains muted due to persistent underemployment and slack in the labor market (Blanchflower, 2019; Bracha & Burke, 2017; Duca, 2016). Despite breaking records, the slow and uneven recovery from the crash of 2008 is evidence of the growing systemic fragility of an increasingly polarized and unequal economy dependent on financial speculation to drive growth (Amountzias, 2019; Gu et al., 2019; Kirschenmann et al., 2016; Mishel et al., 2015).

The upward distribution of wealth, growing precarity, and economic dislocation that the neoclassical policies of the post-1970s formation have produced has, in turn, fueled antagonisms in the political sphere. The American economy is, in the words of Joseph Stiglitz (2018), "rigged," and it is a perspective that is widely shared by the American public and has been a driving force behind much of the political turmoil of recent years (Fingerhut, 2016; Parker et al., 2019). The economic dislocation produced by the free-market policies of neoclassical political economy has fueled a politics of nationalism, xenophobic rhetoric, and resentment that help to explain the rise of right-wing populism in the United States.

The United States increasingly resembles, from an economic point of view, a failed state. The economic infrastructure constructed during the postwar boom, including everything from roads to communication infrastructure, is now in a state of disrepair and is rapidly deteriorating (American Society of Civil Engineers, 2019). The United States is seeing a historic reversal in life expectancy that is largely being driven by so-called deaths of despair, with the greatest increase in mortality being in Ohio Valley Rust Belt states (Woolf & Schoomaker, 2019). The economic domain of this historic moment is defined by economic polarization in which the elite and affluent prosper while the middle classes are increasingly hollowed out and a growing subaltern population experiences ever greater levels of precarity. All of these trends have become even more visible and are accelerating in the aftermath of the COVID-19 pandemic. Unemployment has grown to historic levels while the financial sector quickly recovered from its lows in March of 2020. Indeed, the rapid recovery of financial markets from their lows in March 2020 was driven by technology companies that employ relatively few workers leading one investment group to proclaim a "bear market for humans" (Ponczek, 2020).

Taken together, the evidence points toward a clear conclusion. The United States is entering into a period of economic crisis the seeds of which were planted by the neoclassical counter-revolution in the 1970s. This crisis is not the product of "iron laws" but of a policy regime informed by an ideological discourse that rose to hegemonic dominance in the economic domain from the 1980s forward. It is a policy regime that has advanced economic dislocation, polarized wealth and income, slowed mobility, and fueled precarity and economic antagonisms. It is a crisis that provides the perfect economic seedbed for radical right-wing politics to take root, for a politics that grounds calls to re-embed markets into social norms informed by nationalism, xenophobia, and antidemocratic politics. It opens the door to the fascist solution.

CODA

I endeavored in this chapter to tell a better story about this historical moment of emergent conjunctural crisis through an economic analysis focused on the rise to hegemonic dominance of neoclassical economic theory, the economic policies informed by neoclassical theory, and the emergent economic crisis these policies have engendered. The narrow focus on the emergent hegemonic crisis of neoclassical economic theory informed the historical approach, theoretical framework, and evidence used in the analysis. However, the narrow focus of the analysis bracketed out important stories that are often absent in the narratives of economic history.

Historical narratives of the Bretton Woods system and the post–World War II economic boom too often romanticize this historical era and are often guilty of serious omissions, an observation that very much applies to the one presented in this chapter. The postwar boom was an era of dramatic economic growth and widely shared prosperity (Stone et al., 2019), but it was also an era of exclusion that denied not simply economic but political rights to subaltern classes. African Americans in the Jim Crow South were mired in poverty and political exclusion enforced through a system of white terrorism. Nationally, African American, Hispanic, and Asian populations faced an array of federal, state, and local laws denying them access to the avenues of upward mobility and intergenerational wealth, such as homeownership (Rothstein, 2017). Women were entering the labor market in greater numbers, but they were entering a two-tier economy of career and wage inequality. American Indians faced the same exclusionary legal structure as African Americans and Hispanics but were also often faced with the no-win situation of fighting to maintain the culture and languages of their peoples and live in the isolating poverty of the reservation system or be steered toward low-wage occupations through federal assimilation policies. And, the economic status (and often physical safety) of members of the LGBTQ community could be threatened by exposure of their sexuality. The postwar era may have been a period of widely shared prosperity on the sliding scale of history, but an honest accounting of this period would demonstrate that it was also a period exclusion, exploitation, and inequality that dis-proportionately benefited white, heterosexual males.

It is not surprising then that this era of economic growth and prosperity, often wrapped in the triumph of Western democratic values in the fight against fascism, became the terrain upon which marginalized groups would challenge economic inequality and political exclusion. The long Civil Rights Movement accelerated after World War II as African Americans challenged Jim Crow, school segregation, job discrimination, and housing segregation. The Chicano Movement fought back against exclusionary policies, school and housing inequality, and the abuses of the agricultural industry. The Feminist Movement challenged patriarchal norms that denied women economic opportunity, political power, and reproductive rights. The American Indian Movement fought back against their economic, political, and cultural exclusion and challenged the federal assimilation policies seeking to destroy their cultures. And the Gay Rights Movement began to push back against their marginalization in a culture of heteronormativity and economic exclusion.

The postwar era was, indeed, a period of rapid economic growth and widely shared prosperity. African American men, for example, made solid wage gains in the postwar era (Bayer & Charles, 2018). However, it was also a period of profound economic and political inequality structured along the lines of race, ethnicity, gender, and sexuality. These marginalized groups were by no means passive victims but engaged in political activism to achieve greater economic and political rights and spawned movements that persist to this day. Marginalized groups laid claim to the triumphant Americanism of the postwar era to fight for equal citizenship and prosperity, but the liberatory movements of the 1950s, 1960s, and 1970s were met with a reactionary movement that sought to maintain and restore traditional hierarchies: the modern conservative movement. A new conservative movement was born in the postwar era that would not simply champion the neoclassical counter-revolution against Keynesian political economy but would give rise to a dangerous politics driving an emergent political crisis. Telling a better story about the *emergent crisis of the present* will require an analysis of the political crisis that, in part, defines this historical moment.

What will become clear is that the rise of right-wing populism in the United States cannot be reduced to an economic explanation alone (Cramer, 2016; Hochschild, 2016; Oberhauser et al., 2019). The politics of resentment fueling the rise of right-wing populism in the United States is bound up with a white identity politics, a "racialized economics" (Sides et al., 2018, p. 8) in which race forms "the terrain in which class anxieties generated by a crisis of hegemony are worked through" (Camp, 2016, p. 148). The rise of right-wing populism in the United States is not simply the product of economic crisis and growing economic antagonisms but is being fueled by a politics of resentment against a culturally and geographically distant "other" and the cosmopolitan elites who (supposedly) put the welfare of racial and ethnic minorities ahead of those of "real" Americans in the so-called heartland.

The emergent crisis of the present is, in part, *constituted by* but *cannot be reduced to* an emergent economic crisis. There is simply more to the story. Telling a better story about the rise of right-wing populism will require, therefore, that we attend to the political transformations in the United States.

Chapter 3

Political Crisis

Telling a better story about this historical moment requires an analysis of the right-wing populism making political gains across the globe, but (as I discussed in the introduction) the object of inquiry for such a political analysis is by no means self-evident. Framing the radical right politics of this historical moment as "populism" is quite common in contemporary popular political discourse, and it is the frequency with which this framing is employed that led me to take it up as an object of inquiry. However, the issue with the framing of radical right politics as being populist is that the term "populism" is never adequately defined nor is it acknowledged how the use of this particular framing in popular culture is constitutive of its discursive and social construction.

Populism invokes a politics of the common people or, at least, a politics directed toward the interests of the common people. Its invocation should raise important questions that all too frequently are never asked. Who are the common people? And, conversely, who are not counted to be among them? How is it that right-wing populist movements find their avatars among economic and political elites? Or, how is it that policies pursued by the so-called populist leaders serve the interests of elites at the expense of the less privileged groups in whose name the policies are justified? Telling a better story about the radical right politics of this historical moment requires an unpacking of the populist component of the right-wing populism frame.

The story that emerges from the political analysis detailed in this chapter is a disturbing one with dangerous parallels to the history of the interwar period, a re-framing of right-wing populism that I do not employ lightly. To assert that contemporary trends in the United States and beyond parallel the history of the 1930s is to summon the specter of fascism. Invoking the concept of fascism in political analysis invites charges of hyperbole or, more distressingly, charges of minimizing the horrors of the industrialized genocide perpetrated in Nazi death camps.

There is, of course, a real danger in using the term fascism too loosely. A term that can mean anything has no meaning at all. However, enforcing a strict taboo around the term is dangerous and can only empower the radical right. It disallows the posing of important questions that societies must ask of themselves. Is it, for example, appropriate to label the extrajudicial facilities along America's southern border holding migrant families seeking asylum protections concentration camps? Is it fascist politics when the leader of a republic frequently describes news media as being the enemy of the people? Is it hyperbolic to describe the arrest of protesters by masked federal agents without identifying badges and driving unmarked civilian vehicles as being fascist?

Enforcing a strict taboo around the use of fascism in political analysis contributes to the impoverished manner in which the fascism of the interwar period is discussed in popular political culture. The impoverished story about the rise of twentieth-century fascism is one that involves the rapid seizing of power by charismatic leaders who immediately set about making war and committing genocide. It presents the rise of fascism as an aberration, shock, or sudden break down of the liberal democratic order.

In reality, the rise of twentieth-century fascism was a long process involving the development of an ideological discourse around which individuals and groups could construct political identities, the building of institutions and party organizations, and the construction of propaganda apparatuses to build the necessary popular support to seize control of the state. Once in power, fascist leaders employed this political infrastructure to reshape the instruments of the state in a long process of normalization in which war and genocide were not breaks or immediate shocks but a fait accompli. Taking seriously the call to never forget the horrors and genocide perpetrated by twentieth-century fascism requires constant vigilance, introspection, and a willingness to ask if specific trends, events, and persons are similar to or reflective of the fascist politics of the past (Eco, 1997).

In the United States, right-wing populism is a phenomenon bound up with the Republican party. The election of Donald Trump as president on the Republican ticket in 2016 and his seemingly unwavering support among Republican voters is considered a triumph of the nationalist and xenophobic alt-right and evidence of the populist transformation of the Republican party. The right-wing populism of Trump and the alt-right is frequently presented in popular political discourse as being an aberration or rupture in Republican party politics. However, upon closer examination, this narrative quickly breaks down. The populist rejection of a distant cosmopolitan elite, denouncement of multiculturalism and identity politics, and calls for restoring "traditional American values" have been central to the modern conservative movement and the Republican party since the presidency of Richard Nixon.

The crisis of the 1970s discussed in the preceding chapter was not simply an economic crisis. It was a hegemonic crisis of the postwar social formation that created an opening for the modern conservative movement to achieve hegemonic dominance in the political domain and to take up a position of leadership in the post-1970s social formation. The modern conservative movement rose to dominance by constructing: an ideological discourse oriented around an anti-elite politics; a political infrastructure of knowledge-producing institutions to inform policy development and build popular support for conservative policies; a political strategy to mobilize specific voting blocs through implicit and explicit appeals to white, Christian nationalism; and a media infrastructure to popularize the conservative movement and propagate its ideological discourse. In so doing, the modern conservative movement reoriented the American political landscape transforming not just the politics of the Republican party but the politics of the opposing Democratic Party (Mudge, 2018).

I will argue in this chapter that the right-wing populism of the Trump era is not an aberration or break in Republican party politics but is, in large measure, the driving force behind its electoral success over the past fifty years. In what follows, I will trace how intellectual, economic, and political elites developed an ideological discourse, political infrastructure, electoral strategies, and media structure to achieve hegemonic dominance in the post-1970s social formation. I will conclude this chapter by arguing that the right-wing populism of the Republican party is quickly metastasizing into a dangerous politics paralleling those of the fascist political movements of the interwar period and that these metastasizing politics constitutes an emergent political crisis threatening the post-1970s social formation.

REACTIONARY POLITICS OF CONSERVATISM

The historical origins of political conservatism can be traced to elite opposition to the French Revolution and the intellectual work of Edmund Burke, although he never used the term himself. Indeed, the modern convention of conceptualizing the political as a continuum of left and right has its origin in the various responses to the revolutionary period in France. The Latin root of conservative *conservare* means preserve, guard against, or keep intact with the implication that a conservative is one who seeks to preserve traditional social practices and guard against societal change, or at least swift societal change. It is not surprising then that conservatism is often conflated with a crude traditionalism and a reflexive aversion to change. However, this conflation of conservatism and traditionalism is deeply problematic. Put simply, it masks the diversity and complexity of actually existing conservative movements and political parties as well as the propensity of these movements and parties to pursue radical change in the name of conservatism.

The modern American conservative movement emerged in the post–World War II era as a diverse coalition of traditionalists, fundamentalist Christians, libertarians, statists, and nationalists with considerable overlap among these groups that defy simple conceptualizations of each category. The unification of this diverse and contradictory coalition into a coherent political movement is commonly attributed to the "fusionism" of William F. Buckley Jr. and early conservative media in the 1950s and 1960s that successfully organized these groups around a coherent set of policies associated with "free-market" economics, anti-communism, and traditional social values. There is, of course, a grain of truth to this origin story. However, to understand the unifying forces animating the modern conservative movement and their political significance in this historical moment, one must look beneath the surface of these historically and contextually specific policies.

Corey Robin (2011, p. 7) argues that conservatism is, at its core, a reactionary politics organized around a collective "animus against the agency of the subordinate classes." Conservatism is a reactionary politics that continuously recalibrates itself to either eclipse the democratic challenges from subaltern classes that threaten the private exercise of power in the domestic, economic, and political realms or to recover power and privilege lost in previous political struggle. As such, conservatism is necessarily concerned with and attuned to societal change both actual and potential. Drawing upon the work of Karl Mannheim, Robin argues:

> Conservatism "becomes conscious and reflective when other ways of life and thought appear on the scene, against which it is compelled to take up arms in ideological struggle." Where the traditionalist can take the objects of desire for granted—he can enjoy them as if they are at hand because they are at hand—the conservative cannot. He seeks to enjoy them precisely as they are being—or have been—taken away. If he hopes to enjoy them again, he must contest their divestment in the public realm. He must speak of them in a language that is politically serviceable and intelligible. But as soon as those objects enter the medium of political speech, they cease to be items of lived experience and become incidents of an ideology. They get wrapped in a narrative of loss—in which the revolutionary or reformist plays a necessary part—and presented in a program of recovery. (Robin, 2011, p. 23)

Conservatism is, in Robin's analysis, a reactionary politics oriented around an ideological narrative of loss and restoration that frames the political as an arena of existential conflict, and it is this framing that informs the political programs pursued by conservatives and conservative movements.

What I find most intriguing about Robin's analysis of conservatism is his seemingly paradoxical assertion that conservatism is not simply reactionary but is a form of counter-revolutionary practice that is necessarily radicalizing.

> [Conservatism does not oppose] change in the abstract. No conservative opposes change as such or defends order as such. The conservative defends particular orders—hierarchical, often private regimes of rule—on the assumption, in part, that hierarchy is order. . . . In defending such orders, moreover, the conservative invariably launches himself on a program of reaction and counter-revolution, often requiring an overhaul of the very regime he is defending. . . . To preserve the regime, the conservative must reconstruct the regime. . . . [O]ften it can require the conservative to take the most radical measures on the regime's behalf. (Robin, 2011, pp. 24–25)

Conservatism is animated by the perceived loss of power to the democratic challenges of subaltern classes and, as such, sees itself locked in existential conflict that necessitates making war on the society it wishes to defend. To preserve a regime of power, the regime must be continuously transformed to meet new threats as they emerge. Conservatism is not simply reactionary; it is radicalizing. However, it is a politics that must not be mistaken for an un-thinking, atheoretical reflex.

Robin makes a convincing case that conservatism must be understood as an idea-driven praxis oriented around the generative exercise of power. Conservatism "begins from a position of principle—that some are fit, and thus ought, to rule others—and then recalibrates that principle in light of a democratic challenge from below" (Robin, 2011, p. 18). The hierarchies defended by conservatives are not a function of title or inherited privilege but are a mode of power that must be won or seized in existential conflict with subaltern classes seeking to challenge the hierarchical ordering of society. Conservatism valorizes the archetype of the warrior not in a literal sense (although militarism remains a central feature of American conservatism) but in the sense of achieving power in an economic war of all against all.

> The great men of money are not born with privilege or right; they seize it for themselves, without let or permission. . . . The primal act of transgression—requiring daring, vision, and an aptitude for violence and violation—is what makes the capitalist a warrior, entitling him not only to great wealth but also, ultimately, to command. For that is what the capitalist is: not a Midas of riches but a ruler of men. A title to property is a license to dispose, and if a man has

the title to another's labor, he has a license to dispose of it—to dispose, that is,
of the body in motion—as he sees fit. (Robin, 2011, p. 36)

The economic sphere of capitalist markets constitutes the proving ground
upon which power and privilege are to be won and upon which a "natural"
hierarchy is continually constructed and reconstructed. Power relations
are not fixed but are fluid and contested. The hierarchical ordering of
society that conservatism seeks to defend is not fixed by tradition but is
conceptualized as a field of competition in which the positionality of the
dominant and the dominated are determined on the field of social Darwinian
struggle.

The animating force of modern conservatism is opposition to the
democratic challenge of subaltern classes seeking greater political agency
and a more socially just society. Conservative movements conceptualize the
political as a field of existential conflict over the loss of power and privilege
(both actual and perceived) and the fight for its restoration, not as an exact
replication of a preexisting social formation but in response to the historical
conditions from which conservative movements emerge and in which they
operate. It is a politics that frames the political field in a binary logic of
loss and restoration that can justify radical transformation in the name of
preservation and tradition. Conservatism must be understood, somewhat
counter-intuitively, as a counter-revolutionary politics that is necessarily
radicalizing and that can destabilize the social formation that it intends to
either defend or transform.

The early conservatives of the eighteenth century were not motivated by
a quaint sentimentality for pre-revolutionary France. Theirs was a counter-
revolutionary project defined by its opposition to the exercise of political
agency of subaltern classes during the revolutionary period, and their counter-
revolutionary work contributed to the rise of Napoleon Bonaparte and the
cyclical tragedy of nineteenth-century France just as much as Robespierre
and the bloodsport of the scaffold. In a similar vein, the modern American
conservative movement that emerged during the post–World War II era was/
is not motivated by sentimentality for an imagined Jeffersonian ideal. It is a
reactionary, counter-revolutionary movement that defined itself in opposition
to the democratic challenge of the subaltern social movements of the mid-
twentieth century seeking to advance the political agency of racial and ethnic
minorities, labor, indigenous nations, women, and the LGBTQ community.
American conservatism is a reactionary politics that frames the political in
the binary logic of loss and restoration that, in turn, frames the political field
in terms of existential conflict and the fight to continuously (re)construct
"natural" hierarchies through the generative exercise of power. And, as
with post-revolutionary France, the political projects pursued by the modern

conservative movement are destabilizing and delegitimizing the American republic and are contributing to the rise of illiberal, authoritarian politics.

Conservatism does not seek to preserve or conserve the traditions of a previous historical formation. Conservatism is a reactionary, counter-revolutionary politics that seeks to direct the course of societal change to maintain "private regimes of power—even at the cost of the strength of the state" (Robin, 2011, p. 15). Conservatism is animated by an ideological discourse of loss and restoration and a social Darwinian logics that justify radical projects that seek not stability and preservation but radical transformation to maintain and restore hierarchical social relations.

The political analysis of the modern American conservative movement that follows will take up this conceptualization of conservatism. Accordingly, the analytic focus will not be the historically and contextually specific policies advanced by American conservatism. The focus will be the animating forces and political projects that have propelled the conservative movement to hegemonic dominance in the late twentieth century and the radicalism of this reactionary, counter-revolutionary politics. In what follows, I will demonstrate that the rise of authoritarianism in the conservative movement and the Republican party is not an aberration but a necessary feature of the forces animating the movement and unifying the contradictory groups within the conservative coalition; authoritarianism is not a bug but a feature.

THE NEW RADICALS

George Nash (1976, p. xiii) began his history of the modern conservative movement by stating that "[i]n 1945 no articulate, coordinated, self-consciously conservative intellectual force existed in the United States." The New Deal response to the Great Depression of the 1930s and the prosperity of the postwar era seemingly solidified the dominance of American progressive liberalism as it discredited the laissez-faire liberalism of the nineteenth century defended by conservatives before the war. However, Nash notes that the decade following the war saw the emergence of an inchoate and contradictory new conservative movement made up of three distinct intellectual traditions.

The first intellectual tradition Nash identified is a group of economists that featured prominently in the preceding chapter and will be discussed again in chapter 5: the "classical liberals" or "libertarians." The neoclassical revolt against Keynesianism discussed in chapter 2 was not simply a dispute over economic theory and policy but involved a political struggle over the postwar social formation in toto. The neoclassical theory that took root in the Chicago School of Economics sought to challenge the postwar formation and drew its inspiration from the Austrian School of Economics and the work of Ludwig von Mises.

Writing during the dark days of World War II, Mises argued that the fascism he was forced to flee in 1940 shared a common lineage with Soviet Communism and American New Deal Liberalism, and that all three systems would lead to similar ends. He described this common lineage as a "trend toward government control of business" (Mises, 1944, p. 6). This trend toward intervening in markets was, in Mises' telling, not an altruistic attempt to advance the interests of the public but a consolidation of power in the state that undermined the possibility of human liberty, what he termed etatism.

> Etatism assigns to the state the task of guiding the citizens and of holding them in tutelage. It aims at restricting the individual's freedom to act. It seeks to mold his destiny and to vest all initiative in the government alone. . . . Etatism appears in two forms: socialism and interventionism. Both have in common the goal of subordinating the individual unconditionally to the state, the social apparatus of compulsion and coercion. (Mises, 1944, p. 44)

According to Mises, the state may be a necessary evil, but it is paramount to restrain the intrusion of the state into the economic domain no matter how noble its justification, because it *a priori* involves the centralization of power in the state and the subordination of citizens whose decision-making is eclipsed. In the name of equality and justice, state interventions in the marketplace create new hierarchies within a centralized state more pernicious than the hierarchical organization of the marketplace. It is an economic model of liberty that establishes freedom as being free to choose in a marketplace. Mises argued that technocratic management of the economic sphere (Keynesianism), centralized state planning (Communism), and the subordination of economic production to nationalist goals (Fascism) all fall under the same category of *collectivism* and all lead to a form of tyranny threatening the foundations of Western civilization.

It was a student of Mises, Frederick Hayek, who popularized this binary logic of collectivism versus liberty in *The Road to Serfdom* (Hayek, 1956) and who brought his ideas to the University of Chicago. The political theory that ultimately took root in the Chicago School of Economics framed human liberty as economic liberty realized in a marketplace of competition and consumer choice and framed attempts to intervene in the name of justice as thinly veiled tyranny (M. Friedman, 1962). Hierarchy produced through the Darwinian struggle of the competitive marketplace is a reflection of talent and merit and is, therefore, legitimate. Hierarchy achieved through the machinations of the state intervene in competition and remove consumer choice and are, therefore, illegitimate. Interventions on behalf of the downtrodden constitute the road to tyranny and totalitarianism and inevitably lead to conflict.

Thus, in an era of optimism and prosperity, this group of academic economists viewed the postwar social formation as a society in slow motion civilizational crisis. Their view of the postwar Keynesian economic boom and Fordism was as a period of advancing tyranny just as dangerous as fascism and Stalin's Soviet Union. They understood the era as a period of political conflict between the technocratic elites and intellectual classes working through the state to achieve their capricious aims and a minority of insurgent intellectuals seeking to restore economic-political liberty and the crumbling foundations of Western civilization.

The second intellectual tradition Nash identified is the "traditionalists." The traditionalists attributed the disasters of the mid-twentieth century not to state interventions into the economic sphere but the emergence of a rootless mass society that had replaced objective truth with relativism and materialism. The traditionalists decried the collapse of traditional Western values that had, in their telling, created a moral vacuum that opened a space for fascism, totalitarianism, and world conflict to emerge.

The spirit of the traditionalists is perhaps best captured by the cultural criticism of noted conservative and University of Chicago English professor Richard Weaver (1948). His book *Ideas Have Consequences* offered a stark warning that the postwar era was a period of civilizational collapse and that the root cause for the crisis of the West lay in the transformation of its intellectual culture in the nineteenth and early twentieth centuries, or what he termed the big ideas of the age. Two ideas stood out for Weaver.

First, Weaver argued that the "positivism" of modern scientific and social scientific inquiry had displaced transcendental, objective truths leaving Western societies with a rootless relativism and materialism that made the butchery and global conflict of World War II a fait accompli. Second, Weaver pointed toward the emergence of a politics of equality as unleashing political forces that have upturned the natural order of societies and that fuel a politics of conflict and envy.

> Equality is a disorganizing concept in so far as human relationships mean order. It is order without a design; it attempts a meaningless and profitless regimentation of what has been ordered from time immemorial by the scheme of things. . . . The rule is that each shall act where he is strong; the assignment of identical roles produces first confusion and then alienation, as we have increasing opportunity to observe. . . . It will be found as a general rule that those parts of the world which have talked least of equality have in the solid fact of their social life exhibited the greatest fraternity. Such was true of feudal Europe before people succumbed to various forms of the proposal that every man

should be king. . . . In the present world there is little of trust and less of loyalty. People do not know what to expect of one another. Leaders will not lead, and servants will not serve. (Weaver, 1948, pp. 42–43)

Weaver argued that restoration of a collapsing Western culture can only be achieved by replacing materialism and relativism for objective truths found in the Christian faith and by replacing a politics of equality for the nobility of a democratic elite and natural hierarchy, a model which he located in the Southern feudalism of the Antebellum South (Weaver, 1968).

The traditionalists, such as Weaver, longed for an idealized past rooted in natural hierarchies and Christian orthodoxy. It was an intellectual tradition that rejected modern science and social sciences as a source of knowledge arguing instead for a reliance on transcendence and faith as the organizing principles of society. It was inward-facing, anti-intellectual, antidemocratic, and suspicious of global engagements.

The third intellectual movement Nash identified was made up of a group of former left-wing radicals and Trotskyites who had become stridently anti-communist. Prominent conservative thinkers, such as Irving Kristol and James Burnham, argued that the battle to protect Western civilization from the totalitarian threat did not end with the defeat of fascism but continued on in the Cold War struggle against the Soviet Union and international communism. For the anti-communists, the threat to the United States was two-fold. First, the internationalism of Soviet Russia threatened the nations of the world and, ultimately, the dominant position of the United States in the postwar era. Second, the Red Scare and the McCarthy witch hunt had convinced this group of intellectuals that communists and those sympathetic to communist ideology were common among members of the federal bureaucracy, universities, and the cultural elite.

Burnham argued that the United States was locked in existential conflict with the international communism of the Soviet Union and that the fate of Western civilization would be determined by the outcome of this conflict. As such, the postwar policy of containment was, in the view of anti-communists, an abdication and surrender of our civilization.

Western Civilization has reached the stage in its development that calls for the creation of its Universal Empire. The technological and institutional character of Western Civilization is such that a Universal Empire of Western civilization would necessarily be at the same time a World Empire. In the world there are only two power centers adequate to make a serious attempt to meet this challenge. The simultaneous existence of these two centers, and only these two, introduces into world political relationships an intolerable disequilibrium. . . . For this reason, the United States, crude, awkward, semi-barbarian, nevertheless enters this irreconcilable conflict as the representative of Western culture. The other center, though it has already subdued great areas and populations of the West, and though it has adapted for its own use many technological organization devices of the West, is alien to the West in origin and fundamental nature. (Burnham, 1947, pp. 134–135)

For the anti-communists, the United States must overcome its hesitancy, what Burnham calls its "immaturity," and become a global empire that ensures the survival of Western culture. The anti-communists framed the postwar consensus of containing the spread of communism beyond the Eastern Bloc as a hesitancy born of liberal sympathies to the communist cause. In Burnham's telling, the postwar political leaders came of age under New Deal liberalism and were staunchly anti-fascist, but they were educated by left-leaning intellectuals who subtly influenced their perception of communism as kindred spirits.

The leading carriers of this ideology are men who were born between 1900 and 1914—the generation and in many cases the one-time colleagues of Alger Hiss. . . . The depression left them disillusioned with traditional American capitalism. "Anti-fascism" became the core of their political being, a passion as well as an intellectual attitude. In part, the anti-fascism was a native product of "liberalism" (in the American populist sense) modified by the influence of Marx—touched writers like Vernon Parrington, John Dewey and the early Charles Beard. In part, though most of them did not realize this, the specific content of their anti—fascism was moulded by communist pressures. (Burnham, 1953, pp. 204–205)

Consciously or unconsciously, the liberal elites of the postwar era were failing to meet the challenge of communism, an abdication amounting to "suicide" (Burnham, 1964).

The anti-communists argued that Western democracy and communism were incompatible and cannot coexist. The red menace was both global and national in scope and must be challenged in both arenas. The anti-communists were, therefore, outward-facing advocating for aggressive state action, foreign policy, and military action to ensure the survival of Western culture.

According to Nash, there emerged in the first decade after the war a nascent conservative movement made up of three intellectual traditions that, at first glance, would not seem to be very compatible. The "classical liberals" were cosmopolitan, scholarly, and empirical; more focused on economic issues than cultural ones; and driven by a desire to limit the size and scope of government (more on that in chapter 5). The "traditionalists" were nationalists, anti-scientific, focused on cultural issues, and, while rhetorically suspicious of government, supportive of governmental action that furthered their interests. And, the "anti-communists" were globalists that were primarily focused on the preservation of Western political and intellectual culture and that advocated for a strong, activist state to achieve their goals.

However, there was a shared set of commonalities among these intellectual traditions with which to organize a coherent political ideology and practice. All three traditions believed that theirs was a minority voice in an era dominated by the New Deal progressive liberalism of a technocratic, intellectual elite in government, the academy, and media. They believed that these liberal elites work toward the same ends of equality and justice as do communists and socialists. Accordingly, they believed that the political adversary of conservatism was a unified left that differed only in method but that all fall under the same organizing category: collectivism. Moreover, despite living in an era of postwar optimism and growing prosperity, they believed that the dominance of collectivism was leading the United States down the road to tyranny and Western culture to the brink of collapse. And, finally, all three traditions sought to restore traditional practices and "natural" hierarchies in the name of advancing individual liberties.

Despite the differences among the intellectual traditions of the nascent conservative movement, they shared a common set of beliefs that could form the basis for a shared political ideology and practice; however, these early conservatives faced two major challenges. First, these were elite intellectual projects cloaked in the anti-elite language of populism. To be politically successful, the conservative movement would need to develop a coherent message that squared this especially problematic circle. Second, by their own admission, their ideas did not enjoy popular support. Modern conservatism required not only coherent messaging but also a means of popularizing conservative ideas.

The person for the task was William F. Buckley Jr. Buckley was, in many ways, the embodiment of the three intellectual traditions of the early conservative movement. He was born into a world of privilege and spent many of his childhood years overseas receiving a cosmopolitan education that, in part, explains his unusual and widely noted accent. Buckley was a devout Catholic and traditionalist who attended Yale University, and he served a brief stint in the Central Intelligence Agency, working under E. Howard Hunt who would later play a key role in the Watergate Affair that toppled President Richard Nixon. Buckley was a free marketeer, a traditionalist, and an anti-communist.

Buckley (2002) made a name for himself in 1951 with the publication of *God and Man at Yale*. In it, Buckley developed an ideological discourse that would come to define the modern conservative movement and its challenge to the postwar social formation. Buckley railed against the Keynesianism, collectivism, and secular ideologies propagated by professors during his time at Yale and argued for the restoration of the individualism, free markets, and Christian values that he argued formed the foundation for the American republic and Western culture. In so doing, Buckley constructed an ideological discourse of cultural loss and restoration that positioned conservatism as a radical, anti-elite politics challenging the dominance of a collectivist elite.

> For where public criticism is vocal and intense, it is because *the minority has offended the majority*. Even discounting the disproportionate addiction of the collectivists to propagandize their doctrines at every opportunity, I am forced to conclude from my experience with the Yale Daily News through several years, and from other evidence also, that at least at this college level, the great transformation has actually taken place. The conservatives, as a minority, are the new radicals. The evidence is overwhelming. (Buckley, 2002, p. 95)

God and Man at Yale argued that the elite universities of the United States had been overrun by collectivist intellectuals propagandizing dangerous liberal ideologies. More importantly, Buckley positioned himself and other conservatives at Yale as both a marginalized minority and as political radicals challenging the intellectual hegemony of the collectivists.

What Buckley was able to accomplish in *God and Man at Yale* is that he constructed a unifying ideological discourse around which the three intellectual traditions of the nascent conservative movement could coalesce. *God and Man at Yale* was a widely read and controversial book that generated a significant amount of press, but it alone would not be sufficient to launch a new conservative movement. A successful conservative movement needed a venue through which to publicize this new conservative discourse and weigh in on the issues of the day.

Four years after the publication of *God and Man at Yale* Buckley partnered with Willi Schlamm to publish a new conservative magazine the *National Review*. In its first issue, Buckley published a mission statement demonstrating that he had both refined the ideological discourse constructed in *God and Man at Yale* and expanded its scope to the broader society.

> [S]ince ideas rule the world, the ideologues, having won over the intellectual class, simply walked in and started to run things. Run just about everything. There never was an age of conformity quite like this one, or a camaraderie quite like the Liberals. . . . Conservatives in this country—at least those who have not made their peace with the New Deal, and there is serious question whether there are others—are non-licensed nonconformists; and this is dangerous business in a Liberal world. . . . Radical conservatives in this country have an interesting

time of it, for when they are not being suppressed or mutilated by the Liberals, they are being ignored or humiliated by a great many of those of the well-fed Right, whose ignorance and amorality have never been exaggerated for the same reason that one cannot exaggerate infinity. (Buckley, 1955)

In Buckley's telling, conservatives were now a marginalized minority suffering under the yoke of an intellectual elite in academia, government, media, and a Republican party establishment that had acquiesced to liberal dominance. Buckley called on conservatives to "rise up" and challenge the liberal elite and to transform the Republican party into an effective opposition movement (Buckley, 1968).

To be conservative in the postwar era was to be an anti-elite radical, a radical populist. For Buckley's new conservative movement:

The danger in America lay not in great concentrations of wealth, but in the growth of a political and cultural elite—a new class, centered in the Northeast—that was more cosmopolitan than patriotic. . . . Articulated during a time of rapid expansion of government and higher education, these themes struck a chord, and conservatism was rebranded as a form of populism.(Gross et al., 2011, p. 334)

Initially, the *National Review* struggled financially. However, over the ensuing years, the *National Review* developed into a free-wheeling and often controversial outlet around which a new conservative movement began to organize. It is difficult to overstate Buckley's influence over the new conservative movement or the significance of the *National Review* (Diamond, 1995, pp. 32–35).

In many ways, the history of the modern conservative movement in the postwar era was bound up with the individuals and public intellectuals associated with and discovered by the *National Review* (Bjerre-Poulsen, 2002; Hart, 2007; Nash, 1976). It became an organizing center around which the intellectuals of a nascent modern conservative movement would coalesce and from which would emerge an ideological discourse to inform a collective identity. What this movement lacked, however, was the means of propagating this discourse in the public sphere and to use it as means to achieve political power.

This new conservative movement began to gain steam throughout the 1960s. Arizona Senator Barry Goldwater became a champion of the movement and employed its ideological discourse in his presidential campaign of 1964 (Perlstein, 2001). Lyndon B. Johnson won the election in a landslide, but Goldwater's presidential campaign was a testament to the growing influence of the new conservative movement within the Republican party. It also demonstrated that for the movement to maintain its momentum it would need to build new institutions to construct and advance conservative policies and political strategies to achieve electoral power.

CONSERVATIVE INSTITUTION BUILDING

An important figure in conservative institution building was future Supreme Court justice Lewis F. Powell. In 1971, Powell composed a memorandum for the U.S. Chamber of Commerce in which he implored business leaders to fund a new generation of intellectuals and institutions to counter the liberal dominance of universities, government, and media. Echoing Buckley, Powell argued that American capitalism was under sustained attack by a new intellectual class that had come to dominate universities, popular media, the administrative state, and federal courts. He called for the nation's business elite to band together in a concerted political effort to push back against this attack.

> Business must learn the lesson, long ago learned by Labor and other self-interest groups. This is the lesson that political power is necessary; that such power must be assiduously cultivated; and that when necessary, it must be used aggressively and with determination—without embarrassment and without the reluctance which has been so characteristic of American business. (Powell, 1971)

Powell's memorandum was a call to arms for corporate America to conduct "guerrilla warfare" against the postwar social formation and the "propaganda" of the liberatory movements threatening the capitalist system.

Powell advocated that the business community take up three primary tasks. First, he argued that business elites must fund and cultivate a new generation of public intellectuals to conduct research that support the aims of the conservative movement. Second, Powell thought conservatives should monitor news media and demand equal time for conservative intellectuals and to create new outlets to publicize conservative ideas. And, third, he argued that long-term success for a conservative movement would require that business leaders fund university programs and centers so that conservative intellectuals could bring balance to academia and to fund programs to monitor secondary school textbooks and introduce curricula to advance conservative ideology.

Powell's call to arms was answered by a group of wealthy industrialists and business leaders, many of whom were heirs to vast fortunes, who developed a new model of weaponized philanthropy to build an institutional structure for the modern conservative movement (Mayer, 2017). Private philanthropies linked to wealthy families, such as the John M. Olin Foundation, the Charles

G. Koch Charitable Foundation, the David H. Koch Foundation, the Scaife Family Charitable Trust, the Adolph Coors Family Foundation, the Richard and Helen DeVos Foundation, and the Lynde and Harry Bradley Foundation, began to use their wealth to fund new institutions to fulfill the tasks Powell identified. They built a constellation of think tanks and research institutions to produce new ideas and develop new conservative intellectuals. They created political advocacy groups to promote conservative policies and to build support for new policies. And, they began to leverage their fortunes to influence university programs and curricula.

Private research institutions, commonly known as think tanks, have grown in number since the 1970s and have been transformed from staid institutions catering to the needs of policymakers to public-facing institutions producing advocacy research and marketing their expertise in the public sphere (Rich, 2004; Medvetz, 2012). Think tanks began in the Progressive era of the early twentieth century. They began as private research institutions dependent on funding from the government and large, private foundations, such as the Russell Sage Foundation and the Ford Foundation. The credibility and funding for these early think tanks were predicated on the production of rigorous, relevant, and non-ideological research that could inform policy decision-making. However, changes in the federal budget and a move by the U.S. Congress in the late 1960s to limit the role of private organizations in policy-making fundamentally changed the landscape in ways that would ultimately undermine Congressional intent.

The *Tax Reform Act of 1969* prohibited private foundations from supporting activities designed to influence policy, a prohibition that made the large foundations who had traditionally funded think tanks withdraw resources for fear of losing their nonprofit status. At the same time, federal research funding began to fall from the Cold War highs of the postwar era. It was these shifts in the landscape that opened the door for the wealthy elites who took up Powell's call to arms to enter. Andrew Rich sums it up this way:

> The most obvious constraints posed by the changes in available support were on the continued success of existing think tanks that depended on foundations and government and on the efforts of entrepreneurs motivated to form think tanks that might require their patronage. The changes had the combined effect of diminishing traditional sources of support for relatively long-established organizations and giving a boost to more ideological, particularly conservative, institutions, like the fledgling Heritage Foundation, that rejected value-free expertise and could appeal to a clear conservative constituency in the business sector. Organizations that were ideological—and particularly conservative—became institutionally advantaged; those that were not were challenged. (Rich, 2004, pp. 63–64)

Smaller family foundations with conservative agendas grew in stature as they were increasingly able to leverage their resources to create a new constellation of ideological think tanks and to transform existing think tanks, such as the American Enterprise Institute, into advocacy organizations marketing expertise, advocacy research, and policy analyses in the public sphere. Conservative think tanks became ideological apparatuses (Pautz, 2011).

The number of think tanks grew from 70 in 1969 to over 300 by the 1990s, and the vast majority of these new think tanks were ideologically conservative (Rich, 2004). Today, there are 1,871 think tanks in the United States (McGann, 2019). While there is no direct, mechanistic relationship between the number of think tanks and policy influence, conservative think tanks utilizing private philanthropic and corporate funding have become highly visible institutions that have become an incubator of public intellectuals and act as a government in waiting for future presidential administrations and congressional staffing.

The corporate elite who created and funded this new constellation of think tanks also channeled resources into political advocacy organizations to promote conservative ideology and policies. Americans for Prosperity is a prominent advocacy organization founded by Charles and David Koch and is funded with corporate money that runs media campaigns on behalf of candidates and politicians and libertarian policies on specific issues, such as health care, taxes, and education (The Center for Media and Democracy, n.d.b). The American Legislative Exchange Council (ALEC) was founded in 1973 by Paul Weyrich of the Heritage Foundation (among others) as a member organization of state legislators that receives funding from private philanthropies and corporations (The Center for Media and Democracy, n.d.a). ALEC creates model legislation that politicians can take back and introduce into their state legislatures to become law, and it has grown into an influential organization that coordinates with the State Policy Network of think tanks to achieve legislative goals. Over ten thousand ALEC bills were introduced into state legislatures across the United States and more than two thousand were ratified into law between 2011 and 2019 (O'Dell & Penzenstadler, 2019). The economic elites of corporate America have succeeded not only in cultivating a new cadre of public intellectuals and exerting influence over media but in contributing directly to the legislative process.

Beyond think tanks and advocacy, wealthy conservative elites have made significant inroads to academia. The John M. Olin Foundation was an early leader in funding academic programs at elite universities. The Olin Foundation funded the creation of so-called "law and economics" programs at the University of Chicago, Stanford University, Harvard University, and Yale University (Philanthropy Roundtable, n.d.). The Olin Foundation also provided the initial funding for the Federalist Society, an organization dedicated to cultivating conservative law students at elite institutions for federal courts and (ultimately) the Supreme Court (Hollis-Brusky, 2015). Charles and David Koch have also funded academic centers, such as the Institute for Humane Studies at George Mason University (The Center for Media and Democracy, n.d.c), and economics programs over which they have curricular and faculty oversight, such as at Florida State University (Pilkington, 2014). As state funding for universities and federal research dollars have trended downward, private philanthropies associated with conservative elites have found an opening to proselytize from the ivory tower.

The Powell memorandum employed Buckley's anti-elite new conservative radicalism in a call to arms for the nation's economic elite to engage in "guerrilla warfare" against the postwar social formation. Despite the high profile of contemporary centrist and nominally liberal philanthropists, such as Bill Gates and George Soros, the majority of economic elites in the United States pursue a conservative ideological agenda through a "stealth politics" that is democratically unaccountable (Page et al., 2018). The wealthiest families in the nation are highly active in the political arena, yet they purposefully remain silent on the issues and agendas they pursue by staying out of the public eye. The organizations and institutions they fund are actively at work in media, government, and the public sphere, but they operate behind the scenes making it difficult for oppositional forces to effectively mobilize. One of the primary reasons for this silence is that "many or most billionaires appear to favor, and to quietly work for, *policies that are opposed by large majorities of Americans*" (Page et al., 2018, p. 132). From tax policy to social security to health care, the majority of Americans want higher taxes on the wealthy to pay for social services, education, and infrastructure (Pew Research Center, 2019; Stokes, 2013), policies wealthy conservative elites oppose.

The stealth politics of the modern conservative movement speaks to the fundamental paradox of Buckley's new radicalism. It is an ideological discourse built around a narrative of anti-elite politics and the restoration of "traditional" American values. However, it is, at its core, an elite political project pursuing an agenda to transfer capital, income, and power to the top of the social pyramid or, to use Burnham's turn of phrase, restore a "natural hierarchy." The stealth politics of conservative elites from the 1970s to today has constructed a vast constellation of research, advocacy, and academic institutions that goes a long way in explaining the rise to dominance of the modern conservative movement, but it is not sufficient. Understanding the rise of the modern conservative movement and the dangerous politics it has unleashed requires an analysis of the political strategies the movement employed to win power at the ballot box.

LONG SOUTHERN STRATEGY

The postwar era witnessed the development of a new ideological discourse among conservative intellectuals and the operationalization of this ideological discourse by economic elites in a period of rapid institution building. However, the elite politics of the era are, while necessary, not sufficient to explain the rise to dominance of the modern conservative movement from the 1970s forward. Political revolutions, or counter-revolutions, require a cultural seedbed in which to take root and political strategies to cultivate political power. For the modern conservative movement, that cultural seedbed was to be found in the American South and the growing suburbs of American cities, especially those in Sun Belt states.

Kevin Kruse (2013) argues that the American South and the growing suburbs of the Sunbelt were sites of political innovation that transformed the modern conservative movement and introduced many of the policies associated with contemporary conservatism. The Dixiecrat revolt of state and local Democrats in 1948 against the growing embrace of civil rights policies by President Harry Truman and the national Democratic Party set the spark to political transformation, but it was the Supreme Court decision in *Brown vs. Board of Education of Topeka, Kansas* in 1954 ordering the desegregation of public schools and the passage of the Voting Rights Act in 1965 that set off a conflagration. A wave of political activism swept the South in the 1950s in defense of hierarchy, white supremacy, and segregation organized around the latest iteration of the "Lost Cause" ideology of the post–Civil War period: states' rights.

In the name of states' rights, southern conservative segregationists advocated for new policies such as tuition vouchers for private schools to maintain school segregation, privatization of public services that were no longer the exclusive domain of whites, and tax cuts that both relieve the burden on "tax payers" and limit the scope of governmental activities that benefit African-Americans. And, perhaps more importantly, they set about framing these policies in a discourse of individual liberty and freedom of choice. A reactionary political culture, a "politics of secession" (K. M. Kruse, 2013), was emerging from the South in the 1950s and 1960s that created an opening for the nascent conservative intellectual movement of the postwar era to enter. What was needed was a political strategy to exploit this opportunity.

The political strategy that was to propel the conservative movement to political dominance was first articulated in the 1960s by Republican wunderkind Kevin P. Phillips (Perlstein, 2008). Phillips rose to prominence in the New York Republican party by engineering electoral success in traditionally Democratic districts in the election of 1966. His insight was that shifting racial and ethnic antagonisms in the Bronx and other traditionally

Democratic districts created an opening for Republican politicians willing to exploit them (Boyd, 1970).

Considered an expert in the "practical politics" of ethnic prejudices and historical migration patterns, Phillips' early success in New York led him to a prominent position in Richard Nixon's 1968 presidential campaign where he became one of the architects of the Southern Strategy. Phillips argued that the racial resentments of the white working class in the American South against the civil rights movement created an opportunity for the Republican party to flip the traditionally Democratic South and establish a new political majority that could hold for a generation or more. He advised Nixon and fellow conservatives to use the coded language of economics, states' rights, traditional values, and education to exploit these antagonisms. Following the election of 1968, Phillips explained the success of the Southern Strategy this way:

> Quite simply, as liberalism metamorphosed from an economic populist stance—supporting farm, highway, health, education and pension expenditures against conservative budget-cutting—into a credo of social engineering, it lost the support of poor whites. Equally important was conservatism's adoption of some economic populism to augment its opposition to Negro-oriented social innovation. The Negro socioeconomic revolution gave conservatism a degree of access to Southern poor white support which it has not enjoyed since the somewhat comparable Reconstruction era. (Phillips, 1969, p. 206)

It was a strategy to tap into the racial antagonisms of the South for electoral advantage with the added bonus of mobilizing the disproportionate concentration of evangelical Christians in Southern states, what was to become a key demographic in the conservative movement.

In an unguarded moment in 1981, Lee Atwater, a member of Ronald Reagan's 1980 presidential campaign, future campaign manager for President George H. W. Bush and future Republican National Chairman, clearly articulated the way in which Phillips' Southern Strategy had become the modus operandi of the conservative movement.

Atwater: As to the whole Southern strategy that Harry Dent and others put together in 1968, opposition to the Voting Rights Act would have been a central part of keeping the South. Now [the new Southern strategy of Ronald Reagan] doesn't have to do that. All you have to do to keep the South is for Reagan to run in place on the issues he's campaigned on since 1964 . . . and that fiscal conservatism, balancing the budget, cut taxes, you know, the whole cluster . . .

Questioner: But the fact is, isn't it, that Reagan does get to the Wallace voter and to the racist side of the Wallace voter by doing away with Legal Services, by cutting down on food stamps . . . ?

Atwater: You start out in 1954 by saying "Nigger, nigger, nigger." By 1968 you can't say "nigger"—that hurts you. So you say stuff like forced busing, states' rights, and all that stuff. You're getting so abstract now [that] you're talking about cutting taxes, and all these things you're talking about are totally economic things and a by-product of them is [that] blacks get hurt worse than whites. And subconsciously maybe that is part of it. I'm not saying that. But I'm saying that if it is getting that abstract, and that coded, that we are doing away with the racial problem one way or the other. You follow me—because obviously sitting around saying, "we want to cut this," is much more abstract than even the busing thing and a hell of a lot more abstract than "Nigger, nigger." (Lamis, 1999, pp. 7–8)

Using the coded language of the Southern Strategy, the conservative movement was able to suture "the interests of hostile working-class whites who were suspicious of civil rights with economic elites who chaffed under the New Deal and Great Society federal government" (Inwood, 2015, p. 414).

The Southern Strategy wrapped a politics of hierarchy, white supremacy, and segregation in an anti-elite populist discourse of economics, tax cuts, consumer choice, and fiscal conservatism. More importantly, the coded language of the Southern Strategy held appeal for suburban whites outside of the South.

The transformation of segregationist rhetoric in the postwar era had led south-ern conservatives to reject the traditional appeals to populism and racism and instead embrace a new, middle-class rhetoric of rights and responsibilities. . . . Removed from their obviously racial origins, segregationist phrases, such as "freedom of choice" or "neighborhood schools," as well as segregationist iden-tities, such as angry taxpayer or concerned parent, could be easily shared by middle-class whites who had no connection to the segregationist past but who gladly took part in crafting the suburban future. (K. M. Kruse, 2013, p. 245)

For Phillips, the secret to politics is to understand who hates who and to understand how to exploit those hatreds. His insight was that the racial antagonisms and political innovations emerging from the South in the 1950s and 1960s could be nationalized by exploiting the racial antagonisms between the predominantly white suburbs and the African American cities through issues such as "busing" (Delmont, 2016).

It was a political strategy that would be employed with great effect by movement conservatives and Republican politicians from the 1980s forward, from Reagan's frequent attacks on "welfare queens" to Trump's invocation to "make America great again." The key innovation was the discursive exchange between the nascent conservative movement of the postwar period and the political innovations taking place in the South that congealed into a coherent political strategy to achieve power through the ballot box. There was an almost seamless exchange between elite actors such as Bill Buckley who publicly defended "state rights" to maintain racial hierarchies and the local political activism taking place throughout the South. The anti-elite political discourse of the modern conservative movement found fertile ground in the South and the suburbs of major cities across the United States in which to take root and from the exchange it gained a new set of policies and strategies to gain political power that would prove especially appealing to evangelical Christians.

EVANGELICAL MOBILIZATION

The standard and somewhat apocryphal story explaining the political mobilization of evangelical Christians, or the Religious Right, begins in the 1970s. It goes like this. Evangelical Christians, embarrassed by the negative publicity associated with the Scopes Monkey Trial, withdrew from the public sphere and remained relatively apolitical through the mid-twentieth century. What began to awaken them from their political slumber was the radicalism of the 1960s, such as anti-war protests and the counter-culture, the women's liberation movement, and the supposed breakdown of traditional values, but it was the Supreme Court decision *Roe v. Wade* legalizing abortion that is most often presented as the catalyst of the Religious Right to become one of the primary political forces within the conservative movement from the 1970s onward.

The dramatic shift of evangelical Christians from an agnostic stance toward abortion as a Catholic issue to mass mobilization in opposition goes a long way toward explaining the mobilization of evangelical Christians. However, telling a better story about the rise of the Religious Right requires a more expansive analysis that begins decades before *Roe v. Wade*. Doing so will demonstrate that evangelicals played an important role early on in the modern conservative movement in the mid-twentieth century and challenges the standard narrative about the rise of the Religious Right.

Jeffrey Hadden (1987) locates the historical antecedents of the Religious Right in the urban revivalism of the late nineteenth and early twentieth centuries. Urban revivalism was a reactionary movement to the urbanization of the early modern period and the influx of immigrants into the rapidly expanding cities across the East Coast and the industrial heartland. Evangelicals and mainline protestants alike grew increasingly concerned that these growing cities were becoming engines of secularization and, perhaps more disturbingly, that the new groups of immigrants inhabiting them were Catholic, Orthodox, and Jewish.

The ideology of urban revivalism was organized around the concept of *dominionism*: the mythos that the United States was founded under God's dominion and plays a central role in his divine plan. Urban revivalists sought to restore the dominion of a (protestant) Christian America as a "city on the hill" by bringing the gospel to the city, but theirs was not strictly a religious movement. It was a political movement of social reform.

> The goal of the urban revivalists was not simply to make Christians of the unwashed masses. Rather, they had in mind a more or less explicit image of how Christianizing people transformed their social character. Salvation was viewed as a solution to the problem of urban poverty. Save souls and people will lift themselves out of poverty. . . . [S]alvation begat motivation to work—it was straight out of Andrew Carnegie's "gospel of wealth." (Hadden, 1987, p. 9)

Early evangelists, such as Charles Finney, Dwight Moody, and Billy Sunday, recreated the tent revivals of the Great Awakening within new urban institutions oriented toward social and political activism that were funded by the industrialists and robber barons of the era. They constructed rationally organized institutions modeled after modern industry, honed their rhetorical and theatrical techniques, and quickly adopted new mass media technologies like radio.

Evangelists in the 1930s were able to build on urban revivalism to promote a new gospel of wealth, Christian libertarianism, to win the hearts and minds of not only the urban masses but those of business elites (K. Kruse, 2015). The titans of capital and industry were not held in high regard during the Great Depression for rather obvious reasons. Frequently the object of scorn in Franklin Delano Roosevelt's presidential addresses and "fireside chats," speeches often sprinkled with Biblical quotes and references to a social gospel, wealthy elites spent the 1930s looking for ways to rehabilitate their image and, more importantly, to challenge FDR's New Deal policies and federal regulation.

They found their road to rehabilitation in an address given by James Fifield to the National Association of Manufacturers (NAM) in 1940 in which he argued that free-market capitalism and the titans of industry were not villains whose greed and caprice brought about the Great Depression but were the vanguards of national salvation. Fifield and a new group of prominent evangelists began to promote a new Christian libertarian ideology as both gospel and a means of social reform, and it was exactly the kind of movement industrialists would fund.

> [T]hese ministers claimed that the Democratic administration made a "false idol" of the federal government, leading Americans to worship it over the

Almighty; that it caused Americans to covet what the wealthy possessed and
seek to steal it from them; and that, ultimately, it bore false witness in making
claims about what it could never truly accomplish. . . . In a forceful rejection
of the public service themes of the Social Gospel, they argued that the central
tenet of Christianity remained the salvation of the individual. If any political and
economic system fit with the religious teachings of Christ, it would have to be
rooted in a similarly individualistic ethos. (K. Kruse, 2015, p. 7)

Funneled through NAM and the philanthropies of wealthy industrialists,
Fifield and others used corporate money to construct new institutions to
promote Christian libertarianism to clergy around the nation and to the public
through magazines, books, and electronic media.

Indeed, electronic media played a critical role in the growth of the Religious
Right before and after World War II (Diamond, 1995). Throughout the 1950s,
prominent evangelists and the National Religious Broadcasters lobbied the
Federal Communications Commission for unfettered access to radio and
television. They succeeded in the early 1960s when federal regulations over
paid religious programming were abolished. The effect of this regulatory
change was profound.

Billy Graham was an early innovator in televised ministry, and he laid
the groundwork for the emergence of a politicized evangelical movement in
the postwar era. With a boost from newspaper magnate William Randolph
Hearst who told his editors to "puff Graham," Billy Graham was able to fuse
the spectacle of a tent revival with Christian libertarian and anti-communist
rhetoric that made for both engaging television and that lent respectability to
a politicized evangelical Christianity. Graham became the elder statesman of
a politicized evangelism and minister to presidents, but it was the new breed
of evangelists that followed that would build a radicalized Religious Right
movement.

The media de-regulation of the 1960s opened the door to a new form of
charismatic evangelical ministry that coupled Graham's televised revival
with aggressive fundraising to build media and educational empires. Oral
Roberts and Jerry Falwell recreated the Southern tent revival in nationally televised broadcasts and used the wealth they created to build not only
sophisticated media operations but educational institutions, such as Oral
Roberts University and Liberty University, to develop future leaders in the
Religious Right movement. However, it was Pat Robertson who revolutionized the televised evangelical ministry (Watson, 1997).

Robertson launched his Christian Broadcasting Network in 1961, but it was
the flagship program *The 700 Club* that revolutionized the medium. While
charismatics such as Falwell and Roberts adopted Graham's revival format,
Robertson's *The 700 Club* was modeled after a morning talk show that mixed

information and news with entertainment, self-help, and lifestyle content. Robertson constructed a media ecosystem that took a holistic approach to evangelism that would be copied with great success by the evangelical leaders that followed, such as James Dobson and the mega-churches that proliferated across the Sun Belt states in the 1990s.

What we see is that from the 1970s onward a new group of evangelical ministers began constructing an institutional framework to advance their beliefs and values. The politics of Christian dominionism and Christian libertarianism were a constant feature of early media evangelism, but it was in the 1970s that these religious leaders began to employ their growing resources to politically mobilize evangelicals. The impetus for this mobilization was the handing down of a Supreme Court decision, just not the one the reader might expect. The Supreme Court decision in *Green v Connally* handed down in 1971 upheld an Internal Revenue Service regulation that the racially discriminatory segregation academies proliferating across the South to undermine federal desegregation policies were not charitable organizations eligible for nonprofit, tax-exempt status. The ruling further radicalized Southern segregationists and evangelicals but also mobilized these new evangelical ministers whose own educational institutions, and in their mind their ministries, were potentially threatened.

Paul Weyrich, a co-founder of the Heritage Foundation and ALEC, saw the controversy over private schools and segregation as an opportunity to "split social conservatives from the Democratic party" (Berlet & Lyons, 2000, p. 223). Weyrich worked with Falwell and Robertson to form political lobbies, the Moral Majority and the Christian Coalition, respectively, that worked with evangelical ministries and institutions to mobilize the faithful in opposition to what they termed the anti-religious statism of New Deal liberalism. A new Religious Right movement emerged from the late 1970s and 1980s rallying not just evangelicals but Catholics and mainline Protestants around issues labeled as traditional family values, including the new hot button issue around which all could now unite: abortion.

It is true that the issue of abortion played an important role in the political mobilization of the Religious Right, but the roots of this weaponized Christianity lay in decades of political organizing informed by the theology of dominionism, the natural hierarchy of market capitalism, and white nationalism. Early pioneers partnered with corporate America to build new religious institutions and media outreach that were always already politicized. Those who followed in their footsteps built not just ministries but universities, educational institutions, and media empires to both influence public opinion and train new cadres of religious conservatives. The most significant accomplishment of these evangelical Christian ministers, however, was their development of a politicized Christian ideology around which the faithful could construct a shared identity.

The ideology of the Religious Right is organized around a politics of restoration and recognition (Watson, 1997) and a politics of fear (Fea, 2018). An organizing ideological discourse for the Religious Right is a call to restore the United States as a Christian nation and to fulfill its destiny as both a world power and as an example to other nations. More importantly, this call to restoration positions Christians and, by proxy the United States, as being victims of a "vast humanist conspiracy involving Hollywood producers, Unitarian churches, the American Civil Liberties Union (ACLU), the National Organization of Women, the National Association for the Advancement of Colored People (NAACP), and many more" (Diamond, 1998, p. 70). The politicized evangelism of the Religious Right is organized around a politics of victimization that draws upon the language of recognition often associated with pluralism and anti-racism. Paradoxically, the Religious Right calls upon the language of pluralism to destroy pluralism. "They want 'their place at the table' *and* they want everyone at the table to agree with them. They want a Christian nation *and* religious freedom. As contradictory as it may seem, they want to have their cake *and* to eat it too" (Watson, 1997, p. 175).

It is important to note that this politicized Christian ideology closely aligns with the other strands of conservative ideological discourses in the postwar era discussed thus far in this chapter and, more importantly, that this alignment is not accidental. The leaders of the modern conservative movement from William F. Buckley to the Religious Right positioned conservatives as being marginalized victims of a secular, humanist, collectivist, liberal elite. This alignment can no doubt be partially explained by the exchange of ideas and resources within elite social networks, but this ideological alignment must also be understood as being the product of discursive exchange taking place within a political and cultural milieu structured by a dynamic and technologically sophisticated media infrastructure.

CONSERVATIVE MEDIA

A common feature in the various threads identified in the preceding analysis of the rise to dominance of the modern conservative movement is the use of media. Buckley's fusionism was carried out on the pages of the *National Review* and, from 1966 to 1999, on his weekly public television series *Firing Line*. The think tanks and policy institutes created by wealthy industrialists following the Powell memorandum sought to influence politics through news media and defined success by the degree of media exposure they could generate. The coded language of the Southern Strategy was a political marketing strategy to speak directly to specific groups of white voters and to frame media coverage of presidential campaigns to facilitate that communication. And, the political mobilization of Religious Right was made possible by the religious media empires built by charismatic evangelical ministers. The electoral success and hegemonic rise of the modern conservative movement in the political domain can be explained in no small part by the sophisticated use of technological innovations in mass media, something conservative elites state openly (Viguerie & Franke, 2004).

Richard Viguerie was an early pioneer in direct mail marketing and electoral politics. He built a direct mail marketing company in the 1960s that would not only make him very wealthy but would also transform conservative politics from the 1970s onward. He famously built his first database from a list of twelve thousand donors to Barry Goldwater's 1964 presidential campaign, and he greatly expanded his mailing list after he acquired George Wallace's primary list of almost three million names (Berlet & Lyons, 2000, p. 223). Viguerie developed a sophisticated marketing operation to identify increasingly narrow groups of voters and direct curated messages to them in the form of fliers, newsletters, and magazines. These curated messages informed readers about salient issues and the conservative viewpoint on them, identified important political campaigns and political candidates and solicited money to support the conservative cause. It was a form of self-financed political marketing that was used with great success in Richard Nixon's presidential campaign in 1968 and proved decisive in the 1980 election, which brought Ronald Reagan to the White House, a new crop of movement conservatives to the House of Representatives and a Senate under Republican control for the first time in decades.

The power of direct, narrowcast messaging to rally voters around the coded language of the Southern Strategy was transformative for the Republican party and the conservative movement, but it was American Broadcast Company talk radio host Rush Limbaugh that would popularize a new format of narrowcast political messaging that would prove revolutionary. The nationally syndicated *Rush Limbaugh Show* was a potent mix of hyper-partisan messaging and entertainment that used classic propaganda techniques and irreverent humor to both attack the Democratic Party, politicians, and activists and to promote the Republican party, conservative politicians, and conservative activists associated with think tanks and policy institutes. Limbaugh demonstrated that narrowcast messaging employed in a relatively obscure media format (initially AM radio) could construct a common language and epistemic community among its listeners. His success made him an influential figure in the growing dominance of the conservative movement and Republican party politics (Barker, 2002), as evidenced by his receiving the Presidential Medal of Freedom from Trump in 2020. The *Rush Limbaugh Show* became wildly popular as his vitriolic and often racist and sexist content became controversial, and the format he developed has been copied with great success by national and local radio personalities. Today, political talk radio is the most popular radio format (Nielsen Media Research, 2018) with the biggest names reaching weekly audiences measuring in the millions: Rush Limbaugh 15.5 million, Sean Hannity 15 million, Mark Levin 11 million, and Glenn Beck 10.5 million (Talker's Magazine, 2019).

Kathleen Jamieson and Joseph Cappella (2008, p. 236) describe political talk radio as being an "echo chamber" that isolates and protects "audience members in an informational and attitudinal enclave." They argue that political talk radio hosts seek to stir anger and outrage in listeners in a way that does not produce cynicism and apathy but engagement. It moves audiences to become active in politics. The focal point of outrage are Democratic politicians, the Democratic Party, and prominent political figures (feminists, environmental activists, racial justice groups, etc.) that constitute a liberal elite threatening traditional American cultural, economic, and political values. The hosts construct a politics of existential conflict in which the host, audience, and (importantly) prominent conservatives and the Republican party play the role of protagonists. They do this by framing, re-framing, and interpreting the news of the day into a shared political language that situates hosts and listeners as possessors of almost secret knowledge and as those who can see through the liberal bias of traditional news media. In so doing, Jamieson and Cappellas (2008) argue that political talk radio polarizes its audience and, in turn, the political culture of the United States more generally.

My own analysis of political talk radio took a structural approach to analysis that was focused on the thematic narratives of the medium and the rhetorical tools employed by the hosts (Ellison, 2014). The thematic structure of political talk radio is organized around the grand narratives of the mythic community and the radical other. The mythic community situates the host, audience, and the conservative movement as the defenders of the United States who are locked in existential political warfare with an implacable liberal elite threatening the nation and with whom compromise can only lead to tragedy. Political talk radio hosts employ a set of rhetorical tools to (re)interpret the daily news and situate it within the grand narratives of the medium. Hosts rely on tools such as the following: *affective appeal*, the open display of outrage and anger at the supposed machinations of the liberal elite; *metonymy*, using an extreme or outlier example to represent a larger group or phenomenon; and *catch phrases*, using slogans and (often pejorative) labels as an epistemic shorthand to represent complex issues and often strung together in long associative chains.

What is important to remember is that political talk radio is a news format that collects no news. Hosts must often rely on the traditional news media that they label as "liberal" and "radical" for content. Their principle task is interpretation. The hosts use rhetorical tools to do deep readings of political texts (print, audio, etc.) that situate specific issues, persons, or events into the grand narratives of the medium as it instructs listeners in how to do the same. It is pedagogical. Political talk radio is a pedagogical medium that provides audiences with and instructs them in the use of interpretive tools with which to construct a shared political identity that immunizes them from opposing points of view or information that could challenge their political identities. Political talk radio does not simply polarize and protect its audience (although it certainly does those things) but *radicalizes* and *empowers* them to engage politically.

Elite Republicans and movement conservatives quickly recognized the growing influence of political talk radio in the 1980s and 1990s, but it was Roger Ailes who understand the transformative potential of the medium. Ailes was a television producer who made his fortune producing tabloid journalism in the 1980s. His break into conservative politics came early on in his career when he was asked to help the notoriously uncharismatic Richard Nixon hone his media image for the 1968 campaign. His success with Nixon created opportunities to work with the presidential campaigns of Ronald Reagan in 1980 and George H. W. Bush in 1988, but he never quit working in television.

Ailes understood that incorporating the political talk radio format into television news could transform the political culture and help to solidify the power of the conservative movement. He got his first chance to put this idea to the test in 1993 when he was appointed president of the struggling business news cable network Consumer News and Business Channel (CNBC). In his three years at CNBC, Ailes turned the struggling network into a success by incorporating elements of political talk radio, such as new programming oriented around opinionated hosts with a clear ideological position on economic issues, into a business news as entertainment model. His success led him to launch a syndicated *Rush Limbaugh Show* for television and the short-lived *America's Talking* cable news network while still acting as president of CNBC. Personal conflicts with other executives and growing anger over his side projects eventually led to his ouster as president of CNBC in 1996, but two weeks after he was fired Ailes stood at a podium with Australian media mogul Rupert Murdoch announcing the launch of a new cable news network: the Fox News Channel (FNC).

Murdoch had the ambition to build a cable news network to challenge the established and popular Cable News Network (CNN). It was a daunting task. CNN was an established presence in news media that had bureaus all over the world and a large staff of prominent journalists. Ailes offered Murdoch a format of opinion-based journalism borrowed from political talk radio that did not require significant news-gathering capability. Swint (2008, p. 163) describes the news format Ailes developed at FNC as a hybrid of CNN and tabloid news, but a better description would be political talk radio with video (Sherman, 2014, p. 178).

Daily programming on FNC follows the standard schedule established by CNN. The programming day begins with a morning show that mixes news and information with entertainment and lifestyle segments. The afternoon features traditional, "straight" news reporting, but it is the nightly opinion-based programming that is the ratings and revenue juggernaut for FNC. So-called flagship programs, such as *Hannity* and *Tucker Carlson Tonight*, feature opinionated hosts who interpret the day's news using the narratives and rhetorical techniques of the political talk radio format. In fact, prominent hosts such as Sean Hannity and Laura Ingraham also host daily talk radio shows. Ailes adapted the format of political talk radio to cable news, and it has transformed the political culture of the United States.

FNC has become the nexus of conservative, Republican party politics. It is the leading cable news network in ratings (A. J. Katz, 2019), and it serves as the most trusted (if not only) source of news for millions of Americans and as a vetting operation for Republican politicians (Bartlett, 2015). Success in conservative politics requires favorable coverage on FNC.

Matthew Norton (2011, pp. 325–327) argues that, as with political talk radio, the opinion-based journalism on FNC relies on "deep structures of meaning" that act like a script that ascribes a binary interpretive frame, such as the little guy vs. the system, folks versus elite, rational vs. emotional, and so on, to any one news story or event. What is important for Norton are the ways in which these deep structures are constructed through the dramatic staging of the media text. The opening monologue commonly associated with the format plays an important role in this staging, but the contentious debates and interviews that take up the majority of the program play a central role in the staging of a political spectacle that makes for engaging television. Whether interpreting the news in the opening monologue or arguing with guests over the significance and meaning of specific issues or events, FNC hosts employ the rhetorical tools of political talk radio to stage the spectacle of partisan conflict that renders all complexity and nuance down to a competitive framing of winning or losing, the outcome of which is presented as being significant for both the audience and the nation.

> The argument form on the show encourages a competitive framing with a winner and a loser. Framing interpretive dynamics as a matter of victory or defeat gives added significance and dramatic force to the interaction. . . . If you really feel strongly about the confrontation between Americans and anti-Americans, then an argument where one side represents what to you is sacred, and the other what to you is polluted, then the outcome of the argument is highly dramatic because its meaning matters so much. By staging interpretation as drama, the

show aims to make its determinations of meaning matter more to the audience. (Norton, 2011, p. 330)

It is through the staging of partisan conflict that FNC hosts actively (re)construct the grand narratives of the imagined community and the radical other, and, in so doing, they not only construct deep stories around which individuals can construct a collective political identity but instruct their audiences in the use of interpretive tools to make sense of and act in the world. Taken together, FNC and political talk radio are the dominant forces in a conservative media landscape that also includes elite newspapers, such as the Rupert Murdoch owned *Wall Street Journal*; magazines, such as the *National Review*; and a growing number of online conservative news sites, such as *Breitbart* and the *NewsMax*. One of the key elements in the rise to power of the modern conservative movement has been the development of a coherent media infrastructure that instructs, immunizes, and (increasingly) radicalizes the conservative faithful.

More importantly, the influence of conservative media extends beyond the immediate audience. Polletta and Callahan (2019) argue that consumers of conservative media don't keep what they hear to themselves but share it with friends and family in their social group who, in turn, interpret their own experiences and identity work through what they hear. The grand narratives of conservative media, or what Polletta and Callahan call "deep stories," become part of the shared stories of the group and work to demarcate its boundaries. "They reinforce collective identities, and in particular, partisan identities" (Polletta & Callahan, 2019, p. 64).

The stories shared among the conservative faithful are ones that render complex issues down to existential conflict between the imagined community and the radical others threatening it. Conservative media do not just interpret and (re)frame news within these structural themes but instructs its audience in how to interpret and act in the world. Conservative media do not simply polarize American political culture through the construction of grand narratives. It is a pedagogical device that radicalizes conservatives.

POLITICAL CRISIS

Corey Robin argues that the animating force of conservatism is a collective animus to the political agency of subaltern classes. It is a reactionary politics defined by its opposition to the democratic challenges of subaltern classes and by its framing the political as a field of existential conflict. Conservatism is a politics of "having power, seeing it threatened, and trying to win it back" (Robin, 2011, p. 15). Conservatism is, therefore, a politics oriented around an ideological discourse of loss and restoration, a binary political logic of existential conflict that is necessarily radicalizing. Robin's analysis of conservatism yields a seemingly counter-intuitive conceptualization of its object of analysis as reactionary, counter-revolutionary political practice, but his work offers a compelling theoretical framework with which to understand the modern American conservative movement and the dangerous politics it has engendered.

The modern American conservative movement is a reactionary politics that frames the political as a field of existential conflict between a marginalized majority and a distant, liberal elite. In the ideological discourse of the modern conservative movement, the marginalized majority is the patriotic, hard-working backbone of the United States. They are the standard bearers of traditional, Christian values who are experiencing cultural, economic, and political loss to an undeserving other supported by a distant, liberal elite. The liberal elite is made up of unpatriotic cosmopolitans in academia, government, and media who do not share the values of the majority. They direct resources and undeserved privileges to minorities, immigrants, radical feminists, homosexuals, and so on, in the name of social justice as they vilify and look down upon the marginalized majority and the values they hold dear. The modern conservative movement is predicated on an ideological discourse of cultural loss to a distant elite and the restoration of an imagined community defined by white, Christian nationalism.

The conservative movement achieved power from the 1980s forward by weaponizing this ideological discourse. The conservative movement built knowledge-producing institutions and party organizations, mobilized specific voting populations, and constructed a sophisticated media structure to shift the ideological terrain. It is a political movement predicated on the exploitation and amplification of class, cultural, gender, geographic, racial, and religious antagonisms via a cultural politics of loss and restoration that parallel twentieth-century fascism.

Indeed, the defining characteristic of fascist politics is the use of discursive tools to frame the political as an existential conflict between a mythic community representing the shared values of the nation and the radical other who not only does not share those values but who threatens the existence of the nation. What defines fascism is a political framing of cultural loss to a distant elite and calls for restoration of an imagined community.

> The mechanisms of fascist politics all build on and support one another. They weave a myth of a distinction between "us" and "them," based in a romanticized fictional past featuring "us" and no "them," and supported by a resentment for a corrupt liberal elite, who take our hard-earned money and threaten our traditions. "They" are lazy criminals on whom freedom would be wasted.

"They" mask their destructive goals with the language of liberalism, or "social justice," and are out to destroy our culture and traditions and make "us" weak. "We" are industrious and law-abiding, have earned our freedoms through work; "they" are lazy, perverse, corrupt, and decadent. Fascist politics traffics in delusions that crate these kinds of false distinctions between "us" and "them," regardless of obvious realities. (Stanley, 2018, p. 187)

Fascism is a politics of differentiation and hierarchy predicated on undermining shared understandings and political values that are the prerequisites for deliberative democratic debate and a socially justice society. It is a reactionary politics that requires not just the discursive construction of a radical other threatening the traditions of the common people but the construction of a "mass elite" who rightfully dominate society and who find their avatar in heroic leaders who can restore the traditional order. Fascism is a reactionary politics predicated on the restoration of hierarchies in the face of democratic challenges from subaltern populations, but it is informed by an ideological discourse that is necessarily paradoxical.

Reactionary politics require an endless supply of radical others threatening the mythic community who are, on the one hand, inferior, undeserving and in need of the leadership and domination of the mass elite and, on the other hand, a cunning adversary in league with a liberal intelligentsia that has abandoned traditional values. The radical other is simultaneously subaltern and elite. This paradox is not a barrier to fascist politics but constitutes the discursive energy of its ideological discourse. The radical other is a fluid category that can be adapted to changing circumstances and the movement of historical time ensuring the continuing discursive construction of existential threats and the need for radical programs to restore what is being lost or threatened to be lost.

To be clear, I am not conflating the modern American conservative movement with the fascism of the interwar period. History neither repeats nor rhymes, but applying a historical lens to the study of the modern American conservative movement can be instructive for identifying the significance of contemporary political trends. Like fascism, conservatism is animated by a politics of fragmentation that is necessarily radicalizing, and its increasing radicalism is leading the American republic into a period of political crisis with global implications.

The rise to dominance of the modern conservative movement has corresponded with a rise in political polarization and animosity (Doherty et al., 2016). The American electorate is increasingly defined by partisan hostility and mistrust (Doherty et al., 2017). It is not simply that conservatives are angry at their partisan rivals; they are increasingly hostile to and actively fear those they see as being the enemy. And, it is a hostility that is increasingly being reciprocated by their partisan rivals (and not without justification). The driving force behind growing partisan animosity is the politics of "us" and "them" that have propelled the conservative movement from the 1970s onward, and this fracturing of the American political culture has led to political impasse and governmental dysfunction that will only further fuel partisan hostility and produce support for illiberal policies, democratic back-sliding, and authoritarianism (Abramowitz & McCoy, 2019).

A politics predicated on an antagonistic politics of "us" and "them" requires an endless supply of new enemies, new threats, and new outrages. The modern conservative movement isn't simply radical; it is radicalizing and dangerous. White nationalist and neo-nazi organizations are building on the white supremacy of the long Southern Strategy and are becoming increasingly empowered to commit political violence in places such as Charlottesville, Virginia, and the streets of Portland, Oregon (Tenold, 2018). Paramilitary weaponry and hardware are now commonplace at conservative rallies. So-called Patriot militias patrol the southern border to deter and sometimes detain migrants and asylum seekers, provide armed security for controversial "free speech" rallies, and stage armed takeovers of governmental property (such as the Capitol riot following the 2020 election) as political protest (Crothers, 2019). A politics of "us" and "them" does not simply foster polarization and partisan hostility but justifies the use of political violence in the name of preservation, an issue only magnified by an American cultural that fetishizes firearms and overt displays of militarism.

A more distressing sign of the increasing dangers posed by the conservative movement relates to white fragility in the face of demographic change. The voting base of the conservative movement is predominantly white, male, Christian, rural/suburban, and older, but the population of the United States is becoming increasingly diverse, secular, and urban (Cooperman et al., 2015; Parker et al., 2018; G. A. Smith et al., 2019). Projections indicate that the United States will become a so-called majority-minority nation by 2050, and these projections have led to widespread speculation that the conservative movement and the Republican party face a future of declining power and influence (Frey, 2018). However, the potential effects of demographic change will be felt long before this date. A third of eligible voters in the 2020 election were non-white (Cilluffo & Fry, 2019). The perceived loss of power has long been an animating force within the conservative movement, but the growing awareness and alarm among conservatives that their power could begin to erode due to demographic changes will only radicalize them further. Indeed, the white supremacy of the modern conservative movement and the threat of demographic change is fueling both a rejection of democratic politics and a growing acceptance of political violence among Republican voters, all couched in the language of "loss" and "restoration" of the American way of life (Bartels, 2020).

The modern American conservative movement is, indeed, reliant on a shrinking voter base to win elections and retain political power, and these demographics trends could potentially spell the downfall of the contemporary articulation of American conservatism. However, the conservative historical bloc need not constitute a majority to maintain its position of hegemonic leadership. Two points are relevant here.

First, the uniquely antidemocratic structure of the American republic was designed to eclipse the will of the majority and to facilitate minority rule. For example, each state sends two representatives to the U.S. Senate which means that Wyoming (with a population of approximately six hundred thousand) has the same number of Senators as does California (with a population of approximately forty million). More egregiously, the U.S. president is not elected by popular vote but by an Electoral College that apportions votes for each state (with the exception of Maine and Nevada) based on a "winner takes all" rule that allocates votes to the overall winner of the state. The Electoral College makes electoral inversions in which the winning presidential candidate loses the popular vote an increasingly frequent outcome, and it is an outcome that favors the conservative movement (Geruso et al., 2019). Indeed, the two conservative Republican presidents elected in the twenty-first century thus far both lost the popular vote, and the lifetime judicial appointments they have made will ensure a conservative majority on the U.S. Supreme Court for a generation. Trump lost the popular vote in the 2020 election by over 7 million but came within 73,000 votes of winning the Electoral College and the election (based on his losses in the battle ground states of Arizona, Georgia, and Pennsylvania). The American republic disproportionately favors rural, white conservatives, and its antidemocratic political structure affords numerous veto points to empower a unified minority to thwart the will of the majority. The American republic was designed for minority rule.

Second, the modern conservative movement is well positioned for minority rule. Conservatism is animated by a dynamic ideological discourse that is adaptable to changing circumstances and the flow of historical time. The conservative movement can rely on a sophisticated and well-funded ideological infrastructure of think tanks and policy institutes to shape public discourse and a complex media structure to shape the ideological terrain and propagate an ideological discourse of "us" and "them." The conservative movement has constructed a robust ideological infrastructure that will allow it to effectively mobilize political, cultural, and ideological forces in defense of conservative hegemony.

In short, the conservative movement need only a unified, motivated minority of voters to retain power in the American system, and Trump's strong support among communities of color along the southern border and in South Florida in the 2020 election demonstrate the folly of mapping race and ethnicity onto discrete and fixed political categories. Race and ethnicity are socially constructed, and the conservative movement need only attract specific groups within communities of color to win elections and retain power. The conservative movement is well positioned to reconstruct a historical bloc, retain ideological leadership, and to advance an increasingly dangerous politics of "us" and "them" that could lead to a global catastrophe on a similar scale to the tragedies of the mid-twentieth century. The world system may be entering into a multipolar phase, but the United States remains an economic, ideological, and political power. A political crisis in the United States would necessarily have global implications that are impossible to predict with any degree of certainty.

The politics of "us" and "them" that has defined the modern conservative movement since the 1970s is an elite political project that rose to hegemonic dominance through a long Southern Strategy of White, patriarchal, Christian nationalism that has radicalized a privileged minority (Maxwell & Shields, 2019) and that is working to shore up its dominance through voter suppression and amplifying the antidemocratic structure of the American republic (Brennan Center for Justice, 2019; Hajnal et al., 2017). In response to Trump's loss in the 2020 election, conservative legislators have introduced over 253 bills in 43 states to restrict voting rights (Brennan Center for Justice, 2021). The modern conservative movement champions mass incarceration policies, attacks on voting rights, and political gerrymandering that work to disenfranchise oppositional voting groups and to solidify the power of its white, rural/suburban voting base. Faced with changing demographics and a shifting cultural landscape, the conservative movement is taking increasingly radical steps toward cementing minority conservative rule.

The modern American conservative movement has entered into a period of hegemonic crisis in which it is working feverishly to shore up the crumbling edifice of the post-1970s social formation through a radical political program threatening the institutions of the American republic and undermining the requisite social cohesion required for a functioning society. The United States is entering a period of political crisis driven by a modern conservative movement that is polarizing, antidemocratic, and radicalizing. It is threatened by a politics of fragmentation. More importantly, despite the rhetoric surrounding the 2020 presidential election, the growing radicalism of the conservative movement will not be reversed in one election cycle. The modern conservative movement will remain a viable political force in this period of emergent crisis no matter the outcome of any one election or the electoral fortunes of specific political actors.

Seen in this light, the rise of Donald Trump, the alt-right, and right-wing populism looks less like an aberration and more like the product of a long-term trend. There is a common thread linking Buckley's "new radicalism" and Nixon's Southern Strategy to Ronald Reagan's "morning in America" and Donald Trump's "make America great again" sloganeering. They are iterations of a white cultural narrative employed by conservative political leaders and propagated by a sophisticated ideological structure to exploit the economic anxieties and racism of a disappearing middle class and growing underclass. It is an antagonistic politics driven by white racial, economic, and political resentment (Cramer, 2016; Hochschild, 2016) and predicated on a deep narrative of loss and restoration (Polletta & Callahan, 2019). It is a cultural politics built around an antidemocratic narrative of cultural loss and restoration and is defined by a generative exercise of power that is both internally contradictory and increasingly dangerous.

The contemporary American conservatism of the Republican party is a reactionary, counter-revolutionary movement that is radicalizing the political culture of the United States and that is corrosive to its societal structure (Hacker & Pierson, 2019). The modern conservative movement is an elite project working to subsume social institutions to the project of rolling back progressive political advances achieved in the past and eclipsing the possibility of future progressive change. However, the modern conservative movement rose to power through a cultural politics of white, patriarchal supremacy and Christian nationalism in what is becoming an increasingly diverse society. As its demographic base of support continues to recede, the conservative movement is becoming increasingly radicalized and is implementing draconian, antidemocratic policies to retain power and relevance. The steps conservatives are taking to advance this elite project have made a slide into authoritarianism and the collapse of the American republic a real possibility.

The United States is entering a period of political crisis that will be defined by the policies and practices the conservative movement employs to retain power and relevance (to retain hegemonic leadership) in the political domain and the policies and practices employed by political actors seeking to challenge conservative hegemony from the Left. In many ways, it is a political moment analogous to the interwar period, but this observation should not be confused with a crude historical determinism. The future resolution of the emergent political crisis is yet to be determined. The conservative movement rose to hegemonic dominance from the 1970s onward through a cultural politics of loss and restoration, and it is on the ideological field of popular culture that subaltern populations and justice movements must organize to not just restore democratic gains that have been lost but to advance progressive change toward a new left hegemonic order.

CODA

I endeavored in this chapter to tell a better story about this historical moment of emergent conjunctural crisis through a political analysis focused on the rise to hegemonic dominance of the modern American conservative movement in the post-1970s formation, the counter-revolutionary and radicalizing politics it has engendered, and the political crisis emerging from its potential loss of and work to retain hegemonic leadership. The specific focus was on the ideological discourses animating the conservative movement with the goal of demonstrating the necessarily radicalizing and increasingly dangerous politics threatening the American republic. The rise to hegemonic dominance of the conservative movement and its moves to retain hegemonic leadership are the primary drivers behind the emergent political crisis of this historical moment, and it is for this reason that this was the focus of the political analysis detailed in this chapter. However, two phenomena alluded to but not fully developed in the preceding analysis will play an important role in the story I wish to tell in this book.

The first (and perhaps most important) phenomenon relates to technological change and the conservative media landscape. An important theme in the preceding analysis was the importance of media in the rise to hegemonic dominance of the conservative movement from Buckley's *National Review* to the Fox News Channel. One key to the success of the conservative movement was the ability of political actors to successfully adapt to technological changes in mass media. In my analysis of conservative media, I alluded to the importance of conservative news media websites and online media, but I did not fully develop how the conservative movement adopted these new media outlets and how these technological changes have influenced and transformed the conservative movement. One of the key insights of Donald Trump's campaign manager and former CEO of the conservative news website *Breitbart* Steve Bannon was the power of new technology and social networks as a political tool to achieve electoral success and transform the conservative movement. Indeed, the so-called alt-right is just as much a product of social media as it is the conservative movement.

A second and related phenomenon deals with the center-left opposition in the United States. In the preceding chapter, I indicated that one of the defining moments marking the ascendancy of neoclassical hegemony was the transformation of the opposition Democratic Party in the 1990s. The so-called New Democrats did not simply adopt conservative economic policy but also conservative social policies that contributed to the astronomical growth of the carceral state imprisoning black and brown bodies, the erosion of reproduction rights, and so on. This transformation of the Democratic Party is frequently explained as being the result of changes in economic theory away from Keynesianism toward neoclassical theory and by the need of the Democratic Party to win back Reagan Democrats, former Democratic voters who switched to the Republican party in the 1970s and 1980s. There is some truth to this story, but it leaves out a broader transformation within the Democratic Party born of a seemingly impossible origin story. An under-examined part of the story of how a nominally center to center-left political party shifted dramatically to the political right involves the unlikely synthesis of New Left politics from the 1960s and the technocracy of Cold War military research into a techno-utopian political sensibility that would emerge from Silicon Valley and the technology industry during the 1970s, 1980s, and 1990s.

Both of these phenomena are defined by a cultural transformation that will be analyzed in the next chapter: the technological transformation of popular political culture. The following chapter will present the findings from a cultural analysis oriented around the rise of internet technologies and the ubiquity of social media. What will emerge from the story I will tell in that chapter is that the emergent crisis of the present is defined not just by the conjoining of emergent economic and political crises but also by an emergent cultural crisis.

Chapter 4

Cultural Crisis

Telling a better story about this historical moment requires an analysis of the popular political culture of the contemporary conjuncture. The preceding chapters analyzed the crisis of the 1970s as a transformative period marking the collapse of Keynesian economic theory and the technocratic governance of postwar liberalism and the rise to dominance of neoclassical economic theory and the modern conservative movement. The story told thus far is one in which a specific school of economic thought and a political movement rose to dominance in their respective domains and one in which each has entered a period of emergent crisis. What is missing from the narrative is an analysis of popular culture.

The postwar era is generally understood as being the apex of mass society defined by bureaucratic institutions and a broadly shared political culture. The popular political culture of the era was largely defined by elite gatekeepers in television news rooms and national newspapers. These gatekeepers decided what political knowledge, events, or issues were news worthy, and, more importantly, the ways in which they constructed narratives to communicate what they deemed to be newsworthy framed and sequenced political knowledge for the vast majority of people. Sources of political knowledge and information were relatively limited in scope, and the variation and diversity in the elite opinion conveyed by mass media was similarly narrow.

This is not to say that the political culture of the postwar era was uniform and homogeneous. There were alternative presses and outlets existing on the margins that were constructing political knowledge ranging from the academic and often critical to the conspiratorial and ludicrous. There were also news magazines, radio outlets, and local newspapers, but these media outlets were largely dependent on news wire services and other national outlets as sources of political, national, and global news. News media of the era did not speak with one voice, but there was a great deal of isomorphism among news media outlets that narrowed the scope of political knowledge and debate.

Cracks in the political culture of this mass society began to appear in the late 1960s and 1970s. Anger over mass media reporting of governmental lies about American wars in Southeast Asia and political scandals in Washington (from Watergate to the Church Committee) animated the antiwar movement and fostered a political culture that came to distrust mass media outlets. Public trust in the elite gatekeepers in news media was eroding at the same time that the modern conservative movement began its ideological campaign against the purported "liberal bias" of elite media. Taken together, growing distrust in mass media and the increasingly radical and well-funded actors working to subvert confidence in the information, ideas, and opinions conveyed by mass news media created an opening for radical changes in the political culture of the United States, but it was technological change that would ultimately prove to be transformative.

There was a rapid proliferation in news media outlets from the late 1970s onward. Cable and satellite television became increasingly widespread and ubiquitous in the 1980s. New cable news outlets began to compete with traditional news outlets for a relatively stable population of consumers which encouraged both new and traditional outlets to shape news content to increasingly narrow demographic groupings. Advances in micro-computing in the 1970s made personal computers increasingly affordable, and the development of internet technologies in the 1980s and 1990s fostered the development of an entire new category of news outlets catering to ever more specific demographics. The quantitative increase in the number of news media outlets fundamentally transformed the political culture of the United States from one defined by the broadcasting of political knowledge by elite actors in a small number of national news outlets in the postwar era to the narrowcasting of targeted, often ideological political information to increasingly narrow demographic grouping by the turn of the twenty-first century (Webster, 2005).

Changes in the popular political culture of the United States continued to accelerate throughout the first two decades of the twenty-first century driven by the qualitative shift in media toward user-centric interactivity via networked devices and social media platforms. Social media platforms, such as Facebook, Twitter, and YouTube, have experienced phenomenal growth over the past decade. Facebook is the dominant platform with 69% of Americans reporting using the service in 2019, but there is a wide array of social media platforms that are very popular with younger demographic groups, especially Snapchat and Instagram (Perrin & Anderson, 2019). Amazon has become a retail juggernaut and global marketplace that has expanded into popular media. Google has become, alongside social media networks, the gateway to the internet. The Google search engine has become the dominant tool for individuals to seek out information online, and the range of services it provides, such as Gmail and Google Maps, have become indispensable tools in everyday life. Not surprisingly, all of the new technology giants are moving into new markets from transportation to entertainment and news.

A celebratory discourse emerged alongside these new technologies that highlight the ways in which they open up new worlds of information and knowledge, create opportunities to connect with others around the world, and empower individuals to become civically engaged. There is little doubt that networked computer technologies make available a wealth of information, knowledge, and news like never before. Nor is there doubt that these technologies have empowered activists around the world from Tahrir Square to Hong Kong (Tufekci, 2017).

Technological enthusiasts now proudly proclaim the dawn of a new era of connectivity, cultural exchange, and civic engagement. The technological cheerleaders of Silicon Valley and the academy proclaim that they are, in the words of Facebook founder Mark Zuckerberg, "developing the social infrastructure for community—for supporting us, for keeping us safe, for informing us, for civic engagement, and for inclusion of all" (Wagner & Swisher, 2017). Recent privacy scandals involving Facebook, ongoing controversy associated with the 2016 presidential election, and the so-called Q conspiracy have certainly tarnished the image of Facebook and other technology giants. Still, wide majorities of Americans continue to hold recent trends in the development of networked computer technologies in high regard and see them as broadly beneficial to society (A. Smith et al., 2018).

Online media have become an important source for political information and knowledge, and social network platforms in particular have emerged as a mediated public sphere. Traditional, so-called legacy media (television and print) remain the dominant source of news and political knowledge. However, networked computer technologies increasingly mediate what news and information individuals see, and news outlets across all different media technologies now shape news content to gain visibility on social network platforms and search engines. The significance of these new networked technologies is not simply additive, that is, a quantitative increase, although that is significant in terms of narrowcasting. The import of these technological changes is that they have transformed the ways in which individuals come to know and engage with the issues, events, and ideas at work in the political culture of the United States and, accordingly, that they have transformed the political culture itself.

This chapter will present an analysis of the technological transformation of popular political culture by the introduction and growing ubiquity of networked computer technologies. I define networked computer technologies here as interactive, user-centric technologies including: social media platforms that connect users in online networks; algorithms that determine the content users see on everything from search engine results to social media feeds; data analysis and analytics that target messages, content, and advertising at users based on their previous online activity; global positioning systems employed by applications and devices; and the physical devices through which users connect to the internet, including personal computers, smartphones, personal assistants, and devices falling into the ever-expanding category of internet of things. Importantly, these new technologies blur distinctions between traditional and new media in ways that have reconfigured older media forms (print, television, etc.) and, therefore, are captured by this conceptualization of networked computer technologies. The focus will be on how the quantitative increase in and qualitative transformation of news media made possible by networked computer technologies are reconstructing the popular political culture of the United States.

The story I tell in this chapter will be wildly out of sync with the celebratory discourse surrounding networked computer technologies that has become the dominant cultural ideology of the post-1970s formation. I will use the following pages to trace the outline of an emergent crisis in the political culture of the United States driven by technological transformation. To be sure, networked computer technologies are having a significant impact on the broader culture, but the focus for this analysis will be more narrowly focused on political culture due to its obvious relevance to the object of inquiry for the larger conjunctural analysis.

I will begin by developing a conceptual framework for the chapter that draws upon the classic work of Neil Postman. This will be followed by an historical analysis that traces the unlikely development of cyber-utopian ideology in academia and the technology industry centered around Silicon Valley in California. I will then seek to connect how this ideological discourse informed the design of networked computer technologies and explore the structuring effects of these technologies on how individuals enter into the collective conversation of the political culture. I will conclude by arguing that the technological transformation of the American political culture made possible by the introduction of networked computer technologies is driving an emergent cultural crisis defined by fragmentation, polarization, and political antagonisms, and new forms of cultural violence.

TECHNOLOGY AS IDEOLOGY

Marshall McLuhan (1964) conceptualized modern technological media as an extension of human selves to a global scale that contributes to the compression of both time and space. McLuhan envisioned a techno-utopian future in which advances in media would expand the possibilities of human life and connection and that would ultimately undermine bureaucratic social institutions and transform society. Looking on from the early twenty-first century, it is hard to take McLuhan's optimism seriously, but it would be a mistake to dismiss McLuhan out of hand. McLuhan's opus *Understanding Media* argued that technological media impose patterns of perception that shape human consciousness and social reality, an insight he summarized as the "medium is the message."

> Our conventional response to all media, namely that it is how they are used that counts, is the numb stance of the technological idiot. For the "content" of a medium is like the juicy piece of meat carried by the burglar to distract the watchdog of the mind. The effect of the medium is made strong and intense just because it is given another medium as "content." The content of a movie is a novel or a play or an opera. The effect of the movie form is not related to its program content. The "content" of writing or print is speech, but the reader is almost entirely unaware either of print or of speech. . . . The effects of technology do not occur at the level of opinions or concepts, but alter sense ratios or patterns of perception steadily and without any resistance. (McLuhan, 1964, p. 18)

McLuhan made the controversial, and somewhat reductive, argument that the proper object of analysis for media studies was not the content or discourse taking place within and through media but the technological media itself. The strong version of this argument (that content and discourse are unimportant) is clearly indefensible, however, the weak version that the structuring effects of technological media is under-appreciated in media analyses remains relevant.

Individuals and societies use technological media to communicate and to think about the nature of social reality in ways that influence how individuals act in the world and how societies organize themselves. And the ways in which individuals and societies communicate and think about the nature of social reality is influenced and structured by the technological media that facilitate this collective conversation. McLuhan forces us to recognize that technological media are not neutral but perform an epistemic and, therefore, ideological function in society.

Neil Postman (2006) argued that a culture or society can be understood as a collective conversation. Following McLuhan, Postman argued that electronic media do not simply make this collective conversation possible but also subtlety regulate and structure the nature of this conversation. The medium is not so much the message for Postman as it is a metaphor.

> A message denotes a specific, concrete statement about the world. But the forms of our media, including the symbols through which they permit conversation, do not make such statements. They are rather like metaphors, working by unobtrusive but powerful implication to enforce their special definitions of reality. Whether we are experiencing the world through the lens of speech or the printed word or the television camera, our media-metaphors classify the world for us, sequence it, frame it, enlarge it, reduce it, color it, argue a case for what the world is like. (Postman, 2006, p. 10)

For Postman, media metaphors perform an epistemic function in the collective conversation of a culture or society by shaping the ways in which individuals make sense of their social world. Postman's point here is not that this epistemic function is mechanical but rather reflects a cultural bias about what is and is not recognized as being true.

> [T]he concept of truth is intimately linked to the biases of forms of expression. Truth does not, and never has, come unadorned. It must appear in its proper clothing or it is not acknowledged, which is a way of saying the "truth" is a kind of cultural prejudice. Each culture conceives of it as being most authentically expressed in certain symbolic forms that another culture may regard as trivial or irrelevant. . . . As a culture moves from orality to writing to printing to televising, its ideas of truth move with it. Every philosophy is the philosophy of a stage of life, Nietzsche remarked. To which we might add that every epistemology is the epistemology of a stage of media development. Truth, like time itself, is a product of a conversation man has with himself about and through the techniques of communication he has invented. (Postman, 2006, pp. 22–24)

Conceptualizing a culture or society as a collective conversation invites us to think about the ways in which the technological media through which that conversation takes place regulate and influence the nature of that conversation and, accordingly, its influence on society itself.

Postman's *Amusing Ourselves to Death* offered what he termed a Huxleyan warning that challenges the often celebratory discourses surrounding technological media. Postman argued that the United States had transitioned from a typographic society made possible by the printing press to an age of show business made possible by electronic media. His concern was that the ideal of the democratic citizen has been replaced by the consumer seeking entertainment and, accordingly, that the United States was in a slow descent into authoritarianism made possible by the passive acquiescence to power, that we are being collectively pacified by an electronic form of the soma depicted in Aldous Huxley's *Brave New World*.

What I take from Postman is that electronic media are not a politically neutral matrix through which a culture or society communicates with itself but is a social force shaping society in ways that are as subtle as they are powerful. Technological media structure the collective conversation that constitutes a culture or society and, therefore, performs an ideological function shaping how individuals make sense of and act in the world. Advances in technological media bring with them a program for social change that require critical reflection and praxis.

> To be unaware that a technology comes equipped with a program for social change, to maintain that technology is neutral, to make the assumption that technology is always a friend to culture is, at this late hour, stupidity plain and simple. . . . Introduce the alphabet to a culture and you change its cognitive habits, its social relations, its notions of community, history and religion. Introduce the printing press with movable type, and you do the same. Introduce speed-of-light transmission of images and you make a cultural revolution. Without a vote. Without polemics. Without guerrilla resistance. Here is ideology, pure if not serene. (Postman, 2006, p. 157)

Postman forces us to see electronic media not as politically neutral tools that can be taken up uncritically in media and political analyses. Inquiry focused exclusively on the content and discourses taking place within and through media, although important and necessary, can displace and mystify the ways in which media forms regulate and structure the content and discourse that make up and constitute the collective conversation of a culture and society.

To be clear, I do not intend to employ a reductive, crudely structuralist account of the political culture of the contemporary conjuncture. There are clearly patterns of exchange between and among technological media, popular discourse, and political culture. What I take from Postman is that the role that media forms play in shaping society is an important, and somewhat neglected, object of analysis.

I want to take up Postman's interest in technological media as an object of analysis. Specifically, the focus of analysis will be the dynamic interplay between the regulating and structuring effects of technological media and the celebratory discourses surrounding and, more importantly, *informing* rapid advances taking place in media technology. I am interested here in the ideological structure of media technology and the ways in which it influences, shapes, and structures the political culture of the contemporary social formation. I will begin with an analysis of the ideological function of networked computer technologies by focusing on the cyber-utopian ideology emerging from the technology industry and Silicon Valley. I will then explore how the user design of networked media technologies structure human experience and how individuals interact with their social world. I am interested in understanding how individuals enter into the collective conversation of their culture and society through technological media and how these media influence, structure, and (as I hope to demonstrate) fragment that collective conversation. And, I will conclude with a discussion on the emergent cultural crisis fueled, in part, by the technological transformation of popular political culture.

CYBER-UTOPIANISM

One of the more prominent cultural discourses at work in the contemporary conjuncture is the celebratory narrative revolving around networked computer technologies and social media. The story goes something like this. The rapid development in internet technologies is fundamentally restructuring the social order ushering in a new economic model, a new political order, and a new understanding of community. This popular iteration of technological determinism asserts that networked computer technologies break the power of monopolistic industries by empowering individual entrepreneurs to compete on a level playing field with large corporations; disrupt the monopoly of information held by political elites, political institutions, and news media thus flattening and democratizing the political sphere; and empower individuals to transcend the limitations of geography to form new global communities organized around shared interests.

The historical emergence of this celebratory discourse is commonly attributed to the enthusiasm of Silicon Valley in the 1990s and the widespread adoption of internet technology. The technological enthusiasm of the 1990s can be seen in one of the more popular texts produced during this period: *Cyberspace and the American Dream: A Magna Carta for the Knowledge Age*, colloquially known as the Magna Carta (Dyson, 1996). The Magna Carta proclaimed the emergence of cyberspace as an electronic space that is conceptualized as being both physical and biological. The Magna Carta conceptualizes cyberspace as being the physical infrastructure of computer technology, machine learning, and networks transmitting, receiving, and exchanging information, but the primary focus of the text is the human and social implications of networked computer technology that are framed in biological and evolutionary terms. The Magna Carta argues that the rapid development of networked computer technology is fundamentally transforming human life and human society and driving the emergence of what the authors termed a Third Wave information society.

> The Third Wave has profound implications for the nature and meaning of property, of the marketplace, of community and of individual freedom. As it emerges, it shapes new codes of behavior that move each organism and institution—family, neighborhood, church group, company, government, nation—inexorably beyond standardization and centralization, as well as beyond the materialist's obsession with energy, money and control. (Dyson, 1996, p. 297)

The Magna Carta employed biological terminology to conceptualize cyberspace as an evolutionary force driving the development of new societies and new humans.

Three foundational ideas articulated in the Magna Carta are relevant here. First, cyberspace liberates and democratizes information and, therefore, shifts power away from governmental and corporate bureaucracies toward individuals. In the language of the Magna Cara, the governments, industries, and bureaucracies of the so-called Second Wave industrial society maintained power through the monopolization of knowledge and information. The breaking of this monopoly will therefore foster the radical reordering of power relations in Third Wave society. Second, by empowering individuals to become both producers and consumers of information and knowledge, cyberspace will foster the proliferation of new diverse communities organized around shared interests that transcend the boundaries of time and space and, in so doing, foster the development of new global selves no longer defined by tribalism and political antagonisms. Third, the disintegration of Second Wave industrial society into a new era of economically and politically empowered individuals holds the radical potential to open up a new era of stability and human liberty.

> The complexity of Third Wave society is too great for any centrally planned bureaucracy to manage. Demassification, customization, individuality, freedom—these are the keys to success for Third Wave civilization. . . . [T]o reconstitute democracy in Third Wave terms, we need to jettison the frightening but false assumption that more diversity automatically brings more tension and conflict in society. Indeed, the exact reverse can be true: If 100 people all desperately want the same brass ring, they may be forced to fight for it. On the other hand, if each of the 100 has a different objective, it is far more rewarding for them to trade, cooperate, and form symbiotic relationships. Given appropriate social arrangements, diversity can make for a secure and stable civilization. (Dyson, 1996, p. 302)

The most important factor defining the "appropriate social arrangements" required for the realization of this vision boils down to the one major dictum proposed by the Magna Carta: cyberspace must never be regulated by government. The Magna Carta argues that, left to its own devices, cyberspace will produce new generations of entrepreneurs who will challenge and ultimately destroy monopolistic industries, new generations of democratic individuals who will redefine human liberty and self-realization, and the demassification of human societies that will constitute the dawning of a new historical era. The principle threat to this brave new world is the legacy power of obsolete elites who could wield their influence over governments to regulate cyberspace and retain their monopolistic power.

One of the leading cheerleaders for this cyber-utopian discourse was Nicholas Negroponte (1995), the founding director of the widely celebrated Media Lab at the Massachusetts Institute of Technology (MIT). Adopting the enthusiasm of the Magna Carta, Negroponte's *Being Digital* proclaimed the dawn of a digital age defined by the transition from materialism (atoms) to informationalism (bits). For Negroponte, the growth and rapid development of internet technologies combined with rapid advances in computer processing power and machine learning will make possible a digital future of human freedom and advancement.

The personalization of information made possible by machine learning will allow for the emergence of authentic selves that defy large-scale statistical analysis and mass marketing. The sharing of these authentic selves through networked technologies will give rise to new digital communities, and the atomization of the mass societies of the twentieth century will flatten and democratize human life and social relations in ways that will erode the power of the nation-state and political bureaucracies. Negroponte (1995, p. 231) argued that "[b]eing digital is different. We are not waiting on any invention. It is here. It is now. It is almost genetic in its nature, in that each generation will become more digital than the preceding one." The only threat to this brave new world is, in Negroponte's telling, the same as the one offered by the Magna Carta: the threat of government regulation or the "bit police."

The cyber-utopian discourse of the 1990s has become a ubiquitous feature of early twenty-first-century popular culture. However, this powerful ideological discourse conceals a contradictory politics. On the one hand, cyber-utopian discourse is notable for its liberal appropriation of leftist and communitarian rhetoric. Cyber-utopianism denounces materialism and asymmetrical power relations, lays claim to the radical democratization of economic and political life, and celebrates the radical transformation of human societies made up of newly liberated, autonomous, self-directing individuals. On the other hand, cyber-utopian discourse is paradoxically founded upon computational logics that reinforce institutional power and that advance a radical right-wing political agenda in the name of leftist political impulses (Golumbia, 2009). Cyber-utopian discourse frames societal problems as informational problems to be resolved through an uncritical embrace of technological determinism and an unquestioned faith in unregulated capitalist markets. How this paradoxical discourse rose to hegemonic dominance requires a historical perspective that extends the time horizon beyond the internet enthusiasm of the 1990s.

Fred Turner (2006) traces the historical development of this cyber-utopian discourse to the unlikely intertwinement of two seemingly contradictory social movements in the postwar era. Turner locates the origins of cyber-utopianism in the military research laboratories of World War II and the Cold War. The military-industrial research complex of the Cold War era is not commonly associated with a free-wheeling institutional culture, but that is an accurate description of the new research centers and laboratories developed by the U.S. military during this period. To be clear, the military-industrial research complex was certainly a bureaucratic project that was "Big Science par excellence, the product of planned coordination of teams with structured objectives, expensive discipline-flouting instrumentation, and explicitly detailed rationales for the clientèle" (Mirowski, 2002, p. 17). What is interesting about the military-industrial research complex is the radically interdisciplinary and collaborative research culture developed in these spaces that were organized around the paradigmatic tool of the era: the computer.

The military research centers and laboratories that managed a multi-theater world war and developed nuclear weapon technology quickly transitioned to the tasks of modeling nuclear armageddon and building a space program in the postwar era, and one of the important successes of these research centers was the development and employment of increasingly sophisticated computer technology. Researchers in these laboratories and centers developed a free-wheeling approach to research that sought to flatten institutional structures and encourage collaboration across disciplinary divides, such as physics, biology, mathematics, operations research, neuropsychology, economics and computer science to name just a few. What emerged from this intellectual milieu was systems theory and cybernetics informed by the logics of computation.

Cybernetics can be understood as a systems management theory primarily concerned with automatic systems, such as communication systems, ecological systems, and neurological systems. Accordingly, cybernetics conceptualizes these automatic systems (whether natural, social, or technological) as organisms made up of dynamic processes yet tending toward steady, homeostatic equilibria. Cybernetics blurs distinctions between the natural, social, and technological domains and conceptualizes research questions as informational problems understood through the paradigmatic logics of computation.

Philip Mirowski (2002, p. 12) terms the research projects that emerged from the military-industrial research complex of this era cyborg sciences, which he defines as a "complex set of beliefs, of philosophical dispositions, mathematical preferences, pungent metaphors, research practices, and (let us not forget) paradigmatic *things*, all of which are then applied promiscuously to some more or less discrete preexistent subject matter or area." Cybernetics conceptualized the material world and human societies as automatic systems tending toward equilibrium and homeostasis and societal problems as technical issues to be managed through data collection, computational analysis, and technocratic solutions. Societal problems were framed by cybernetics as informational issues of inefficiency, ambiguity, and disorder that are to be resolved through technical processes of rationalization. More importantly, cybernetics and the cyborg sciences quickly expanded beyond the U.S. military and became one of the primary tools employed by the technocratic state of the postwar era.

From Robert McNamara's technocratic management of the Viet Nam War to President Lindon Johnson's *Great Society*, a new approach to research that conceptualizes societal problems as informational problems that can be resolved with data and computation rose to dominance, and the researchers who developed cybernetics and systems theory quickly spread these intellectual practices to the rapidly expanding university system and technology industry of the postwar era.

> These men (and they were almost exclusively men) would go on to found numerous university computer science departments, to set up MIT's Project MAC (which introduced computer time-sharing), to help establish key computer companies (such as the Digital Equipment Corporation), and even to help initiate the ARPANET, which would become the basis of the Internet. As they created the military-industrial-academic infrastructure out of which individualized and networked computing would emerge, these engineers . . . brought with them not only a habit of entrepreneurship and interdisciplinary collaboration, but also the discourse of cybernetics and systems theory and the computational metaphor on which it depended. (Turner, 2006, p. 28)

The free-wheeling style of collaborative, interdisciplinary research as well as the cybernetic theory of the postwar military-industrial research complex became a fixture of university culture in the 1960s and, somewhat paradoxically, had a profound impact on the emerging counter-culture and the New Left politics of the era.

The counter-culture is, in common folklore, most closely associated with the antiwar movement and a cultural bohemianism that rejected institutional bureaucracies and the psychologically hollow, fragmented institutional humans they produced. Emerging from San Francisco and spreading to college campuses across the nation, the counter-culture explicitly rejected what it saw as the ultimate inhuman bureaucracy, the Pentagon's institutional war machine, and sought to build a new culture to heal a war-torn world, restore ecological balance, and liberate individuals from stultifying institutions. However, the counter-culture movement also emerged from a university milieu dominated by systems theory and cybernetics, and (somewhat surprisingly) it was the back-to-the-land communards of the New Communalist movement that would most readily take up this technocratic approach to resolving societal problems.

The New Communalists emerged from the 1960s as a back-to-the-land movement that embraced the use of small-scale technologies (from garden tools to amplifiers to LSD) "to bring people together and allow them to experience their common humanity," to enable the psychologically hollow institutional man of the twentieth century "to become both self-sufficient and whole once again" (Turner, 2006, p. 4). Turner argues that, as the enthusiasm of the 1960s waned in the decades that followed, the communards turned away from politics and came to see themselves as a scientific avant-guard working to heal a fragmented world by readily taking up the technocratic orientation, collaborative ethos, and systems theory of cybernetics that emerged from the military-industrial complex they had once rejected.

The counter-culture New Communalists moved from the communes of the 1970s to elite universities and Silicon Valley in the 1990s, and they brought with them the peculiar and paradoxical ideological discourse of cyber-utopianism.

[C]yber-utopianism . . . stems from the starry-eyed digital fervor of the 1990s, when former hippies, by this time ensconced in some of the most prestigious universities in the world, went on an argumentative spree to prove that the Internet could deliver what the 1960s couldn't: boost democratic participation, trigger a renaissance of moribund communities, strengthen associational life, and serve as a bridge from bowling alone to blogging together. (Morozov, 2011, p. xiii)

The communards turned their backs on politics in pursuit of individual liberation through the promiscuous commingling of computer technologies and information systems with a communitarian ethos of self-sufficiency and cooperation. In so doing, they transposed McLuhan's techno-optimism of radical liberation through the seamless integration of technology and human life to a technocratic solutionism that would take root in the technology sector of Silicon Valley (Morozov, 2013).

Turner points toward the work of technological entrepreneurs, such as Stewart Brand, Esther Dyson, and John Perry Barlow, as the prophets of cyber-utopian discourse who successfully transported the communitarian ethos of the Haight-Ashbury district of 1960s San Francisco to the military-industrial-academic complex of Silicon Valley in the 1990s. For these entrepreneurs and the technological enthusiasts of Silicon Valley:

> the early Internet seemed poised to model and help bring into being a world in which each individual could act in his or her own interest and at the same time produce a unified social sphere, a world in which we were "all one." That sphere would not be ruled through the work of agnostic politics, but rather by turning away from it, toward the technologically mediated empowerment of the individual and the establishment of peer-to-peer agoras. For the prophets of the Internet, as for those who had headed back to the land some thirty years earlier, it was government, imagined as a looming, bureaucratic behemoth, that threatened to destroy the individual; in information, technology, and the marketplace lay salvation. (Turner, 2006, pp. 248–249)

The cyber-utopians of Silicon Valley from the 1990s onward have sought to wage war on inefficiency, ambiguity, and disorder through the rationalization of human behavior in the name of liberation, freedom, and market democracy, a politics that bears a marked resemblance to right-wing political ideology. From this paradoxical commingling of the military-industrial research complex and the communitarianism of the counter-culture emerged the contradictory politics of the cyber-utopian discourse at work in the contemporary conjuncture.

The politics of this cyber-utopian discourse has been described as cyber-libertarianism (Golumbia, 2013, 2016; Winner, 1997) or the Californian ideology (Barbrook & Cameron, 1996). Winner (1997, p. 14) defines cyber-libertarianism as "a collection of ideas that links ecstatic enthusiasm for electronically meditated forms of living with radical, right wing libertarian ideas about the proper definition of freedom, social life, economics, and politics in the years to come." What is significant about the paradoxical politics of cyber-utopian discourse is that the adherents of this ideological discourse often do not identify themselves as libertarian or understand their political commitments as aligning with a radical right politics.

> [O]ne of cyberlibertarianism's primary social and epistemic functions is to yoke what would have previously been seen as at least liberal if not actually leftist political energies into the service of the political far right, with enough rhetorical padding to obscure at least partly, even to adherents, the entailments of their beliefs. In other words, cyberlibertarianism solicits anticapitalist (or at least

anti-neoliberal) impulses and recruits them for capitalist purposes, to such as degree that many believers often do not notice and even disclaim these foundations. (Golumbia, 2013, pp. 3–4)

Cyber-libertarianism is an ideological discourse of technological determinism that envisions the realization of anarcho-communitarian ideals through the rapid development of networked computer technologies even as it works to advance a radical right politics of market democracy and radical individualism.

Cyber-utopianism speaks the language of leftist politics, but its adherents work to advance free-market policies and a libertarian ethos that situates government as a Leviathan all while ignoring corporate power and the penetration of technology companies into our personal lives, culture, and politics. In the name of liberating humanity from rigid governmental bureaucracy and monopolistic industry, the denizens of Silicon Valley are delivering humanity into the loving embrace of technology giants (such as Google, Facebook, etc.) and governments (from the nominally democratic to authoritarian) that are increasingly adept in employing networked computer technology to manage populations and retain power (Morozov, 2011). The rhetoric of Silicon Valley may be steeped in the language of disruption and transformation. However, beneath the rhetoric and propaganda, we find historical continuity (Daub, 2020). More importantly, for the purposes of the present analysis, it is important to note that cyber-utopian discourse is not simply a curious sociological phenomenon that emerged from the paradoxical commingling of the military-industrial research complex and the communards of the New Communalist movement but is an ideological discourse that informs the *design* of social media platforms, computer devices, software, and so on (Turner, 2006, p. 262) with profound implications for how individuals *come to know* and *enter into* the collective conversation of a society.

THE DESIGN OF NETWORKED TECHNOLOGY

Adam Greenfield (2017, p. 9) points toward the smartphone as being "the signature artifact of our age." The smartphone has become increasingly ubiquitous in American society and, for many users, it is often the first thing they look at in the morning and the last thing they look at before sleep. The smartphone is, by itself, little more than an expensive paper weight. However, once connected to a network, the smartphone becomes a powerful tool that can perform a large number of tasks that are shaping our lives in untold ways. The smartphone can help an individual navigate an unfamiliar city with ease, pay bills and manage bank accounts, monitor health and well-being, take and store family photos, or access a world of information at the touch of a finger (just to name a few). It would be difficult to deny that the introduction of the smartphone enables individuals to easily carry out a large number of tasks that once would have been much more difficult or prohibitively expensive, if not impossible, prior to their introduction. It is by no means hyperbolic to say that they are quickly becoming a "universal, all-but-indispensable mediator of everyday life" (Greenfield, 2017, p. 9).

What is often under-appreciated is, first, the sophisticated processes smartphones perform unbeknown to users that are made possible by a wide array of sensors, antenna, and software and, second, the ways in which smartphones are designed to shape human experience in ways that are as profound as they are subtle. The everyday activities of human life, from taking back-to-school photographs of children to hailing a cab to making a dentist appointment to keeping in touch with friends and family, are increasingly mediated through one electronic device that, by design, links the user to a distributed network of actors, from the manufacturer of the device to software developers to social media algorithms to (potentially) hackers. And, each of these network actors utilize the sophisticated set of sensors and applications operating within the device as well as algorithms, global positioning tracking systems, and so on, to surveil not only how users interact with their smartphones but also to develop sophisticated data profiles on their consumer habits; their tastes, preferences, and desires; their social network of friends, and so on. It is safe to say that the smartphone is the most sophisticated and widely distributed data collection device produced to date.

> When we move through the world with a smartphone in hand . . . we generate an enormous amount of data in the course of our ordinary activities, and we do so without noticing or thinking much about it. In turn, that data will be captured and leveraged by any number of parties, including handset and operating system vendors, app developers, cellular service providers, and still others; those parties will be acting in their own interests, which may only occasionally intersect our own; and it will be very, very difficult for us to exert any control over any of this. (Greenfield, 2017, p. 27)

More importantly, the distributed network of actors to which an individual user is connected are not passive actors who simply vacuum up data about a user's daily activities. They are actively working to shape the behavior of users. These actors design their devices, software, algorithms, and so on, to stimulate and encourage users to interact with their devices, platforms, or applications to build more complete data profiles.

A simple vibration can alert a user to an incoming text message or notify her that someone uploaded a picture of her to a social media platform.

These stimuli are now taken for granted as being "how smartphones work," but the simplicity of these stimuli belie both their sophistication and the complexity of the processes taking place behind the scenes. The designers of smartphones and social media platforms, for example, use notifications to subtly nudge users to interact with their smartphones or to log on to social media, all the while sophisticated machine learning algorithms are operating in the background to build a comprehensive data set on not just how users interact with the smartphone or the social network but on their total being, including their tastes and preferences, desires and dreams, geographic location and movement, health and well-being, social network of friends and family, and so on. The primary purpose of networked computer technology is to generate actionable data on users to help them successfully complete a task and continue to use the device, platform, software, and so on; identify the needs and wants of users to both market existing goods and services to them or (potentially) develop new goods and services to meet unmet needs; or to simply monetize personal data by selling it to other networked actors.

These distributed networks of actors are now dominated by a small number of large technology companies, such as Alphabet, Amazon, Apple, and Facebook, that are actively pursuing a "strategy of vertical integration by which each of them seeks to control the network, as well as the platforms, applications, physical devices and content that run on and are connected by it" (Greenfield, 2017, p. 275). The significance of this observation isn't simply to point toward the contradictions of a technology industry wrapped in the language of anti-corporatism creating the monopolistic enterprises of this New Gilded Age, although that is certainly relevant to the analysis at hand. What I find significant in this observation is that, no matter whether their core business is ostensibly online retail, advertising or selling physical devices, the business plans of the corporate giants of the technology industry are predicated on collecting data about its users and to use sophisticated data analysis techniques to monetize the day-to-day experiences of human life.

These increasingly monopolistic companies seek to construct vertical systems (that they conceptualize as ecosystems or organisms) to meet if not every human need imaginable at least the majority, and it is through the collection and analysis of data on its users that these companies seek to accomplish this ambitious goal. The business models of the technology giants, not to mention the endless stream of Silicon Valley start-ups seeking integration into larger ecosystems, is predicated on data collection to identify how to meet a wide range of human needs and, more importantly, to steer the users of networked computer technologies into a vertically integrated ecosystem of services, goods, news, and entertainment. The anti-systemic and communitarian narratives of cyber-utopianism lives on as rhetorical flourishes, investment pitches, and advertising campaigns, but the cybernetic logics of this ideological discourse are actualized in networked computer technologies as a technocratic system of atomization, data collection, and behavior modification.

The principle goal for technology companies is to foster user engagement with networked computer technologies, and one of the more well-known models for increasing user engagement was developed by technology entrepreneur Nir Eyal (2014) at Stanford University. Drawing upon the cyborg sciences of psychology, behavioral economics and systems theory that dominate the corporate culture of Silicon Valley and the academic culture of nearby Stanford University, Eyal's *Hooked* model involves four phases: trigger, action, variable reward, and investment. A *trigger* is a call to action that can be either external or internal. An external trigger can be something as simple as an image on a webpage, the buzz of a smartphone, or a notification from a social media platform. In each case, the goal is to stimulate the user to engage with networked computer technologies so as to generate meaningful data. An internal trigger relates to ways of being and emotions, such as boredom, curiosity, stress or loneliness, that can be used to move individuals to action. The goal for technology companies is to identify these internal triggers through data collection and analysis and to connect them to a product or service. The next phase seeks to initiate *action* by making it easy for the user to engage with the technology. If the *trigger* phase motivates then it is the *action* phase that creates the means for the user to perform the desired action with minimal effort. The *variable reward* phase seeks to give the user immediate gratification for engagement by allowing him to easily complete a task in a manner that reinforces his motivation for doing so again in the future, whether that be through social rewards that foster a sense of belonging, a reward for effort and the thrill of the hunt, or a stronger sense of self through feelings of mastery and competence. And, finally, the *investment* phase requires that technology companies employ sophisticated data collection and analysis systems to improve the product or service the more it is used and to identify and exploit new triggers to begin the process all over again. Eyal admits that his model can be used for nefarious purposes, his book is titled *Hooked* after all, but he wants to believe that the potential good of his model, assuming its judicious use by technology giants, outweighs any potential risks.

Adam Greenfield does not share this optimism and with good reason. He argues that the networked computer technologies of the twenty-first century are dominated by massive technology companies and that the complex network of distributed selves and vertical systems made up of devices, software, sensors, social media platforms, and so on, constitutes a hegemonic technosocial structure that increasingly mediates human experience and sociality. He deserves to be quoted here at length:

It resides in the smartphone that is the last thing many of us look at before we sleep, and the first thing we turn to upon waking; in the apps with which we manage time and attention, negotiate the city, and pursue the ends of mobility, sociality and productivity; in the algorithms that parse our utterances, model the flow of our bodily and psychic states, and prepare strategies in response to them; and in the cloud that binds these things together, as indispensable as it is ubiquitous and hard to see clearly. Like any hegemony, that of the [technology industry] actively reproduces itself, sustaining and being sustained by a continuous and all but unquestioned framework of assumptions about what technology is for, how it is developed, and who makes it. And in doing so, it tends to deny the space in which alternatives might be nurtured, to the extent that those alternative have all but literally become unthinkable. In our time, even the most seemingly transgressive visions of technology in everyday life invariably fall back to the familiar furniture of capital investment, surplus extraction and exploitation. We don't even speak of progress any longer, but rather of "innovation." (Greenfield, 2017, p. 313)

For Greenfield, networked computer technology constitutes a hegemonic structure that mediates how individuals enter into the collective conversation of their culture and society. Consciously or unconsciously, users share their desires, needs, daily activities, and so on, with a technological structure that seeks to frame, shape, and cultivate new desires, needs, daily activities, and so on. Networked computer technology has become what is perhaps the most sophisticated surveillance and behavior modification system yet invented and has made possible new modalities of power producing distributed, networked subjectivities.

The individual networked in this way is no longer the autonomous subject enshrined in liberal theory, not precisely. Our very selfhood is smeared out across a global mesh of nodes and links; all the aspects of our personality we think of as constituting who we are—our tastes, preferences, capabilities, desires—we owe to the fact of our connection with that mesh, and the selves and distant resources to which it binds us. How could this do anything but engender a new kind of subjectivity? Winston Churchhill . . . famously remarked that "we shape our buildings, and afterwards our buildings shape us." Now, we make networks, and they shape us every bit as much as any building ever did, or could. (Greenfield, 2017, pp. 27–28)

Mirroring Postman's "Huxlean warning," Greenfield convincingly argues that networked computer technologies, not just the smartphone but networked devices more generally and the distributed networks to which they connect, are fundamentally transforming the texture of everyday life and (accordingly) human subjectivity.

The cyber-utopian discourse that took root in Silicon Valley in the 1990s constituted the hegemonic structure of the technology industry, and it informed the ways in which its champions and adherents constructed the networked technologies of the twenty-first century. It is, after all, a short step from cybernetic logics that see every societal problem as being a data problem to seeing every business plan as being data driven. More importantly, the increasing ubiquity of networked computer technology in daily life has transposed cyber-utopian discourse onto the larger society. Cyber-utopianism constitutes a hegemonic technostructure in which individual subjects move within and through feedback loops of data collection and analysis and behavior modification systems that seek to shape the everyday practices and activities of human life. For the present analysis, this observation raises important questions about how these distributed, networked selves enter into and participate in the collective conversation of society. Specifically, how does the hegemonic technostructure of cyber-utopianism mediate and shape the ways in which individuals become politically engaged in their communities and societies?

CURATED FLOWS AND ENDOGENEITY

Citizens of the early twentieth century entered into the collective conversation of their political culture primarily through print media that became increasingly displaced and supplanted by new forms of electronic media, first radio and then television. In the early twenty-first century, citizens enter into this collective conversation through networked computer technologies. There are, of course, other means by which individuals can become politically engaged both then and now. Political engagement oriented around social movements, community organizing, labor unions, and so on, have long played and continue to play an important role in the ways individuals acquire political knowledge to inform their civic engagement. However, for the majority of people, the primary means to acquire the necessary knowledge and information to become politically engaged is within and through networked computer technologies.

Defining what is meant by political engagement is, of course, imprecise. A common metric frequently used to discuss the relative disengagement of American citizens is voter turnout which was 53.4% in 2018 (US Census Bureau, 2019). However, if you expand the criteria to include activities such as attending political meetings or protests, volunteering or donating to a political campaign or even express political opinions online, then American citizens appear to be more politically engaged than voter turnout would suggest (Doherty et al., 2018). Regardless, no matter how you define political engagement, one of the primary means through which individuals enter into the collective political conversation is within and through networked computer technologies. This observation raises the question of how these technologies structure the ways in which individuals obtain political knowledge, construct a political identity, and becoming politically engaged.

Kjerstin Thorson and Chris Wells (2016, p. 310) argue that the "fundamental action" of a media environment defined by networked computer technologies is *curation* which they define as the "production, selection, filtering, annotation, or framing of content." There are five sets of curating actors in this framework: journalistic curators, strategic curators, social curators, algorithmic curators, and personal curators. For Thorson and Wells, individuals inhabit a fluid space of intersecting information flows curated to varying degrees by a range of political actors.

Journalistic curators continue to play an important role in the dissemination of political knowledge. Despite the now-common refrain that networked computer technologies are displacing the gate-keeping function of traditional news media, journalists and editors continue to play an out-sized role in establishing the political salience of events (what counts as news) and framing political information (defining political problems, making causal diagnoses, and establishing what are "realistic" solutions). It may be common to describe print, radio, and television news as being legacy media, but these media outlets remain primary sources of political information and knowledge.

Strategic curators seek to "bypass conventional newsmaking processes and speak directly to publics" (Thorson & Wells, 2016, p. 315). Strategic curators employ sophisticated social scientific and marketing research to identify increasingly narrow demographic groups and to construct narrowcast messaging targeted to them. There are a wide range of strategic actors from well-funded political organizations pursuing broad political agendas to corporations seeking to influence governmental regulation to issue-specific organizations seeking to raise public awareness. What unifies these actors is that they employ targeted messaging to achieve specific political goals.

Social curators refer to networks of friends, family, acquaintances, and so on, that shape the information and media individual actors access through sharing on social media platforms, text messages, email, and face-to-face interaction. News pieces posted by friends on social media constitute an important source of political information. Likewise, the sharing of political memes or the use of hashtags establishes the political salience of specific events or issues, frames political knowledge, and draws distinctions between different ideological viewpoints in ways that subtlety shape the political information and knowledge to which individual actors are exposed.

Algorithmic curators are the complex, opaque, and proprietary mathematical and machine learning models that determine what information or content is presented to an individual through a search engine or social media platform. Search engines (such as Google or Bing) and social media platforms (such as Facebook and Twitter) collect data on previous online behavior and social networks to build complex data sets on individuals' preferences, beliefs, emotions, concerns, and states of being to curate the information they access. Facebook's News Feed is perhaps the most common and powerful example of algorithmic curation.

> [T]he News Feed is not just a weighted formula with thousands of inputs, but rather a constantly updated, personalized machine learning model, which changes and updates its outputs based on your behavior, the behavior of people you are connected with, and the behavior of the affinity and personality-based sub-group of users the system judges you to belong to. Facebook's formula, to the extent that it actually exists, changes every day. (DeVito, 2017, p. 768)

The principle goal of algorithmic curation is to foster continued engagement with networked computer technologies and to steer individuals into vertical systems of goods and services offered by a technology company. So, for example, when a user clicks on a YouTube video dealing with a specific political issue, the YouTube algorithm will suggest other videos dealing with similar topics, and Google (which owns YouTube) will use this data to curate the information the user accesses from a search on that topic, including related products and services to purchase through Google or an affiliated retailer or media company.

Personal curation refers to the individual choices made by actors in what information they access and the format in which they access it. Networked computer technologies offer an over-abundance of choice in information outlets. Individuals actively curate the political information they access in ways that reflect their own personal preferences that are informed by their political ideology, personal interests, media preferences, and so on. Individual actors have the ability to curate the political information they access from the ever-expanding number of media outlets made possible by networked computer technologies. However, it is important to note that "the effects of personal curation do not occur in isolation from other flows of content" (Thorson & Wells, 2016, p. 316).

Individual actors seek out and access political information by working within and across curation flows. Social curators have a significant influence on the political information individuals access (Anspach, 2017), and the information sources individual actors access is the product of increasingly polarized and partisan journalistic and strategic curation flows (Mitchell & Weisel, 2014). More importantly, the political information curated by journalistic, strategic, and social curators is itself curated through algorithms employed by social network platforms and search engines that tailor the content one sees based on previous online behavior (Pariser, 2011).

Thorson and Wells' conceptualization of curation flows challenges the rational actor or marketplace models frequently employed in mass communication studies and journalism research that too often assumes that individual tastes, preferences, beliefs, and so on, are exogenous to technological media and networked computer technologies. It is often assumed that agents' preferences, beliefs, and so on, exist independently of the various forms of technological media with which they interact. Conceptualizing individuals as inhabiting a dynamic space of intersecting curation flows points toward the "possibility that media preferences are 'endogenous'—that they arise from within the system" (Webster, 2017, p. 358). One of the ways in which individual agents come to know their social world is through curated flows that, on the one hand, reflect their ongoing identity work within specific social contexts and social networks while, on the other hand, are also the product of sophisticated data analysis and machine learning employed by networked computer technologies to not simply give the agent more of what she wants but to powerfully shape and modify her identity work and behavior in pursuit of monetization and commodification.

Pointing toward the importance of curation flows should not be construed as an attempt to construct a crudely deterministic model to understand a popular political culture in the United States that is increasingly defined by networked computer technologies. One of the most important contributions of cultural studies inquiry has been to examine the creative, novel, and (potentially) transgressive ways in which individuals engage with electronic media via the circulation of discourse (Hall, 1993). At the same time, one of the principle weaknesses with how this line of inquiry was operationalized in subsequent research has been to position consumers and users of electronic media as being on relatively equal footing with the producers and owners of electronic media outlets and platforms. The political discourse circulating within and through the networked computer technologies of the twenty-first century necessarily reflect hierarchies of power and the interests of "power elites" who have "special access to discourse: they are literally the ones who have most to *say*" (Dijk, 1993, p. 255). More importantly, in a popular political culture increasingly defined by networked computer technologies, it is not just that this power elite have more to say but that they possess tools to powerfully shape human consciousness, modify human behavior, and (accordingly) to structure human societies in the continual reproduction of power relations. The power they wield is not totalizing; power is always already negotiated and contested in myriad ways. However, it is also the case that networked computer technologies do not magically position individual agents outside of fields of power.

The concern here is not, however, the degree to which individual agents do or do not possess agency within the curated flows afforded by networked computer technologies. The focus of the present analysis is how, *in the aggregate*, individuals navigate these curated flows and the implications of the structuring effects of networked computer technologies for the political culture of the United States. Curation flows are bound up with networked computer technologies that structure the collective conversation that constitutes American political culture and, following Postman, perform an ideological function shaping how individuals make sense of and act within it. Networked computer technologies are not politically neutral but come with a program for social change. It is through critical reflection on the structuring effects of networked computer technologies that the increasingly dangerous trends in American political culture come into clear focus.

STRUCTURING EFFECTS

Recent scholarship has identified three interrelated and increasingly disturbing trends in American political culture related to the rising importance of networked computer technologies in the political domain. The first trend involves the formation of relatively closed epistemic communities online and the fragmentation of the political culture. Two processes are relevant here: homophily and echo chambers. Homophily refers to the tendency of individuals to congregate with others whom they consider to be like themselves. Echo chamber refers to ways in which the opinions and viewpoints of individuals are "echoed" back to them through online social networks and thus reinforcing those beliefs. The primary issue or concern in this body of literature is that the self-segregation of individuals into epistemic bubbles online will fragment the political culture into increasingly hostile political groupings impervious to counter-veiling information or differing viewpoints.

The political media landscape of the United States is highly polarized (Mitchell & Weisel, 2014), and, as discussed in chapter 3, this polarization is the product of long-term political processes driven by the growth in the number of news outlets and the rise of the modern conservative movement. It is not surprising then that social network sites are politically polarized as well (Faris et al., 2017). The issue raised by recent scholarship is whether networked computer technologies further contribute to and amplify these trends by facilitating the development of epistemic bubbles and echo chambers, and it would appear that this is indeed the case.

Large-scale analyses indicate that social network platforms, such as Facebook, Twitter, and YouTube, facilitate and encourage the formation of echo chambers (Bessi et al., 2016; Del Vicario et al., 2017; Garimella et al., 2018; Himelboim et al., 2014). Much of this fragmentation and sorting is being driven by ideology with those on the extremes of the political divide being the ones who inhabit the most isolated bubbles (Bright, 2018). More distressingly, when individuals are exposed to opposing views on social media, this exposure does not moderate partisanship or lead individuals to question their own beliefs but seemingly reinforces and amplifies their ideological commitments, and this effect is most pronounced among those associated with right-wing ideologies (Bail et al., 2018). The fragmentation of American political culture may not be a new phenomenon, but it is increasingly clear that networked computer technologies are opening up new spaces that can facilitate and amplify political fragmentation through the formation of closed epistemic communities.

The second trend involves the growing importance of networked computer technologies as vectors for the spread of misinformation and propaganda. The echo chambers facilitated by networked computer technologies encourage the spread of viral misinformation (Del Vicario et al., 2015; Tornberg, 2018; Vosoughi et al., 2018). Misinformation and conspiracy theories thrive online and are readily spread through social networks and by algorithmic curators. It is not simply that misinformation and conspiracy theories are reductive and debase the quality of debate within a political culture, although that is certainly important. The issue is that it is polarizing. The spread of misinformation and conspiracy theories within echo chambers act as emotional contagions that foster and amplify political antagonisms (Del Vicario et al., 2016). The relatively closed epistemic communities and echo chambers made possible by networked computer technologies create openings for new modes of political propaganda that flood popular political discourse with misinformation and conspiracy (Tufekci, 2017), and it is becoming increasingly clear that the viral spread of misinformation has a tangible impact on the beliefs and opinions of individuals both within and outside of online echo chambers (Bessi & Ferrara, 2016; Marwick & Lewis, 2017; Ruck et al., 2019).

Third, networked computer technologies have created new opportunities for reactionary forces to organize and have made possible new forms of cultural violence against the marginalized. Social media platforms are the sites where racial justice activists are organizing around the hashtag Black Lives Matter, but these platforms are also where a reactionary white nationalist backlash is organizing around the hastags of All Lives Matter and Blue Lives Matter (Carney, 2016) and is working to frame coverage in traditional media of issues related to police violence against persons of color (Kil, 2019). Public criticism of the misogyny in video games and gamer culture by women in the technology industry and media was met with a violent backlash organized on social media platforms and online discussion boards that was mainstreamed by Milo Yiannopoulos on the right-wing news site *Breitbart* (Massanari, 2017; Salter, 2018). The radical, reactionary right has proven to be quite adept at using networked computer technologies to organize and mobilize around anti-immigrant, misogynistic, and white nationalist rhetoric and to mainstream radical ideas into traditional news media and American political culture (Heikkilä, 2017).

The analysis offered in this chapter may not be welcomed by those with left-leaning politics who have, often justifiably, felt empowered by recent online activism, but it is imperative that we critically reflect on the ways in which the structure and design of networked computer technologies foster the development of closed epistemic communities online, empower powerful actors to silence or drown out activists and social movements, and create opportunities for reactionary forces to organize and advance politics that cement traditional hierarchies. Zeynep Tufekci sums up the darker side of networked computer technologies this way and deserves to be quoted at length:

> [Corporate platforms] entrench echo chambers because hearing only those views one agrees with makes people feel more comfortable and thus more likely to spend more time on the site. But these platforms also encourage polarization because people whose views are strengthened in these echo chambers then find people from the other side to argue with online. All of this creates a spectacle more people want to watch, and corporate platforms can use this opportunity to bombard users with more ads and gather more behavior data to help profile users for the benefit of advertisers. . . . Activists find themselves battling their opponents' harassment and counter-movements, and although the authorities may not as easily censor their speech formally, the need to battle armies of abusive and threatening trolls can lead to self-silencing and self-censorship. What started as a space of free expression and free assembly has increasingly become a danger to social movement activists who find themselves targeted, their private information leaked as a means to intimidate them, and their voices drowned out or distorted by ad-friendly algorithms. At the same time, movements based on ethnosupremacy or extremism also spring to life online as those on the fringe find one another and set their own narrative, recruit followers, and push the boundaries of acceptable discourse. (Tufekci, 2017, pp. 271–272)

Tufekci's comments should not be mistaken for the passing of a value judgment about networked computer technologies (i.e., good vs. bad) but should be read as acknowledging the dangers and blind spots associated with an uncritical embrace of techno-utopian discourse. Telling a better story about the cultural landscape of the contemporary formation requires critical reflection on cultural and ideological fields increasingly mediated and structured by networked computer technologies. Doing so troubles the often celebratory discourse surrounding these technologies and, more importantly, elucidates the cultural and ideological fields upon which the radical right is gaining power.

CULTURAL CRISIS

The introduction of networked computer technologies has had and continues to have a profound cultural impact on American society. The social lives of Americans are increasingly mediated by social network platforms and networked devices that not only connect individuals to friends and family but to the larger world. Networked computer technologies now frame and sequence the texture of everyday life in ways that are both subtle and powerful, but these changes have been met with precious little resistance or critical reflection (Greenfield, 2017).

The celebratory discourse that emerged alongside these technological transformations positioned networked computer technologies as a force of empowerment liberating individuals from the stultifying bureaucracies of the state and large corporations. It offered a narrative of personal liberation and the promise of networked subjectivities linked to one another in diverse networked communities. It is true, of course, that networked computer technologies make available a previously unimaginable wealth of information and that activists have used networked technologies to organize social movements and topple regimes in places like Egypt and Tunisia. Indeed, as I write this chapter, democratic activists in Chile, Hong Kong, and Lebanon are not only organizing political actions using networked computer technologies but are using these technologies to exchange ideas, tactics, and slogans.

However, there is nothing inherently empowering about networked computer technologies (Morozov, 2011, 2013). In fact, critical reflection on the structuring effects of these technologies should give pause to even the most ardent of techno-enthusiasts. The enormous amount of data produced by individuals as they interact with networked computer technologies in their daily lives opens them up to a dystopian level of surveillance and manipulation. These same technologies also empower authoritarian state actors to develop new modes of propaganda and to drown out democratic activists through a flood of disinformation. The governments of China and Russia, for example, have proven to be adept at using networked computer technologies to temper the radical potentialities they may facilitate.

To the extent that networked computer technologies do displace state power, it is transferred to a corporate sector organized around the commodification and manipulation of the daily lives of millions. This sector is dominated by a technology oligopoly unified by a shared cyber-utopian ideology that wields power over nation-states and trans-national institutions alike. Networked computer technologies may contribute to the development of distributed power structures, but they are bureaucratic power structures just the same. Indeed, their distributed character makes democratic accountability perhaps an even more distant dream.

The analysis presented in this chapter sought to take seriously Postman's call to critically reflect on the ways in which technological media structure the collective conversation of a society. I began with an analysis of cyber-utopianism to identify the ideological discourse informing the design of the networked computer technologies that increasingly frame, sequence, and mediate the ways in which individuals enter into the collective conversation of American political culture. I then turned to an analysis of how the curation flows that define networked computer technologies structure the daily lives of individuals and the ways in which they engage with their social worlds. What I take away from this analysis is that the celebratory narratives of cyber-utopian discourse belie a dangerous politics of atomization, surveillance, measurement, and behavior modification that are not well understood.

Telling a better story about the political culture of the contemporary conjuncture requires a critical engagement with the networked computer technologies that increasingly structure and mediate political discourse. The story offered here challenges the celebratory ways in which networked computer technologies are often discussed and points toward the uncomfortable reality that they do not encourage a coming together of humanity as much as a fragmenting of political culture in dangerous ways. The technological transformation of political culture structures societal communication in ways that foster closed epistemic communities, encourage political polarization and radicalization, and open new arenas in which dominant groups can exercise power over the marginalized. Indeed, attempts by the Russian state to use networked computer technologies to influence the 2016 presidential election has been a topic of considerable debate in the United States, but large-scale analyses indicate that the feedback loops and closed epistemic communities made possible by networked computer technologies were far more significant (Benkler et al., 2018).

A political culture increasingly defined by the quantitative increase in media choice and the qualitative shift toward networked computer technologies constitutes not a coming together but a tearing apart. In this light, Postman's "Huxleyan" warning appears prophetic. Technological shifts in political culture constituted by the emergence of social media and the blurring of distinctions between old and new media forms foster a set of relations, modes of communication, and subjectivities defined by fragmentation.

I argue that the analysis offered here traces the outline of an emergent crisis in a hegemonic order defined by cyber-utopian ideology. Networked computer technologies have made possible a computational politics of surveillance and targeted messaging that threaten the already crumbling facade of liberal democratic society in the United States (Tufekci, 2014). Individuals are now subject to opaque forms of surveillance and manipulation that may not be necessarily new but are unprecedented in both scale and sophistication. The broad messaging techniques of mass society have been replaced with narrowly targeted and polarizing messages that work to heighten political antagonisms. This observation is not a lament for a lost golden age but is an acknowledgment of structural change. Powerful actors now have the ability to micro-target messages at progressively more narrow groupings to influence political knowledge and behavior and to flood the public sphere with micro-targeted disinformation to fuel political antagonisms.

The explosion of disinformation and conspiracy theories associated with the global COVID-19 pandemic is perhaps a perfect example of this emergent cultural crisis. Online platforms are a battleground of information and disinformation about the origin, risks, possible treatments, cures, and so on, associated with the novel coronavirus. This space is contested by everyone from state actors to think tanks and political organizations to medical organizations to individual users, and the messages they propagate, the stories they tell, are not just meditated but *curated* by networked computer technologies. It is not surprising that disinformation is spreading; the structure and design of networked computer technologies do not simply make it possible but foster it. It is also not surprising that disinformation has taken root in popular consciousness is ways that reflect larger divisions within American society, such as political partisanship, race and ethnicity, social class, and so on (Schaeffer, 2020). The so-called politicization of the COVID crisis has revealed the underlying antagonisms of American political culture and the ways in which those antagonisms are produced, reproduced, and contested through a political culture mediated by networked computer technologies.

Fascist fantasies of a coming race war and a second American civil war are flourishing online, and these new digital communities are not confined to 4chan and social media platforms. The so-called Boogaloo movement and militia organizations (such as Oath Keepers and Patriot Prayer) are growing online and are organizing violent street protests using networked computer technologies. Largely peaceful Black Lives Matter protests are increasingly being met by heavily armed militia groups, and the violent clashes between these radical right actors and leftist activists shift public attention away from and ultimately undermine popular support for a vital protest movement challenging the murder of African Americans by law enforcement. These fascist political actors are, in many ways, a direct product of the increasing radicalism of the modern conservative movement, but it is the technological transformation of popular political culture that has fostered their growth and their ability to organize into a political force influencing state and Republican party politics.

Cyber-utopian ideology advances computational politics that is fueling the fragmentation of political culture with, following Postman, profound epistemological and ontological implications. Networked subjects are indeed forming new communities around shared interests, but these affinity groupings are organizing around shared ideologies that establish rigid in-group and out-group identifications. The danger here extends well beyond psychological constructs such as confirmation bias. Networked computer technologies have engendered the development of closed epistemic communities in which misinformation, conspiracy, propaganda, misogyny, racism, heteronormativity, and so on thrive. The subsequent demarcating of political lines fuels political antagonisms in ways that are fluid and not adequately captured by categories such as liberal, conservative, and so on. What is important for the story I am attempting to tell here is that the fragmentation of the political culture within the contemporary conjuncture has not simply made a space for the rise to power of the radical right, although that is certainly the case. What is significant is that the fragmented political landscape of the contemporary social formation is *radicalizing* and that this radicalization has benefited reactionary forces defending traditional hierarchies and advancing the interests of elite power.

CODA

I endeavored in this chapter to tell a better story about this historical moment through a cultural analysis of the contemporary conjuncture that was focused on the structuring effects of networked computer technologies on the popular political culture of the United States. I hope that it is clear to the reader that this chapter was not intended to be a polemic seeking to frame these technologies in a positive or negative binary. The task for this chapter was to challenge the cyber-utopian ideology that has risen to hegemonic dominance not just in Silicon Valley but the larger political culture, including its widespread and uncritical adoption by left-leaning activists and scholars around the globe. I have attempted to demonstrate here that the structuring effects of networked computer technologies are contributing to the fragmentation of the political culture of the United States into closed epistemic communities that is fueling political antagonisms and new modes of cultural violence against the marginalized. I believe that the analysis demonstrates that recent technological transformations are contributing to an emergent crisis in the political culture that is conjoining with crises in the economic and political domains in this historical moment of emergent conjunctural crisis. However, this does not mean that an implication of the analysis presented in this chapter necessitates the blanket rejection of computer technology. I do not see myself as being a twenty-first century Ned Ludd calling for the destruction of machines.

Indeed, this book project was made possible by many of the cyber-utopians that were the subject of critique. This book was written on a personal computer running a Linux operating system using the following open-source applications: LaTex, Texmaker, JabRef, LibreOffice, Inkscape, and GIMP. I may not share the libertarian and anarcho-capitalist politics of the cyber-utopians in the open-source community, but the idea that the tools of knowledge creation and artistic expression should be freely available to all is one that this leftist scholar can support. Although, it should be noted that the "flattened" communities that develop and maintain open-source and free software are in fact hierarchical and deeply misogynistic, as recent controversies involving Linus Torvalds and the Linux Foundation demonstrate (more on this in chapter 5).

I also hope that it is clear to the reader that the decision to focus on popular political culture as opposed to the larger cultural domain of the United States was an analytic decision due to its relevance to the larger conjunctural analysis I am pursuing with this book. It is clear that the structuring effects of networked computer technologies extend well beyond the narrow framing of political culture. The distributed subjectivities at work in a cultural domain increasingly defined by networked computer technologies are immersed within distributed systems of power that are opaque, if not invisible, at the individual level (Greenfield, 2017). Individuals are now immersed within technologically mediated regimes of surveillance, comparison, and self-regulation that are unprecedented in scope and scale, and they take a significant toll on the emotional lives of people in ways that we are only now beginning to comprehend (Fox & Moreland, 2015; Kramer et al., 2014). The broader cultural impact of networked computer technologies may be beyond the scope of the present analysis, but it is a topic in need of critical reflection and analysis by education scholars.

Finally, I hope that it is clear to the reader that the analysis presented in this chapter overlaps with the analyses presented in chapters 2 and 3. Indeed, all three of the analyses presented thus far have traced societal transformations taking place over the same two historical periods: the post–World War II formation and the post-1970s formation. It should go without saying that changes in the economic, political, and cultural domains are each bound up with the other and that there are complex patterns of exchange across and between these domains. However, while the preceding analyses hint at those patterns of exchange, these connections remain underdeveloped. This is to say that the larger conjunctural analysis that is the goal for this project remains inchoate and incomplete. Advancing this conjunctural analysis will require a move toward recovery and synthesis to establish connections and patterns of exchange across the preceding analyses and to build a foundation for the construction of a problem space to inform educational inquiry and practice. Or, put more simply, telling a better story about this historical moment requires that I begin to synthesize the various pieces of the puzzle I have constructed thus far into a more coherent narrative. It is to this task that I now turn.

Chapter 5

The Neoliberal Political Project

The primary task for this project is to tell a better story about this historical moment of emergent crisis. I began with the problem of right-wing populism as an emerging political force in the world system and called into question the crude economic explanations at work in popular discourse. I argued that, while economic change is a driving force behind the rise of so-called right-wing populism, a narrow focus on the economic sphere erases the complexity of the object of analysis, an observation with important implications for activists and scholars doing left-liberatory work.

Put simply, bad stories make for bad politics. The task I set for myself is to tell a better story about this historical moment to understand the rise of right-wing populism as a complex societal phenomenon being driven by an array of social forces operating within and across the economic, political, and cultural domains. My goal is to conceptualize right-wing populism as a problem space and to think through the implications of this conceptualization for pedagogical and scholarly practice.

The story I have told thus far presents the findings from a conjunctural analysis of the contemporary formation. The story traced the emergence of crises at work in the economic, political, and cultural domains conjoining in this historical moment through an analysis of the collapse of the postwar formation and the rise of the post-1970s formation. The narrative gestures toward the emerging crisis of the present as a crisis of hegemony in the post-1970s formation, but it remains in its present form an incomplete and unfinished story.

An attentive reader will surely have identified clear points of overlap and patterns of exchange among the actors, movements, and ideological discourses identified in the preceding chapters. It makes sense analytically to tease out the societal processes at work in the economic, political, and cultural domains. However, doing so risks reifying those analytic categories and opens the door to overly reductive, narrow analyses that posit unitary and discrete domains or, more reductively still, the possibility of one domain determining the operation of the others. To tell a better story conjunctural analysis must not only tease out the complex movement of forces within the relatively autonomous economic, political, and cultural domains and the emergent crises within each but must also trace the patterns of exchange among and between those domains and crises. Telling a better story about this historical moment will require a move toward synthesis.

This chapter will attempt to complete the conjunctural analysis of this historical moment by teasing out these patterns of exchange through a recovery of the neoliberal political project, the last element of the story I wish to tell. The reader may balk at this call for recovery and not without justification. Scholarship across a wide array of disciplinary fields are replete with analyses of and references to neoliberalism, but it is its seeming ubiquity in scholarship that has led to conceptual slippage that is problematic. And, in the spirit of full disclosure, I must confess that my own work has contributed to this mystification.

Neoliberalism is too often employed in scholarship as if it were an economic theory of globalization, financialization, and deregulation that displaces and erodes the power of the state through privatization and that reworks the cultural sphere through the discursive production of homo economici. Neoliberalism is frequently discussed in academic circles and in the public sphere as an economic theory promoting laissez-faire governance, self-regulating markets, the conflation of free market capitalism with democracy, and a single world market without borders undermining the legitimacy and power of the state. It is certainly the case that the neoliberal project is animated by an economic imaginary and that neoliberal policies have contributed to the transformation of the global economic system. However, "the fallacy of identifying neoliberalism exclusively with economic theory becomes apparent when we notice that the historical record teaches that the neoliberals themselves regarded such narrow exclusivity as a prescription for disaster" (Mirowski, 2009, p. 427).

In this chapter, I will work to tell a better story about this historical moment by recovering the neoliberal political project as a transformative force working within and across the economic, political, and cultural domains and as an animating force contributing to the emergent crises within each. This chapter will present a materialist analysis that conceptualizes neoliberalism not as a unified, totalizing force but as a political project made up of agents, movements, and ideological discourses that engage with, compliment, and contradict other agents, movements, and ideological discourses at work in the various societal domains (Clarke, 2008). A materialist analysis of the neoliberal political project will tease out the spaces, contradictions, and hybridizations that define the neoliberalism of the contemporary conjuncture and that will inform a move toward synthesizing the emergent crisis of the present as a "rich totality of many determinations and relations" (Marx, 1973, p. 100).

The chapter will begin by developing a theoretical model of neoliberalism using the work of Philip Mirowski. I will then retrace the steps of the preceding analysis examining the patterns of exchange between and among neoclassical economics, the modern conservative movement, cyber-utopianism, and the neoliberal project. And, I will conclude the chapter with a first move toward synthesizing the preceding analysis by developing a new conceptualization of the neoliberal political project and reflecting on the implications of this new conceptualization for politically engaged scholarship and pedagogy.

THE RUSSIAN NESTING DOLL MODEL

The analysis presented in this chapter will conceptualize neoliberalism not as economic theory or even political theory but as a political project with multiple histories at work within and across the economic, political, and cultural domains. Accordingly, neoliberalism is not a unitary object of analysis with a simple, straightforward definition but must be understood as a constellation of dynamic and mutating forces operating in patterns of cooperation, contestation, and contradiction. It is perhaps best to think of neoliberalism as a political project made up of an array of political projects that rose to hegemonic dominance from the 1980s onward. My goal in this chapter is to untangle this Gordian knot through a materialist analysis that draws upon two lines of thought in the historical work of Philip Mirowski (2014a, 2009): his Russian nesting doll model of neoliberalism and his concept of double truth.

Mirowski uses the conceptual model of a Russian nesting doll to understand neoliberalism as an elite political project made up of discrete political projects at work across the economic, political, and cultural domains each connected to the other in complex networks. This model conceptualizes the neoliberal political project as a series of nested dolls (or embedded shells) that are, on the one hand, relatively discrete and autonomous while, on the other hand, being defined by patterns of exchange, cooperation, competition, and contradiction across and between various shells. Each doll or shell is made up of a network of agents that are, in turn, bound up in larger networks of other dolls and shells. In Bourdieuian terms, each doll can be understood as a network of elite agents often working across multiple social fields who are each connected to other networked agents and social fields in complex patterns of exchange and competition.

Mirowski argues that a historical analysis of the neoliberal political project must begin with its innermost shell: the Mont Pèlerin Society (MPS).
The story of the MPS begins in 1938 Paris with the convening of the Walter
Lippmann Colloquium (WLC). The colloquium was organized by the French
philosopher Louis Rougier and brought together what would become some of
the most influential intellectuals of the twentieth century, including Ludwig
von Mises, Frederick von Hayek, Wilhelm Röpke and Alexander Rüstow, to
discuss Walter Lippmann's book *The Good Society*.

The convening of the colloquium reflected the elite anxieties of the interwar period over both the perceived crisis of liberalism brought on by the
Great Depression and the perceived threats posed by the rising tide of "collectivism" in the form of socialism and Keynesian social democracy. These
intellectuals saw liberal society as being threatened by the growing demands
of democratic publics and the collapse of empire, this was especially true for
Mises whose early work in the 1920s was animated by the collapse of the
Austro-Hungarian Empire. Participants discussed and debated topics such as
the relationship between capitalist economies and democracy, the ideals and
possibilities for authentic human freedom, and the nature and limitations of
human knowledge.

The debates that began at the WLC were interrupted by the outbreak of
World War II, but many of the same actors reconvened in 1947 in Mont
Pèlerin, Switzerland to begin the work anew. Organized by Hayek, the
meeting at Mont Pèlerin was attended by many of the same participants
from the WLC, such as Mises, Röpke, and Rüstow, but expanded in
size considerably to include intellectuals from across Europe and North
America, such as Karl Popper, Milton Friedman, and George Stigler. The
thirty-nine participants at the first MPS agreed that liberal society was in
a state of crisis and concluded with a formal statement of principles and a
vision for future study.

- The analysis and exploration of the nature of the present crisis so as to bring
  home to others its essential moral and economic origins.
- The redefinition of the functions of the state so as to distinguish more
  clearly between the totalitarian and the liberal order.
- Methods of re-establishing the rule of law and of assuring its development in such a manner that individuals and groups are not in a position to
  encroach upon the freedom of others and private rights are not allowed to
  become a basis of predatory power.
- The possibility of establishing minimum standards by means not inimical
  to initiative and functioning of the market.
- Methods of combating the misuse of history for the furtherance of creeds
  hostile to liberty.

- The problem of the creation of an international order conducive to the safe-guarding of peace and liberty and permitting the establishment of harmonious international economic relations (Mont Pèlerin Society, 1947).

More importantly, the drafting of these statements marked the founding of the MPS and with it the neoliberal political project.

The MPS was founded as a political society with the goal of constructing "a functional hierarchical elite of regimented political intellectuals" (Mirowski, 2014a, p. 43). The goal was to create a safe space out of the public eye to both debate ideas and to coordinate political action. Membership in the society was by invitation only so as to ensure that the work of the MPS remained out of the limelight and to ensure that debate stayed within relatively narrow bounds. Interestingly, the political project that developed at the MPS mirrored, in many ways, that of one of its perceived ideological enemies, the Fabian Society, in that its primary objective was to influence elite opinion with the ultimate goal being the gradual transformation of society. The founders of the MPS set out to construct a *new liberal* society through the propagation of ideas that have material consequences (M. Friedman, 2002, pp. xiii–xiv).

The neoliberal project enjoyed its earliest successes in spreading neoliberal ideas in the university economics departments associated with MPS members. Constituting the innermost shells of the neoliberal nesting doll, these economics departments developed into the various "schools" of neoliberalism, such as the Chicago School, the Virginia School, the London School of Economics, the Geneva School and the Freiburg School. The economic imperialism (Lazear, 2000) of the twentieth century ensured the spread of neoliberal thought to other influential academic disciplines, such as Business Management, Law, Public Policy, and Political Science, creating more nested dolls within the neoliberal political project. Over time, new shells emerged from the development of generalized think tanks funded by philanthropies and corporations to influence political parties, first on the Right and later the Left, and specialized think tanks organized around specific issues and policies. Neoliberal intellectuals also worked to develop new media outlets and to gain access to popular political media forming the outer shells of the neoliberal project. It is these outer shells of the nesting doll that constitute the public face of the neoliberal political project, but it is important to not reduce the constellation of forces at work in the neoliberal project down to the veneer that is most easily visible.

The strength of Mirowski's nested doll model is that it offers a historical perspective on the development of the neoliberal project that does not fall prey to a reductive erasure of complexity. Mirowski begins with what he terms the neoliberal thought collective that first developed at the MPS and traces the

historical development of the neoliberal project as it continues to expand out-
ward in the production of new nested dolls. The primary function of these shells
is to "amplify and distribute the voice of any one member throughout a series
of seemingly different organizations, personas, and broadcast settings, lending
it resonance and gravitas, not to mention fronting an echo chamber for ideas
right at the time when hearing them [is] most propitious" (Mirowski, 2014a,
p. 49). Each of the shells is discrete and relatively autonomous, yet they work
to promote and advance a relatively uniform set of political ideas and policies.

In Gramscian terms, the members of the MPS were and continue to be
public intellectuals operating on the contested field of ideological struggle.
Their goal was and remains to propagate their ideas to influence elite opinion
to re-engineer society from the top-down. Mirowski deserves to be quoted
here at length:

> The MPS construction of neoliberalism was anchored by a variety of mainly
> European and American roots, encompassed a variety of economic, political,
> and social schools of thought; and maintained a floating transnational agora for
> debating solutions to perceived problems and a flexible canopy tailored with
> an eye to accommodating existing relations of power in academia, politics, and
> society at large. The unusual structure of the thought collective helps explain
> why neoliberalism cannot be easily defined on a set of 3 by 5 cards and needs to
> be understood as a pluralist organism striving to distinguish itself from its three
> primary foes: laissez-faire classical liberalism, social welfare liberalism, and
> socialism. . . . [N]eoliberal intellectuals understood this general goal to imply a
> comprehensive long-term reform effort at retatting the entire fabric of society,
> not excluding the corporate world. The relationship between the neoliberals
> and capitalists was not merely that of passive apologists or corporate shills.
> Neoliberals aimed to develop a thoroughgoing reeducation effort for *all par-
> ties* to alter the tenor and meaning of political life: nothing more, nothing less.
> (Mirowski, 2009, p. 431)

The public intellectuals of the MPS sought to market neoliberal ideas across
the various nested shells of the neoliberal project to construct a new elite
consensus and to contribute to the continual formation of an ever-expanding
array of new nested dolls as a *political project* with global ambitions. Thus,
Mirowski's model traces the historical development of neoliberalism from
the development of its innermost nesting dolls to hegemonic dominance, and,
in so doing, it develops a conceptualization of the neoliberal political project
that does justice to the complexity, diversity, and diffuse networks that constitute the object of analysis.

The diverse and diffuse nature of the neoliberal political project is not
a weakness or handicap but is, instead, perhaps its greatest strength. The

flexibility and malleability of neoliberalism make possible a nimble political project that is able to shift and mutate in response to economic, political, and cultural change. It is a political project that can reflexively respond to societal change while advancing a relatively coherent set of political ideas (Mirowski, 2009, pp. 434–440).

The first of these ideas is what Michel Foucault (2010) identified as the neoliberal rejection of the "naturalism" of classical liberalism. Neoliberals reject the idea that the market society they envision will emerge spontaneously when freed from governmental interference. Markets and the market society must be *constructed*. The neoliberal political project does not seek to dismantle the state, as its critics from the Left frequently charge, but seeks to transform and recalibrate the state to serve neoliberal ends.

Second, neoliberalism conceptualizes markets as vast information processors and market participants as nodes in a distributed computational system. Market actors continuously signal information to other market participants through the price system that, in the aggregate, generates a spontaneous rational order that is greater than the sum of its parts. Individual market actors may not behave rationally, but their behavior is rationalized by markets. Neoliberals envision a strong state facilitating markets as a mode of technocratic management to *rationalize* society. Markets are the solution to every societal problem, including those created by markets.

Third, the neoliberal political project endows capital with "natural rights" that it seeks to strip from individuals. The principle role for the state is to safeguard the rights of capital. National borders, social norms, nor anything between should be allowed to hinder or restrict the ability of capital to seek profit. Neoliberals envision no such freedom of movement for individuals.

Fourth, neoliberals view economic and political inequality not as a bug in the capitalist system but a feature of a rational market society. Inequality is not an unfortunate byproduct of markets but is the engine driving the capitalist system. Ambition, envy, and greed shed their traditional framing as vices and become in the neoliberal world view the motivating force behind entrepreneurship, innovation, and human progress. It is fuel for the market society. The neoliberal political project posits a social Darwinian moral code that naturalizes and defends hierarchy from the democratic challenges of subaltern populations.

Finally, the neoliberal project rejects the political legitimacy of democratic practices. Democracy is, at best, tolerated but must be constrained. Neoliberals view socialism and Keynesian social democracy (both "collectivist" projects in neoliberal jargon) as a democratic challenge from below that threaten markets, the "natural rights" of capital, and the possibility of a rational society. The purest expression of human liberty and rationality is located in the marketplace, and any move to subsume the market to the will of the majority is an existential threat to human freedom and the possibility of a just and rational society.

These are the political ideas that constitute what Mirowski calls the neoliberal thought collective and that give shape to the neoliberal project. They inform the shared language of neoliberal intellectuals and shape the nature of internal debates among them. However, it is important to distinguish between this internal discourse and the public-facing discourse of neoliberalism.

Mirowski notes that there is a disconnect between the internal discourse among neoliberal intellectuals and the popular political discourse they champion in the public, what he terms the double truth of neoliberalism. Specifically, Mirowski draws a distinction between the exoteric and esoteric discourses of neoliberalism.

> What I shall refer to here is the proposition that an intellectual thought collective might actually concede that, as a corollary of its developed understanding of politics, it would be necessary to maintain an exoteric version of its doctrine for the masses—because that would be safer for the world and more beneficial for ordinary society—but simultaneously hold fast to an esoteric doctrine for a small closed elite, envisioned as the keepers of the flame of the collective's wisdom. Furthermore, whereas both exoteric and esoteric versions would deal with many similar themes and issues, the exoteric version might appear on its face to contradict the esoteric version in various particulars. (Mirowski, 2014a, p. 68)

The popular political discourse of neoliberalism mythologizes the naturalism of free markets, argues for curbing the power of the state to interfere in the lives of individuals, positions itself as defending human rights and equality, and champions market democracy. It is an exoteric discourse that stands in contradistinction to the esoteric neoliberal discourse of state activism and technocratic management, the privileging of capital and corporate rights, the embrace of inequality and hierarchy, and a distrust of democracy.

The founding members of the MPS understood that elite opinion wields significant influence over popular consciousness. The neoliberal project developed from its founding at Mont Pèlerin into complex networks, or nested dolls, held loosely together by an elite esoteric discourse, but neoliberalism advanced to a dominant position in the post-1970s formation through the promotion of an exoteric discourse that spoke and continues to speak to the lived experiences of the masses living within late capitalism (Hall, 1988a). The founding members of the MPS took up a Gramscian project to drive societal transformation via ideological leadership.

The task for this chapter is to recover the neoliberal political project as an animating force at work in the emergent crisis of the present. I will present an analysis that takes seriously Mirowski's nested doll model to conceptualize neoliberalism as a complex political project made up of networks and networked actors operating within and across nested shells, and I will take care to distinguish between the esoteric and exoteric discourses of the neoliberal project. I hope to trace the influence of the neoliberal project across the economic, political, and cultural domains and as a force at work in the emergent crises within each. My goal is not to identify how the neoliberal project is the primary cause of the economic, political, and cultural crises identified in preceding chapters but is to trace the patterns of exchange between the three domains. I will seek to tease out the spaces, contradictions, and hybridizations that are inherent to the neoliberal project to open up news spaces for political and cultural criticism and activism. Telling a better story about the emergent crisis of the present requires a materialist analysis of the neoliberal project and a synthesis of the movement of forces at work in the contemporary conjuncture.

RECONSTRUCTING THE ECONOMIC DOMAIN

The analysis in chapter 2 identified an emergent economic crisis in the contemporary conjuncture through a historical analysis of long-wave secular trends in the world system. The postwar A phase of the world system and the Keynesian political economy of the era collapsed in the crisis of the 1970s. The crisis created an opening for the rise of neoclassical economic theory to hegemonic dominance in the United States and, accordingly, the world system from the 1980s forward. The neoclassical hegemony of an American-dominated world system fundamentally restructured the world economy and successfully restored capital accumulation in a B phase of secular stagnation. However, as I attempted to demonstrate, the neoclassical restructuring of the global economy has produced ever-growing economic fragmentation and antagonism that is fueling a hegemonic crisis in the economic domain.

The reader will surely have noted that many of the actors associated with the neoclassical counter-revolution against Keynesian political economy in the postwar era, such as Friedman and Hayek, were also central actors in the founding of the neoliberal political project at Mont Pèlerin. The reader would be justified in thinking that there is little difference between neoclassical economics and the neoliberal political project or even in conflating the two. S/he would certainly not be alone in doing so. It is quite common for critics on the left to blur the distinction between the two, but the failure to distinguish between neoclassical economic theory and neoliberalism is a serious mistake (Mirowski, 2014b).

It was Thorstein Veblen (1900) who first attached the term "neoclassical" to the economic science of his day, and the targets for his critique, such as the concept of utility, remain relevant to contemporary critiques of orthodox economics. The neoclassical theory at work in the contemporary conjuncture conceptualizes economics as an axiomatic social science reliant on mathematical modeling for a deductive, positivist approach to inquiry. Neoclassical theory asserts the primacy of the mostly rational individual pursuing a utility function and the primacy of the "free market" tending toward a stable equilibrium when freed from government intervention.

Put simply, neoclassical theory posits that a lightly regulated free marketplace of utility-maximizing individuals will lead to the efficient allocation of scarce resources and a stable equilibrium. Neoclassical theory does acknowledge the possibility of market failure, when the utility-maximizing behavior of individuals fails to produce efficient or rational outcomes, as well as light touch regulations to correct market failure, but neoclassical economics fetishizes the naturalism of markets. For orthodox neoclassical economists, market failures are most likely to occur due to outside interference from the state.

The founding members of the MPS largely rejected the laissez-faire naturalism of neoclassical theory. This rejection was not necessarily universal; Friedman was committed to neoclassical economic science. But, it was a conceptualization of markets and the state that was dismissed by the neoliberal thought collective, "with Hayek, the Austrian School, and the Ordoliberals all rejecting the legitimacy of neoclassical economic theory as an appropriate framework within which to understand how the market worked" (Mirowski, 2014b, p. 9). They understood the lesson that Polanyi had learned from his historical analysis of the long nineteenth century: the free market must be planned by a strong state. Indeed, Polanyi's brother and intellectual sparring partner, Michael, was a founding member of the MPS.

The neoliberal political project at work in the contemporary conjuncture differs from the neoclassical theory dominating the field of economics in important ways. Neoliberals do not conceptualize individuals as being mostly rational agents pursuing utility nor markets as natural, homeostatic systems to be overseen by a limited state. Individual actors must be *rationalized* through the imposition of market logics across all domains of human life, and markets must be constructed through political and ideological work. Indeed, in the neoliberal world view, humans are essentially collectivists and are therefore a continual threat to the market society envisioned by the neoliberal project. Markets must be *constructed* and *protected* from democratic demands by a strong state.

[T]he distinguishing characteristic of neoliberal doctrines and practice is that they embrace this prospect of retasking the strong state to impose their vision of a society properly open to the dominance of the market, again, as they conceive it. The fact that neoliberals from Friedrich Hayek to James Buchanan to Richard Posner to Walter Rüstow (who invented the term *Vitalpolitik* which Foucault translated as "biopolitics") to Jacques Rueff, not to mention a plethora of figures after 1970, all explicitly proposed policies to strengthen the state, seems to elude almost anyone approaching the MPS from the outside. Friedman's own trademark proposals, like putting the money supply on autopilot, or replacing public schools with vouchers, required an extremely strong state to enforce them. (Mirowski, 2014b, p. 10)

The neoliberal political project requires a strong state to construct and expand markets and, more importantly, to protect markets from democratic challenges from below that might distort market processes and disrupt the hierarchies that are a necessary precondition for their vision of a market society.

Another important difference between neoliberalism and neoclassical economics is epistemological. Neoclassical economists employ statistical models to produce precise, "scientific" knowledge about markets, the behavior of market actors, and the outcomes of market processes. Hayek, in particular, flatly rejected the scientific pretenses of neoclassical economics to precise knowledge about the functioning and future outcomes of market competition.

The necessary consequence of the reason why we use competition is that, *in those cases in which it is interesting*, the validity of [an economic] theory can never be tested empirically. We can test it on conceptual models, and we might conceivably test it in artificially created real situations, where the facts which competition is intended to discover are already known to the observer. But in such cases it is of no practical value, so that to carry out the experiment would hardly be worth the expense. If we do not know the facts we hope to discover by means of competition, we can never ascertain how effective it has been in discovering those facts that might be discovered. All we can hope to find out is that, on the whole, societies which rely for this purpose on competition have achieved their aims more successfully than others. (Hayek, 1978, p. 180)

Hayek was especially keen to differentiate between market equilibrium, which implies a phenomenon that can be precisely measured and known, and market order, which is beyond measurement. The neoliberal conceptualization of the market and market competition is that of an ineffable, spontaneous order. The neoliberal project is primarily concerned with the political and in developing the means by which to introduce and foster market competition without the pretense of a positivist social science.

The conflation of neoclassical economic theory and the neoliberal political project by critics on the Left is perhaps best explained by a failure to distinguish the esoteric and exoteric discourses of neoliberalism. The exoteric discourse of neoliberalism adopts the language of neoclassical economics. Neoliberals expound on the power of "free markets," the need to limit the power of the state, the goal of freeing individuals from government and bureaucracy, and the realization of authentic freedom through consumer choice. The exoteric discourse of neoliberalism constructs a narrative of human liberty linked to the free markets mythologized by neoclassical economics. The esoteric discourse of neoliberalism, however, constructs a narrative of elite societal engineering operating at the global, national, and individual levels.

Quinn Slobodian (2018) describes the neoliberal political project as elite social engineering operating at a global scale. Slobodian traces the development of the neoliberal political project through a historical analysis of the Hayekian influenced Geneva School that points toward decolonization as being one of the animating forces driving the neoliberal project. The early work of Mises in the interwar period was motivated by the collapse of the Austro-Hungarian Empire, but it was the period of rapid decolonization following World War II that became a primary concern within the intellectual core, or inner shell, of the neoliberal political project.

The neoliberals looked on in horror as new global institutions were constructed after World War II. They viewed the United Nations (UN) and the Bretton Woods institutions as providing a framework for newly empowered democratic publics across the global South to pursue a politics of redistribution and social justice. The neoliberals of the MPS possessed a sophisticated understanding of their political context and understood that once constructed, these institutions would be difficult if not impossible to dismantle. So, they set about re-engineering them to achieve their political goals.

The neoliberal political project sought to influence elite opinion and policymakers as a means of transforming these new institutions into a global framework to limit and constrain the autonomy of individual nations and to circumscribe the power of the newly liberated nations of the global South. Neoliberals envisioned a global constitutional order of multilayered governance operating outside of direct democratic decision-making, the trade dispute settlement mechanism of the WTO, and the structural adjustment policies of the IMF and World Bank being the most prominent examples. Slobodian traces a line "from the end of the Hapsburg Empire to the foundation of the World Trade Organization" to outline the civilization ideal envisioned by the neoliberal political project.

It was necessarily global, designed with institutions to contain potential disruptions from the democratically empowered masses. It was a world without empires but with rules set by supranational bodies operating beyond the reach of any electorate. It was a world where the global economy was safely protected from the demands of redistributive equality and social justice. (Slobodian, 2018, p. 264)

Drawing upon Weberian language, Slobodian uses the metaphor of *encasement* to understand the imaginary teleos of the neoliberal project as insulating the global economy from the desires of democratic publics.

Neoliberalism is here a theory of law and statecraft that envisions a world civilization of competitive federalism defined by a global set of rules imposed by a technocratic institutional framework. The neoliberal political project sought to develop an institutional framework to construct and protect the global market from democratic publics and to use the global economy to discipline national politics. "In the neoliberal vision of world order, the world economy exercises discipline on individual nations through the perpetual threat of crisis, the flight of investment that punishes expansion of social policy, and speculative attacks on currencies in reaction to increases in government spending" (Slobodian, 2018, pp. 270–271).

Despite the differences and disputes within the neoliberal thought collective, it was the globalist orientation of the Geneva School that came to define the neoliberal political project at work in the contemporary conjuncture. Neoliberalism is, at its core, a political project oriented around multilayered global governance in which the state is far from being obsolete or expendable. In fact, the state is indispensable to the neoliberal project.

It is not just that state power in the global North constructed the global institutions of the postwar era and transformed them toward neoliberal ends in the wake of the 1970s, although that is certainly the case. The power of the state (both in the global North and South) is required to maintain constant vigilance in regulating and reforming the global framework in response to societal change. State power is the primary mechanism through which the neoliberal political project regulates national economic structures to ensure the free movement of capital, construct political legitimacy to neoliberal policies, and manage populations to blunt democratic challenges from below.

There is, however, no one archetypal model for the neoliberal state. As neoliberalism expanded from the MPS core to its outer shells, the ideas and practices of the neoliberal project were adapted to and, in turn, influenced by the local contexts of individual states. The neoliberal state is defined by adaptation and divergence, but it is also defined by the general privileging of business and the financial industry "over the well-being of the population or environmental quality" (Harvey, 2007, pp. 70–71).

The neoliberal state is perhaps best understood as an ongoing process of reform and reconfiguration organized around a politics of withdrawal and intervention that serves the interest of capital over that of the masses. The neoliberal reconfiguration of the state involves the removal or non-enforcement of environmental, financial, and labor regulations; the lowering of taxes on business and wealthy individuals; the privatization of state services; the cutting and limiting eligibility for social security services; and the reconfiguration of legal structures to ensure elite impunity to the law, for example, the lack of prosecutions for financial crimes in the aftermath of the 2008 financial crisis. At the same time, the neoliberal state intervenes in the economy by negotiating free trade agreements; offering large corporations tax credits that effectively transfer capital from the state to private coffers; assisting corporations in the externalization of workforce training and environmental cleanup costs onto the public sector; limiting risks for financial institutions through bailouts and financial backstops; constructing new markets through so-called public-private partnerships that transfer profit to the private sector and risk to the public sector; introducing work or volunteer requirements for eligibility for state services that ensure a steady supply of low-cost labor; and disciplining consumers by limiting their ability to challenge finance and business through legal channels, such as the enforcement of fraudulent financial contracts on homeowners in the aftermath of the financial crisis of 2008.

Indeed, despite its exoteric discourse of individualism and liberty, neoliberal practice is organized around the management of individuals and, accordingly, entire populations. The neoliberal political project posits the primacy of the private sphere and individual choice, but the private sphere it envisions stands in marked contrast to its exoteric discourse.

> "[P]rivatisation" is not merely a process of transfer to an unchanged private space. The private is re-worked in the process—subject to processes of responsibilisation and regulation; and opened to new forms of surveillance and scrutiny. Both corporate and state processes aim to "liberate" the private—but expect the liberated subjects to behave responsibly (as consumers, as parents, as citizen-consumers). (Clarke, 2004, p. 33)

The neoliberal political project advances a model of governance informed by managerial logics of responsibilization and rationalization. It is a political project of societal engineering.

The neoliberal reform and reconstruction of both the public and private spheres work to subject individuals to increasing levels of surveillance, measurement, quantification, and accountability policies that regulate human behavior through rewards and punishments. Neoliberalism works to responsibilize individuals by constructing regulatory structures that establish performance metrics, measure performance, and hold individuals "accountable" for reaching those metrics and by constructing neoliberal subjectivities informed by concepts developed from positive psychology, such as "growth mindset," "mindfulness," and "positive organizational behavior," that maximize entrepreneurial behaviors while minimizing critical questioning of the regulatory structures surrounding daily activity. Neoliberal rationalization seeks to shape unconscious behavior through gamification strategies designed to influence human activity without the individual understanding how they are being regulated. The neoliberal project constitutes a new technocratic paternalism that employs "nudges" to rationalize human behavior (Thaler & Sunstein, 2003, 2009).

A paradigmatic example of neoliberal managerialism can be found in the so-called gig economy, a sector of the economy often wrapped in the celebratory language of entrepreneurship. Gig work requires the worker to take on risks that would have previously been borne by the employer, such as the purchase of tools necessary for the job, and subjects the worker to a regulatory structure built around networked computer technologies. These technologies measure performance and dole out rewards and punishments in real-time, such as giving more gigs to workers who have high customer reviews or who are willing to take low paying-jobs while withholding work for low ratings or failure to take jobs. Networked computer technologies not only responsibilize workers but are also designed to influence or gamify worker behavior through interface design geared toward engagement and symbolic rewards.

The "gig economy" may be the paradigmatic example, but the managerial logics of neoliberalism permeate public and private life. The health exchanges established by the Affordable Care Act work to responsibilize and rationalize individual behavior in myriad ways, from eligibility and reporting requirements to interventions designed to subtly steer individuals toward healthy behaviors. The neoliberal political project works to influence individual behavior and construct new subjectivities within a regulatory structure of surveillance, measurement, and quantification.

Scholarly work in the Foucaultian tradition has made the strongest contribution to understanding the regulatory structures of the neoliberal political project. This work has focused on governmentality and the managing of populations through perpetual intervention across all spheres of human life. Within this theoretical framework, neoliberal discourses are regimes of truth (Foucault, 2010) informing practices of responsibilization and rationalization across all domains of human life that is informed by an economic imaginary that corresponds with but cannot be reduced to neoclassical economic theory.

Neoclassical economic theory is the dominant model informing orthodox economic research in the contemporary conjuncture. The privileged status of the economics discipline in the university facilitates the diffusion of neoclassical theory and methods to other social science disciplines and (ultimately) to public institutions. Neoliberalism is an activist political project concerned with issues of governance and law. It is a political project of elite societal engineering operating at global, national, and individual levels.

Neoclassical economic theory and the neoliberal political project are distinct from one another, but it is also clear that they work in tandem (Mirowski, 2014a, p. 13). It is perhaps best to think of neoclassical economic theory and neoliberalism as two complimentary forces that have been restructuring the world economy since the crisis of the 1970s and that are animating an emergent crisis of fragmentation and growing economic antagonism. The challenge for scholars and activists on the Left is to think through the patterns of exchange, cooperation, contradiction, and competition between neoclassical economics and the neoliberal political project, and it will require a new liberatory imagination and politics working toward the transformation of economics and social science departments in universities, a prerequisite for any hope of transforming neoliberal regulatory structures operating at the global, national, and individual levels. A Left response to the emergent economic crisis at work in the contemporary conjuncture will require shifting economic theory and research away from deductive, positivist mathematical modeling that eschews philosophical questions around methodology or distributive justice toward an economics of structural transformation oriented around human emancipation as a normative value (Lawson, 1997, p. 277). It will also require interrogating the technocratic and elitist politics of the neoliberal project and to imagine a new politics of distributive justice and democratic decision-making in economic policy.

RESTORATION OF HIERARCHY

The analysis presented in chapter 3 traced the rise to hegemonic dominance of the modern conservative movement understood as a reactionary, counter-revolutionary movement animating a neofascist politics reminiscent of Carl Schmitt's friend-enemy binary. The modern conservative movement rose to power on a politics of "us" and "them" that re-energized patriarchal white nationalism and used these energies to build a base of political power that is antidemocratic and increasingly dangerous. The modern conservative movement played an instrumental role in constructing the post-1970s social formation, but the forces that it unleashed now threaten the republic it claims, at least rhetorically, to save.

The modern conservative movement may have played a critical role in the development of the post-1970s formation and the emergent crisis into which it is entering, but its rise to dominance coincided with and was, in part, made possible by the parallel rise to hegemonic dominance of the neoliberal political project. It may not be readily apparent, at first glance, how these two projects came to work together. The cosmopolitan, globalists who founded the MPS would appear to have very little in common with fervent nationalists and religious conservatives. Indeed, prominent neoliberals, such as Hayek (1960) and Buchanan (2005), went out of their way to differentiate the neoliberal project from conservatism. Neoliberals charged that conservatism's traditionalism made it resistant to the social changes inherent to their vision of a market society, that its nationalism threatened the global order envisioned by the neoliberal project, and that its paternalism inevitably leads it to embrace the "coercion and arbitrary power" of the state "so long as it is used for what [conservatism] regards as the right purposes" (Hayek, 1960, p. 401). However, despite protestations to the contrary, the neoliberal political project and the modern conservative movement are each bound up with the other. Understanding the emergent political crisis of this historical moment requires that we think neoliberalism and conservatism together (Brown, 2006).

The first way that we need to think neoliberalism and conservatism together is to acknowledge that neither the modern conservative movement nor the neoliberal political project are unitary objects of analysis. I have attempted to make clear in both chapter 3 and the present chapter that the modern conservative movement and the neoliberal political project are composed of a diverse set of actors, movements, and ideological discourses working in complex relations of cooperation, competition, and contradiction. Both projects must be understood as complex and multifaceted and as being in a constant state of flux. These two political projects are not fixed in time and space but are constantly shifting their thinking and political practices in response to societal changes and to shifts in the power relations among constituent groups.

Second, it is important to acknowledge that there is considerable overlap between the neoliberal political project and the modern conservative movement. They are both reactionary political projects that share common enemies: Keynesian political economy and economic regulations, the democratic challenges of subaltern groups, civil rights legislation and jurisprudence, and redistributive social welfare policies. Put simply, they share a common goal of restoring what they consider to be "natural" hierarchies.

The neoliberal political project and the modern conservative movement were both made possible and continue to advance thanks to the largesse of elite philanthropic funding. The Powell memorandum issued a call to arms that mobilized elites for the nascent conservative movement. Elite philanthropic funding was also instrumental to the funding of the MPS. The Volker Fund financed the first meeting of the MPS and continued to finance seminal thinkers like Hayek long after he had fallen from favor with neoclassical economists.

The neoliberal political project and the modern conservative movement share networks of elite political actors, think tanks, and philanthropic foundations. The Trump administration, for example, included both neoliberal elites, such as Steven Mnuchin, and conservative white nationalists, such as Steven Miller. However, the two camps are by no means mutually exclusive. Friedman was both a founding member of the MPS and was active in conservative politics all of his life. More importantly, neoliberal and conservative elites maintain formal and informal connections to a shared network of influential think tanks and philanthropic foundations. These shared networks facilitate the continuous exchange of ideas and personnel, and they ensure that both of these reactionary political projects are able to reflexively respond to societal change.

Third, the neoliberal political project and the modern conservative movement both engage in ideological-political work. They work to influence elite opinion through think tanks, universities, and government, and they also work to influence popular opinion through ideological work in popular culture. Buckley's *God and Man at Yale* and the *National Review* were aimed at relatively elite audiences, but it was the media empires of the Religious Right and a constellation of conservative media outlets that fueled conservatism's rise to hegemonic dominance. Mises and Hayek argued that neoliberal ideological work should be aimed at influencing elite opinion through think tanks, universities, and government, but Friedman pioneered neoliberal ideological work in popular culture (Brandes, 2020). Today, the conservative media landscape serves up a steady diet of both conservative and neoliberal discourses.

And, finally, there is a high degree of resonance between neoliberal and conservative discourses. The inward-facing, or esoteric, discourse of neoliberalism and the modern conservative movement advance hierarchical order, antidemocratic politics, and the use of state power to achieve political aims. The outward-facing, or exoteric, discourse of neoliberalism and modern conservative movement advance a utopic imaginary of individual liberty, market freedom, and limited governance.

Thinking the neoliberal political project and the modern conservative movement together does not, and indeed should not, conflate these two reactionary projects. Neoliberalism and conservatism adhere to two different political rationalities. Neoliberalism adheres to a market-political rationality while conservatism adheres to a moral-political rationality (Brown, 2006). However, even here, the distinction between these two rationalities is not always clear cut.

Recent work by Wendy Brown (2019) and Melinda Cooper (2017) identifies a strain of moral-political rationality at work in neoliberal discourse, especially in the work of Hayek. Brown identifies two forms of privatization within the neoliberal political project. The first is the economic privatization discussed in chapter 2. The second form of privatization relates to responsibilization which she terms familial privatization. Cooper (2017, p. 21) describes familial privatization this way:

[T]he strategic reinvention of a much older, poor-law tradition of private family responsibility, using the combined instruments of welfare reform, changes to taxation, and monetary policy. Under their influence, welfare has been transformed from a redistributive program into an immense federal apparatus for policing the private family responsibilities of the poor, while deficit spending has been steadily transferred from the state to the private family.

Hayek (1979) argued that traditional values, which he conceptualized as a spontaneous order separate from any guiding hand, must supplement free markets to sustain and secure societies from the disruption of the global marketplace (Brown, 2019, p. 90). This is not to say that neoliberalism is conservative. Hayek was very clear about this. It is, instead, evidence of the resonance between these two projects as well as discursive exchange between conservatives and neoliberals. After all, Hayek made his argument for the role of traditional values in the neoliberal project after decades of working alongside prominent conservatives in the United States and Europe.

The point I am trying to make here is that the neoliberal political project and the modern conservative movement are, on the one hand, distinct political projects informed by unique political grammars and, on the other hand, are each bound up with the other in complex relations of cooperation, competition, and contradiction. Thinking the neoliberal political project and the modern conservative movement together requires that we attend to the patterns of exchange between these two reactionary political projects. These patterns of exchange operate as both discursive and governmental practices.

Neoliberal and conservative discourses call upon a broadly shared set of cemented norms, moral structures, and national symbols, but each reworks them in the process. This ensures that there is a necessary resonance between the discursive practices of these two political projects while also being reflective of their very different political grammars. There is resonance as well as divergence and contradiction. Understanding the emergent political crisis of this historical moment requires that we jettison the search for a coherent, unified ideology that has achieved hegemonic dominance within the contemporary conjuncture and think instead of ideological discourses and hegemonies in the plural.

Ideology is always contradictory. There is no single, integrated "ruling ideology"—a mistake we repeat again now in failing to distinguish between conservative and neoliberal repertoires. Ideology works best by suturing together contradictory lines of argument and emotional investments—finding what Laclau called "systems of equivalence" between them. Contradiction is its *métier*. . . . [F]ew strategies are so successful at winning consent as those which root themselves in the contradictory elements of common sense, popular

life and consciousness. Even today, the market/free enterprise/private property
discourse persists cheek by jowl with older conservative attachments to nation,
racial homogeneity, Empire, tradition. "Market forces" is good for restoring the
power of capital and destroying the redistributive illusion. But in moments of
difficulty one can trust "the Empire" to strike back. (Hall, 2017b, p. 326)

The resonance and dissonance between neoliberal and conservative discourses structure the political landscape of the contemporary formation. It
is the discursive tension between these ideologies that is the driving force
behind the continuing salience and vitality of both the neoliberal political
project and the modern conservative movement. It is a discursive tension that
allows for a "big tent" politics encompassing radically different and often
contradictory groups empowering individuals to construct disparate political identities while working to advance a relatively uniform set of political
goals. The discursive power of the neoliberal political project emanates from
a suturing of this ideological discourse to a conservative ideology of nationalism, white supremacy, American exceptionalism, and "traditional" values
that arose alongside and in concert with the rise of neoliberalism.

The governmental practices borne of the suturing of these two ideological discourses draw upon the technocratic orientation of neoliberalism and
the paternalism of conservatism. Neoliberals sought to construct and protect
the market society they envisioned through processes of marketization and
responsibilization, a mode of technocratic governance that drew upon the
patriarchal white nationalism of the modern conservative movement. Despite
the exoteric discourses of limited government advanced by both neoliberals and conservatives, the suturing of the neoliberal political project and the
modern conservative movement has reconfigured and expanded the scope
of the state, and it has retasked the state with cementing rigid hierarchies
through what Foucault termed "permanent vigilance" or "governmentality."

The neoliberal political project and the modern conservative movement
rose to hegemonic dominance together, but there is no reason to believe that
this historical settlement is fixed or permanent. The marketization of the
post-1970s social formation has led to extreme concentrations of wealth and
political power, an outcome that was both anticipated and welcomed by the
neoliberal intellectuals who founded the MPS. However, this concentration
of wealth and power has given rise to plutocratic politics undermining both
the free market envisioned by neoliberals and the historic settlement between
neoliberals and conservatives. The neoliberal political project rose to power
in concert with the modern conservative movement, but the "traditional"
values espoused by conservatives have failed to hold society together in
the face of massive economic and political dislocation, as Hayek had envisioned. Instead, its historical settlement with the conservative movement has

unleashed a virulent, anti-elite politics threatening the post-1970s social formation just as the collapse of nineteenth-century liberalism set the stage for the rise of the fascist politics of the interwar period. The emergent political crisis of this historical moment is not simply the product of the logics of the modern conservative movement. The present political crisis has two fathers: neoliberalism and conservatism.

The Left must think the neoliberal political project and the modern conservative movement together (Brown, 2006). This requires developing a synthetic perspective of these two projects that take into account the complex patterns of exchange, areas of overlap, and points of departure between these two elite political projects. Such a synthetic perspective will empower the Left to identify and exploit potential divergences between these two projects and to advance a new counter-hegemonic politics centered around liberatory logics.

MANAGING POPULATIONS

Chapter 4 presented an analysis of the technological transformation of American popular political culture. It traced the development of cyber-utopian discourse informing the design of networked computer technologies and their structuring effects on how individuals enter into the collective conversation of a political culture. I argued in that chapter that the rise to dominance of cyber-utopian discourse to hegemonic dominance in the post-1970s social formation has produced a fragmented and radicalizing political culture that ultimately serves the interests of reactionary politics.

Cyber-utopianism emerged from the seemingly paradoxical co-mingling of the military-industrial research complex and New Left radicalism in elite universities. The founding members of the MPS sought to shift elite opinion within elite universities, but they were not alone in doing so. The Cold War turned the university into an ideological battleground over not just politics or political systems but also over the nature of scholarly inquiry. "In a deliberate and also largely covert effort to resist the possibility of communist/ Marxist encroachment on the US *conceptual* establishment . . . individuals, government entities including the military and intelligence bodies, and private foundations like the RAND Corporation, promoted values like objectivity and rationalism over against subjectivity, collectivity, and shared responsibility" (Golumbia, 2009, p. 32). The federal government, U.S. military establishment, and corporate America became increasingly involved in elite universities in the postwar era, and their intervention made for some interesting bedfellows. For example, Noam Chomsky may have been a strident critic of American foreign policy and militarism, but his early linguistic work was both grounded in the computational cybernetic logics of the military-industrial research complex and was funded by the U.S. military and Eastman Kodak (Chomsky, 1957). It was in the strange intellectual cultural milieu of the postwar university that cybernetics, systems theory, and the cyborg sciences emerged, and it would influence both the neoliberal political project and the Left radicalism of the era.

Hayek was especially interested in cybernetics and systems theory. His imperial intervention into psychology, *The Sensory Order* (Hayek, 1952), drew upon cybernetics to theorize individual psychology within his conceptual model of spontaneous order, specifically the role of negative feedback loops in stabilizing a dynamic system following exogenous shocks. What Hayek saw in cybernetics was scientific proof for both his conceptualization of spontaneous order and the impossibility of social justice.

> It may be difficult to understand, but I believe there can be no doubt about it, that we are led to utilise more relevant information when our remuneration is made to depend indirectly on circumstances we do not know. It is thus that, in the language of modern cybernetics, the feedback mechanism secures the maintenance of a self-generating order. It was this which Adam Smith saw and described as the operation of the "invisible hand"—to be ridiculed for 200 years by uncomprehending scoffers. It is indeed *because* the game of catallaxy disregards human conceptions of what is due to each, and rewards according to success in playing the game under the same formal rules, that it produces a more efficient allocation of resources than any design could achieve. (Hayek, 1978, pp. 63–64)

Social justice, in the Hayekian system, requires the impossible: perfect knowledge. The only possibility for the efficient allocation of resources, just outcomes, and human liberty is to relinquish control to the Hayekian model of the marketplace as spontaneous *computational* order. Hayek's desire to reframe societal processes and human psychology within the structural logics of computation was a reflection of the dominant model of inquiry within elite universities just as much as Chomsky's universal grammar.

The Left Communalists of the 1960s and 1970s also looked to cybernetics and systems theory for scientific validation. New communalists, such as Charles Reich (1970), sought to construct a new consciousness beyond the bureaucratic man of the postwar era, what Reich termed Consciousness III. Reich's communalism was not a rejection of the technologies made possible by industrial society but, instead, embraced those technologies as tools to create new humans and to dismantle industrial society.

> The new consciousness seeks new ways to live in light of what technology has made both possible and desirable. . . . Consciousness III could only have come

into existence given today's technology. And only Consciousness III can make possible the continued survival of man as a species in this age of technology. (Reich, 1970, p. 308)

Fred Turner notes that the new humans envisioned by the New Communalists were connected to one another not through traditional politics or bureaucratic structures but through natural, spontaneous systems that valorize the atomized neoliberal subject.

> By turning to consciousness as the source of social change, Reich and the New Communalists who put his ideas into practice turned away from the political struggles that preoccupied both the New Left and the Democratic and Republican parties. But, even as they did, they opened new doors to mainstream culture, and particularly to high-technology research culture. If the mind was the first site of social change, then information would have to become a key part of countercultural politics. And if those politics rejected hierarchy, then the circles-within-circles of information and systems theory might somehow make sense not only as ideas about information, but also as evidence from the natural world for the rightness of collective polity. . . . [I]ndividual lifestyle choices became political acts, and both consumption and lifestyle technologies— including information technologies—would have to take on a newly political valence. (Turner, 2006, p. 38)

Like Hayek and the exoteric discourse of neoliberalism, the new communalists sought to liberate the individual from the bureaucratic state and conceptualized individual action as having macro-level effects in the production of a spontaneous computational order defined by looping circuits of energy and information.

Indeed, computationalism is the unifying metaphor conjoining the neoliberal political project and the cyber-utopians of Silicon Valley, and it is a political metaphor that has become woven into the social fabric of the post-1970s formation. Neoliberals envision the capitalist marketplace as a spontaneous, computational order that can liberate the individual from the state and bureaucracy. Cyber-utopians envision cyberspace as a spontaneous, computational order that can liberate the individual from the state and bureaucracy. They may frame their rhetoric in the anti-elite language of free speech, democratization, and well-worn platitudes that "information wants to be free," but cyber-utopians advance a neoliberal politics fetishizing a social space, cyberspace, dominated by corporate and institutional power.

The cyber-utopians of Silicon Valley can therefore be understood as an outer shell of the neoliberal nesting doll (Golumbia, 2019). Cyber-utopianism advances the exoteric discourse of neoliberalism but with a strategic substitution of cyberspace for the marketplace as its paradigmatic system. Networked computer technologies become tools in the cyber-utopian imaginary that can liberate individuals from the heavy hand of government, corporate monopoly, and elite power. Networked computer technologies flatten and democratize social structures empowering newly liberated subjects to become entrepreneurs, to construct new global communities, and to generate new spontaneous orders that maximize human liberty. However, as with the exoteric discourse of neoliberalism, the social spaces into which newly liberated subjects are positioned are ones dominated by corporate and institutional power and are defined by a dangerous politics of atomization, surveillance, measurement, and behavior modification.

The esoteric discourse of neoliberalism at work in the technology sector advances a politics that does not seek to dismantle the state but works to reorient and restructure governmental and legal power to achieve the political and economic goals of elite groups. The cyber-utopians of Silicon Valley have constructed complex networks of advocacy organizations and lobbying groups, such as the Electronic Frontier Foundation and The Center for Democracy and Technology, that employ the exoteric language of freedom and democracy to advance an esoteric neoliberal discourse.

> Again and again, the effect of these efforts is to lessen the ability of governments to restrain corporations in particular and capital in general . . . to grant governmental and quasi-governmental powers to corporations; to chip away at national sovereignty in so far as it threatens corporate power; to mitigate against labor organization of many sorts; and to promote a corporation-centered, deeply reactionary and even algorithmic notion of absolute free speech that forces minorities of all sorts to "just deal with" hatred and intimidation of many sorts. (Golumbia, 2019, p. 8)

Cyber-utopianism is fundamentally a neoliberal project that does not eschew state power or flatten hierarchies. It is a political project that seeks to use state power to create a legal framework that advances capital accumulation and constructs distributed, networked hierarchies.

Philip Mirowski (2014a) points toward the open-source movement as a prime example of the neoliberal logics at work in cyber-utopian discourse. Open-source software is created by distributed networks of individuals who volunteer their time and expertise to develop applications and even entire operating systems, such as Linux and OpenBSD. Open-source advocates speak of their work using the language of anarcho-hacker culture, but it is a language that conceals the hierarchies within open-source projects and the corporate ends they often serve.

A look at the Linux operating system is instructive. The Linux kernel was released by Linus Torvalds in 1991 under a General Public License that allows users to modify the kernel. Since its release Linux has proliferated into an ever-expanding array of Linux distributions from those that are individually maintained, such as Slackware Linux, to corporate Linux distributions, such as Red Hat. Linux is widely celebrated as a radical democratization of the tools for knowledge creation and entrepreneurship, and this is true to a certain extent. Remember, the text you are reading was created with open-source software on a Linux operating system. However, this celebratory rhetoric works to conceal both the hierarchical structure of Linux and the corporate ends it often serves.

The Linux kernel is overseen by the Linux Foundation, a nonprofit organization reliant on corporate funding. The Linux Foundation is embedded in the cyber-utopianism of Silicon Valley, and this is visible in a number of ways. The Linux Foundation is a hierarchically organized institution that oversees the day-to-day development of the Linux kernel, and it operates much like a large technology company and exhibits many of the same pathologies associated with the corporate culture of Silicon Valley. The foundation is overseen by wealthy executives with often over-sized egos who create a toxic, male-centric culture. Torvalds stepped back from the foundation in 2018 after the New Yorker began to investigate his abusive and often misogynistic behavior toward developers (Cohen, 2018).

Technology companies, such as Amazon, Google, and Microsoft, contribute to the Linux Foundation, because they use Linux to run the servers that are the core of their business model. Linux, and the open-source movement more generally, is built on a foundation of unpaid labor in the name of cyber-utopian dreams, but it ultimately works in service to capitalist accumulation.

> [In the open source movement], people are recruited to provide the fruits of their labor gratis in the guise of a rebellion against the market system, which is then reprocessed by other parties into fungible commodities. Although promoted under the banner of "freedom" the process is much more attuned to fostering the self-image of the insolent anarchic hacker, while averting participants' gaze from the sheer amount of hierarchical coordination that is required to invest any such project with a modicum of persistence and continuity. . . . This strange hybrid of voluntarily unpaid labor and hierarchical control and capitalist appropriation has become so prevalent in the current neoliberal era that some have suggested it actually constitutes a novel form of economic organization. . . . Perhaps it deserves to be called "unprimitive accumulation." (Mirowski, 2014a, pp. 142–143)

Linux and open-source technology are perhaps the best examples of the material realities of cyber-utopian discourse. The exoteric discourse of

cyber-utopianism speaks of liberating individuals from government bureaucracy and corporate monopoly, but the esoteric discourse employed by the
cyber-utopians in Silicon Valley reveals a neoliberal political project to
reconstruct hierarchies in service to capitalist accumulation.

The liberated subjects of cyber-utopian discourse are delivered into a distributed network of institutional power that dwarfs even the most dystopian
visions of the postwar industrial society.

> "It is clear . . . that not merely individual human beings but also institutions
> are empowered by computerization; many of the most pernicious effects of
> computerization," such as surveillance, measurement and control, "stem exactly
> from this form of empowerment. . . . Our computers are built to enable exactly
> the kinds of bureaucratic and administrative functions that are by and large the
> provenance of institutions." (Golumbia, 2009, p. 182)

From the office worker whose computer usage is monitored by supervisors to
the gig worker being measured and "nudged" by an application operating on
a mobile device to the YouTube user being recommended ever more extreme
content to foster continued engagement, the networked computer technologies of this cyber-utopian era introduce new mechanisms of surveillance,
measurement, and governmentality made all the more powerful by their
seeming invisibility. The outer shell of the neoliberal nesting doll inhabited
by the cyber-utopians of Silicon Valley advances a computational politics of
neoliberal population management that advances elite power as it both com-
modifies and contributes to the economic precarity of human life.

Neoliberalism is an elite political project that seeks to construct and protect a
market society that rationalizes human behavior. The Left must take account of
the ways in which the ideological discourse of cyber-utopianism advances neoliberal logics within popular logics. More importantly, it must also take account
of the new mechanisms of disciplinary power made possible by the networked
computer technologies being produced by the technology sector that are quickly
being woven into the fabric of everyday life (Greenfield, 2017).

MUTATING, REVANCHIST NEOLIBERALISM

Telling a better story about this historical moment of emergent crisis and
an ascendant radical right politics requires that scholars and activists on the
political Left think conjuncturally. This call to conjunctural thinking requires
scholars and activists to both tease out analytically the movement of forces
in the economic, political, and cultural domains and the emergent crises they
produce *and* to identify the movement of forces and patterns of exchange

between and among those domains. Put another way, it requires an analytic synthesis of the emergent crisis of the present that takes into account the accumulating crises emerging within the contemporary social formation *and* a recovery of the movement of forces linking these crises one to another. In attempting to tell a better story, this chapter sought to recover the neoliberal political project as a common thread linking the emerging crises in the economic, political, and cultural domains identified in the preceding chapters.

Neoclassical economics did not achieve hegemonic dominance in the academy, among policymakers, and within the popular imagination based on the strength and rigor of economic research. It was the neoliberal project that elevated this scholarly practice. The neoliberal political project may have had a conflicted relationship with neoclassical economics, but there were clear patterns of exchange between the two. Prominent neoliberals, such as Milton Friedman, may have been neoclassical economists, but there were/are significant differences between the two that are reflective of the various "schools" of thought within the neoliberal project. The esoteric discourse of neoliberalism departs from neoclassical economic theory in important ways, but the exoteric discourse of the neoliberal project elevated neoclassical theory to become the common sense logics of the post-1970s formation. Despite their differences the two rose to hegemonic dominance together, but their rise would not have been possible without the modern conservative movement.

It might appear to the casual observer that the neoliberal political project would have little in common with the modern conservative movement. The conservative movement is made up of a contradictory coalition of economic elites, traditionalists, religious conservatives and evangelical Christians, and neoconservatives that are unified by a shared sense of American exceptionalism, traditionalism, and white supremacy. Such a movement would appear to be wildly out of sync with an intellectual, cosmopolitan movement with global ambitions, but it was the modern conservative movement that brought the neoliberal project to ascendancy in the United States. Prominent conservatives, such as William F. Buckley and Ronald Reagan, readily took up the exoteric discourse of the neoliberal project and incorporated its esoteric discourse into their own political practice. The neoliberal political project sought to influence elite opinion to achieve its goals, but it was the modern conservative movement that popularized the exoteric discourse of neoliberalism and cemented it within the popular imagination.

The neoliberal political project was also propelled into the popular imagination by another equally unlikely vector: the cyber-utopians of Silicon Valley. Cyber-utopian discourse took root in the epicenter of a counter-culture experimenting with drugs, technology, and Eastern mysticism. The counter-culture spoke the language of freedom and liberation from mid-century industrial society, often couched in the language of anarchism and anti-capitalism. However, the shift of the counter-culture in the 1970s from mass politics to a narcissistic focus on self-transformation took place hand in glove with the growing salience of the exoteric discourse of neoliberalism in popular culture and the rapid growth of the technology industry. Indeed, the co-mingling of radical individualism, technology, and the cut-throat business culture of late capitalism in Silicon Valley was perhaps the perfect cultural milieu for the neoliberal project to take root.

Neoclassical economics, the modern conservative movement, and cyber-utopianism advanced relatively autonomous ideological discourses that achieved hegemonic dominance in the economic, political, and cultural domains, respectively, and that are now entering into crises of hegemony in this historical moment. They are distinct societal phenomena, but they also share key points of ideological symmetry, people, and practices that are conjoined by the neoliberal political project (figure 5.1).

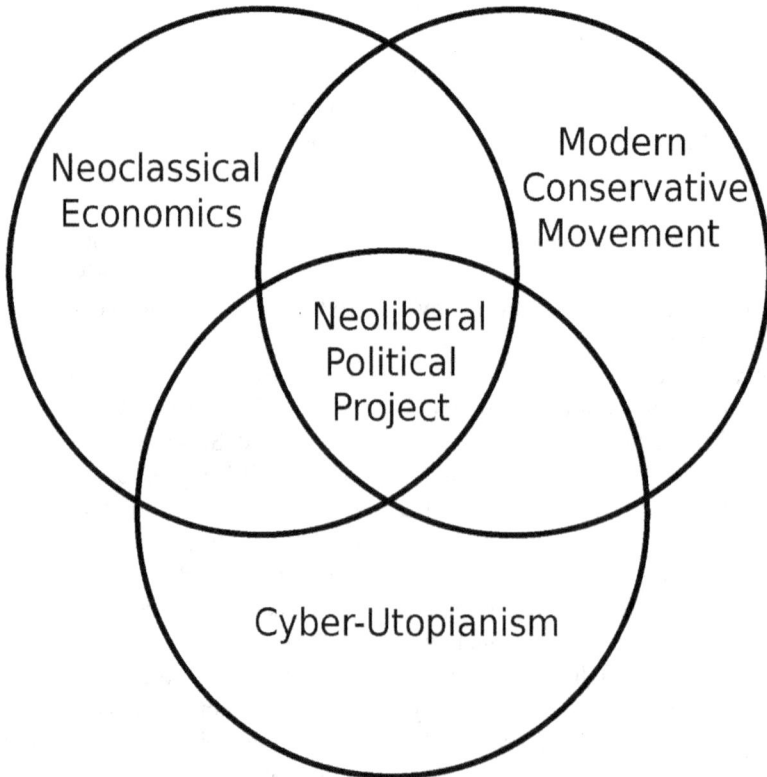

Figure 5.1 **Re-conceptualizing the Neoliberal Political Project.** *Source:* Author-created figure.

The conjunctural analysis presented here demonstrates that each are bound up with the other and that the conjoining of these hegemonic crises is the animating force behind the emergent crisis of the present. One interpretation of this observation is that the emergent crisis is a crisis of neoliberal hegemony, and there is no shortage of public intellectuals making just this argument.

Cornell West (2016), for example, argued in the aftermath of the 2016 presidential election that Trump's victory should be understood as a rebuke of neoliberal hegemony over the American two-party political system. West points toward growing economic insecurity as creating an opening for neofascist rhetoric to capture the imagination of the white working and middle classes and threaten the dominance of neoliberal hegemony. There is some truth to his argument. However, it suffers from an overly simplistic conceptualization of neoliberalism as a unitary and primarily economic project. Trump's use of state power to enforce intellectual property rights in his trade war with China, for example, is but one example of how his administration pursued neoliberal goals.

Nancy Fraser (2019) adds a layer of sophistication to this argument by differentiating between reactionary neoliberalism on the Right and progressive neoliberalism on the Left. According to Fraser, the original reactionary neoliberalism on the Right was supplanted by the progressive neoliberalism of the New Democrats which reached its apotheosis during the presidency of Barack Obama. The election of Trump was, in this telling, a rebuke of progressive neoliberalism at the hand of neofascist rhetoric. Fraser's argument addresses a notable absence in the present analysis: transformations in the progressive left-liberal politics of the post-1970s social formation. However, her bifurcation of neoliberalism still falls prey to a reductive conceptualization that fails to adequately account for the complex patterns of exchange between and among a constellation of actors, movements, and ideological discourses operating within and across the various economic, political, and cultural domains identified in the preceding conjunctural analysis.

Jamie Peck (2010) adds another layer of complexity to our thinking about neoliberalism. He argues that neoliberalism should not be understood as a set of commandments brought down from Mont Pèlerin to the masses but is, instead, a political project that is defined by neoliberal governance and statecraft. The practice of neoliberal politics over time has produced an ever-growing number of contradictions and multiplying crises that has rendered neoliberalism a discredited project that could, nevertheless, continue to lumber forward like the undead in a zombie movie for the foreseeable future. Peck's "Zombie Neoliberalism" depicts neoliberal governance as having reached a point where it is attempting to resolve and ameliorate issues and problems produced by previous neoliberal reforms. Peck correctly notes that neoliberalism is a mutable project that has historically advanced from crisis to crisis and that there is no reason to believe that this zombie neoliberalism will collapse in toto of its own accord in response to the present crisis.

These are important observations by Peck that closely align with my own thinking about the neoliberal project, but I do take issue with his undead framing. If neoliberalism advances from one crisis to another then why should the emergent crisis of the present be any different? If neoliberalism is a mutable, dynamic political project then who is to say that it has lost its vitality? As Peck observes, his undead neoliberalism can only be toppled by sustained counter-hegemonic political work. The right-wing populism rising to power across the global North and South could be understood as just such a counter-hegemonic politics. However, there is little reason to believe that this is the case. And, it is difficult to see (as of the time of this writing) any substantive counter-hegemonic Left politics on the horizon.

This digression into differing ways of thinking about neoliberalism and neoliberal crisis may appear to be an exercise in pedantry, but the stories that we tell about this historical moment inform both political practice and work to establish the horizon of what is possible. It establishes what we can collectively dream. I would like to contribute my own conceptualization based on the preceding analysis. I argue that neoliberalism must be conceptualized as a *politics of permanent revolution that is forever mutating and revanchist in character.*

It was Stuart Hall (2017b) who first conceptualized neoliberalism as permanent revolution. He observed that a hegemonic order is not fixed but is defined by continual adjustment to societal change. "No victories are permanent or final. Hegemony has constantly to be 'worked on', maintained, renewed, revised" (Hall, 2017b, p. 334). Neoliberalism must be understood as a reflexive political practice constantly revolutionizing in response to societal changes produced by both its own governmental practice as well as exogenous shocks from outside the system. It is for this reason that I have taken care to describe neoliberalism in the preceding text as a *political project*. Neoliberalism must be understood as a reflexive praxis informed by a common set of political goals that are animated by a liberal, neoclassical economic imaginary.

Thinking about the neoliberal project as political praxis means that it is constantly mutating as it interacts with other dominant logics at work in the conjuncture. A social formation is not a unitary, undifferentiated structure but is made up of a historic bloc of dominant groups and competing logics. A social formation is not a singular hegemonic order but is a structure of hegemonies.

Neoliberalism has always existed alongside other ideological and discursive formations such as neoclassical economics, conservatism, and cyber-utopianism. It exists in tension with and in league with these other discursive formations and readily appropriates oppositional narratives within its exoteric discourse. There are clear patterns of exchange between the neoliberal project and the dominant logics operating within and across the economic, political, and cultural domains. Neoliberalism influenced and was influenced by neo-classical economics. The same is true for the modern conservative movement and cyber-utopianism. The neoliberal political project has emerged alongside the rise of these dominant logics, or hegemonies, at work in the economic, political, and cultural domains and each are defined by the complex relations of exchange among and between them. "If we understand neoliberalism as embodying less a credo than an injunction—to defend capitalism against democracy—then mutations should be expected" (Slobodian & Plebwe, 2020, p. 105). Neoliberalism is defined by that which it defends against and by the hybridizations and mutations that develop through political practice.

The neoliberal political project emerged as a reactionary elite politics to defend capitalism from the democratic challenges of socialism, Keynesian political economy, organized labor, civil rights, and post-colonialism. What unifies this messy, mutating praxis is the reactionary policing of democratic and subaltern challenges to the natural hierarchies of capitalism. Jordan Camp (2016) draws upon the concept of revanchism, or revenge, to understand the underlying dynamic driving the neoliberal carceral state. He demonstrates that neoliberalism tapped into the white counter-insurgency against the radi-cal challenge of the Long Civil Rights Movement in its rise to power. Camp argues that this dialectic of insurgency and counter-insurgency is a defining characteristic of neoliberalism. Neoliberalism works to define subaltern chal-lengers as being enemies of the nation which justifies the use of state violence to restore what has been lost or threatened. Indeed, Stuart Hall (1988b) was prescient in describing the neoliberal political project as a form of authoritar-ian (often racialized) populism (Hall et al., 1978).

There is a long history of neoliberals embracing reactionary authoritarian movements to violently crush democratic challenges to capitalist hierarchies. Mises initially lauded Mussolini for having saved European civilization, and he was eager to work with the Austrofascist Christian Socials before ultimately fleeing to Switzerland and the United States (Wasserman, 2019). Hayek and Friedman (not to mention Margaret Thatcher and Ronald Reagan) praised Augusto Pinochet for having saved liberalism from the collectivist threat of Salvador Allende. In other words, revanchism is a term that applies more broadly to the reactionary politics of the neoliberal project in general. It is one of its defining characteristics.

Conceptualizing neoliberalism as a mutating, revanchist political project of permanent revolution points toward the conclusion that the emergent crisis of the present is as much an opportunity for neoliberal advancement as it is a threat to its continued dominance. The elite networks that make up the various shells of the neoliberal nesting doll remain well-positioned to shift with the movement of societal change, and this observation holds equally true for the public intellectuals propagating the dominant ideological discourses at work in the economic, political, and cultural domains. Neoclassical theory remains the dominant model of economic inquiry in the academy and among policy-makers, and even the supposed challengers to neoclassical orthodoxy, such as behavioral economics and game theory, retain the core ideas of the neoclassical model (Mirowski, 2011). The modern conservative movement retains its institutional structure and media infrastructure, and it has demonstrated itself to be quite adept at shifting with changing circumstances, for example, the rapid shift from opposing deficit spending to prop up the economy following the crash of 2008 to proposing massive stimulus in response to the economic shock of COVID-19 to again opposing deficit spending once the opposition Democrats won back the presidency. Networked computer technologies are fully integrated into daily life, and, despite criticism in the wake of the 2016 election, the cyber-utopians of Silicon Valley remain poised to offer technological solutions to novel problems as they arise.

The resiliency of the neoliberal political project is perhaps best explained by its ability to mutate and respond to societal change. Thinking about the neoliberal project as a nesting doll of distributed networks operating in patterns of exchange defined by cooperation, competition, and contradiction gestures toward a flexible and malleable political project that is, on the one hand, unified by a reactionary politics dedicated to the restoration of hierarchy and the eclipse of the demos while, on the other hand, influenced and shaped by competing material and discursive forces. This malleability and mutability can be located in the very founding and structure of the MPS as a debating society. The elite actors at the early MPS meetings did not think or act in unison. Indeed, the often profound disagreements among them defined the various "schools" of neoliberal thought, and the ways in which they worked to advance the project in their various nations reflected the unique circumstances of each. American neoliberalism and German ordoliberalism each reflect the unique cultural, economic, and political contexts of those nations.

The point I am trying to make here is that the neoliberal logics animating the contemporary social formation are more stable than they may appear, and the emergent crises within the economic, political, and cultural spheres identified in the preceding analysis present new opportunities for a mutating political praxis to revolutionize itself. Contra Peck, neoliberalism "is not on its deathbed, but is instead splintering and mutating to survive changing circumstances—with potentially devastating effects for human and planetary life. As political ruptures yield unexpected lines of alliance and enmity, prevailing strategies of market rule are also being reprogrammed" (Callison & Manfredi, 2020, pp. 26–27). Conceptualizing neoliberalism as a unified object of analysis that is primarily economic in character means that we fail to grasp not simply its complexity but its resiliency. Indeed, I would argue that the political Left has much to learn from the neoliberal political project (Hall, 1988a, 1988b). I will offer three lessons here.

First, the Left must develop a dynamic political project that works across the economic, political, and cultural domains. It must operate from a core set of ideas, such as the elimination of scarcity, the fundamental equality of all human beings and ecological sustainability, and strategically seek out opportunities created by crises to achieve radical change. Friedman famously stated that it was during a crisis that change can occur, and the nature of the changes that take place depends on the ideas that are at work within a social formation. The Left must do that foundational work within the various domains of the formation to take advantage of opportunities as they arise.

Second, the Left must guard against rigid utopian politics that demand ideological or theoretical purity, what is in effect a retreat from the political. The neoliberal project is shot through with contradictions. Hayek argued, on the one hand, that the economy is ineffable and beyond measurement while, on the other hand, advocating for the technocratic engineering of a global framework using state power. Friedman was one of the primary architects of an exoteric discourse that framed the state as a sclerotic bureaucracy incapable of managing the economy, yet his neoclassical monetarism endowed the state with almost perfect knowledge to manage the money supply. These contradictions were/are not a barrier to the advancement of the neoliberal political project. In fact, contradiction is the discursive energy that animates the neoliberal project and allows it to mutate in response to societal changes. The same observation applies to neoclassical economics, the modern conservative movement, and cyber-utopianism. The Left must develop a coherent political project informed by a core set of values that is flexible enough to respond to opportunities as they arise. The Left must remain flexible and attend to societal changes as they emerge.

Third, the Left must not look to the dead languages of the past (Marx, 1978), a mistake progressive liberals make in attempting to resurrect the Keynesian political economy of the twentieth century as though nothing had changed. The Left must reflexively shift and move with the flow of historical time. Following Gramsci, Hall argues that the Left must attend "violently" to the discipline of the conjuncture, onto things as they are and not as they were or as we want them to be. The Left must develop a political project that both contests and grounds itself in "the root values, the root concepts, the root images and ideas in popular consciousness without which no popular socialism can be constructed" (Hall, 1988a). Even now, the neoliberal political project is reflexively responding to societal change by capitalizing on popular anger at the European Union, an institution considered by many as an almost perfect example of Hayekian neoliberal governance, by working with right-wing populists to advance the neoliberal project (Slobodian & Plebwe, 2020).

I want to argue that a reinvigorated Left must tell better stories about this historical moment of emergent crisis that, in Hall's words, *attend to the discipline of the conjuncture.* This is not a call to construct utopian visions of a future beyond this historical moment. It is a call to attend to the dynamic movement of forces and patterns of exchange at work in the contemporary formation. It is a call to radical contextualization, to radical inquiry that situates social problems, issues, and so on, within a problem space that poses its own questions and makes its own political demands. It is a call to radical contextualism as a necessary precondition for doing liberatory work.

I began the preceding analysis with the problem (the simple determination or chaotic conception) of right-wing populism as an emerging force within the world system, specifically focusing on the radical right politics in the United States. The radical right is often represented in popular culture as a growing populism taking root among the newly precarious middle and working classes that are rejecting five decades of neoliberal globalization. The analysis presented here demonstrates that there is a kernel of truth in this popular conceptualization, but the analysis also demonstrates that this conceptualization tells an ultimately reductive story about this historical moment.

I have endeavored in the preceding to conduct a conjunctural analysis of the contemporary social formation and the emergent crisis into which it is entering. My goal is a radical contextualization of right-wing populism so as to re-conceptualize this immediate problem as a critical problem space. My goal is to tease out through analysis the questions being posed and political demands being made by the contemporary conjuncture.

Is this historical moment a crisis of neoliberal hegemony? I am doubtful. If it is at all meaningful to conceptualize the contemporary conjuncture as a moment of neoliberal crisis then it must be conceptualized as a condensation of multiple crises, a neoliberal crises of hegemonies. This is a clumsy conceptualization at best. Labeling the emergent crisis of the present, or even the contemporary formation, neoliberal erases neoclassical economics, the modern conservative movement, and cyber-utopian discourse.

I believe that there is a better story to tell here. I have collected all of the elements for a better story; I must now assemble them onto the storyboard. I must move toward synthesizing these elements into a coherent story that radically contextualizes the problem of right-wing populism as a problem space and to think through the scholarly and pedagogical implications of this contextual work. It is to this task that I now turn.

Chapter 6

A Problem Space

I now want to make sense of the preceding conjunctural analysis to begin telling a better story about this historical moment of emergent crisis. I would suspect that, by now, the reader will surely know that the story I wish to tell is neither neat nor tidy. In fact, the preceding analysis would seem to militate against a story with a linear, evolutionary timeline. It militates against telling a story that seeks to establish a causal chain of development of primary elements and their determinants. To be clear, I will begin to synthesize the various elements from the preceding analysis into a narrative, but I will attempt to do so in a way that troubles any notion of linearity or of one primary element determining the others.

My goal here is not to focus on any one element identified in the preceding analysis and establish a linear chain of development but to attempt to make sense of the broader societal context of this historical moment. I want to think about how I can theorize this context as a problem space. However, by theorize, I do not mean a precise cartographic mapping of this social formation that captures every element and that offers easy, compelling answers to every question in advance. A social theory is not reality but a tool to talk about, think about, and act in the world.

I want to pull back the analytical perspective of this project to the necessary level of abstraction to think about the contemporary social formation and the emergent crisis of the present as a totality, as an ensemble, as an articulated structure, as a *problem space*, without succumbing to the fiction that this abstraction fully captures every element, phenomena, movement, discursive practice, ideology, structure, and so on. I want to develop a short-hand, so to speak, to think about this problem space without erasing complexity, contradiction, and the dynamic movement of social forces. I want to map the terrain of political struggle upon which this historical moment of conjunctural crisis will play out. The value of this theorizing will be determined by its utility for informing the scholarly and pedagogical work I develop in subsequent chapters. I do not, therefore, intend to present the reader with a fully formed social theory in this chapter but to *theorize*, to develop a kernel of a theory or a rough sketch of a map that will be developed further through practice.

In this chapter, I will take what Stuart Hall termed a "necessary detour through theory" to make sense of the preceding conjunctural analysis (Grossberg, 2010a, p. 210). I will begin by examining the work of two seminal thinkers, Ernesto Laclau and Henry Giroux, whose work has much to contribute to our understanding of the contemporary conjuncture. I will attempt to tease out the important contributions these two thinkers make to understanding the context of political struggle in this historical moment of emergent crisis. I will then attempt to build on the lessons learned from Laclau and Giroux to tell a better story in the form of a narrative synthesis of the preceding conjunctural analysis. And, I will conclude the chapter by theorizing the contemporary conjuncture as a problem space defined by fragmentation.

EMPTY SIGNIFIER

One of the foremost theorists of populism is Ernesto Laclau (2018), and his book *On Populist Reason* has much to contribute to making sense of the preceding analysis. Laclau and Chantel Mouffe are considered the pioneers of post-Marxist theory that retained the political concerns of Marxism while rejecting its economic determinism and theory of history (Laclau & Mouffe, 2014). They argue that complex social formations are not determined in the last instance by the economic base and that the engine of history is not defined by the necessary conflict between labor and capital. For Laclau and Mouffe, the emergence of a relatively stable formation is the product of articulatory discursive practice, and it is on the field of discursive practice that political struggle takes place.

The touchstone for Laclau's analysis of populism is Gramsci's theory of hegemony and historical bloc. Gramsci understood that dominant forces construct and maintain power not only through the threat of state-sanctioned violence but through persuasion and ideology, and he understood the need to construct a counter-hegemonic historical bloc out of diverse classes and groups organized around new liberatory ideologies. Laclau largely adopts and seeks to advance Gramsci's project, but he differentiates his own work from Gramsci in two ways. First, Laclau rejects what he sees as the primacy that Gramsci attributes to the working class in political struggle. For Laclau, the globalized capitalism of the twenty-first century is defined by "a multiplication of dislocatory effects and a proliferation of new antagonisms" that trouble traditional class categories (Laclau, 2018, p. 230). Second, he shifts the concept of hegemony from an ideological construct or structure to a discursive practice constructing a contingent unity out of a diversity of social demands.

Laclau argues that populism is not a unitary, delimitable phenomenon. Populism is a social logic that literally constructs the political. The question that Laclau urges us to ask is not whether or not a particular movement is populist but to what extent a movement is populist. The populist discursive construction of "the people" is, for Laclau, the sine qua non of the political. All politics is populist to some extent. The object of analysis for Laclau is the populist rupture in which a new articulation of heterogeneous groups emerges and redefines the political field.

The basic unit of analysis for Laclau is the social demand. He differentiates between two different types of social demands: those that can be resolved through established practices and institutions, demands that follow what he terms the logic of difference, and those that cannot be resolved within the constraints of a social formation, demands that follow what he terms the logic of equivalence.

> The logic of difference implies that social agents have different demands which are claimed through normal social and political processes (e.g., negotiation; construction of alliances and coalitions etc.). Populism arises, argues Laclau, when a large number of these demands remain unfulfilled for a long time, and a political leader or movement emerges in the political scene and manages to portray all of these demands as equivalent and undifferentiated—this is the logic of equivalence. (Zembylas, 2020, p. 154)

The populist rupture emerges when an articulatory force in the form of a movement or charismatic leader unifies the various unfulfilled social demands of heterogeneous groups around a symbol, what Laclau terms an empty signifier, establishing a "frontier" between "the people" and the powerful.

> Since the construction of the "people" is the political act *par excellence*—as opposed to pure administration within a stable framework—the *sine qua non* requirements of the political are the constitution of antagonistic frontiers within the social and the appeal to new subjects of social change—which involves . . . the production of empty signifiers in order to unify a multiplicity of heterogeneous demands in equivalential chains. (Laclau, 2018, p. 154)

One of the examples that Laclau uses in *On Populist Reason* is especially pertinent to my project: the collapse of New Deal liberalism and the rise of conservative hegemony in the United States.

Laclau argues that New Deal hegemony was organized around populist themes, such as the working man, positioned across a frontier from the monied classes. The transformation of New Deal liberalism into bureaucratic institutions increasingly focused on the redress of racial, ethnic, and gender inequalities created an opening for a right-wing articulation. George Wallace and Richard Nixon spoke to a "Middle America" that "felt underrepresented—asphyxiated between an almighty bureaucracy in Washington and the demands of several minorities. . . . The crisis of representation which is at the root of any populist, anti-institutional outburst was clearly in embryo in the demands of these people. Some kind of radical discourse had to emerge which was able to inscribe those demands" (Laclau, 2018, p. 137). More importantly, Laclau argued that the populist signifiers of the New Deal were not abandoned or supplanted but were "hegemonized" by a new conservative movement. Or, to put it another way, right-wing populism disarticulated New Deal hegemony and re-articulated its empty signifiers into a new articulated formation.

Laclau has much to contribute to the present analysis. I will make three observations on what I take away from Laclau's work. First, Laclau complicates and advances Gramsci's theorizing of political ideology. He shifts theorizing ideology away from structural analysis toward the discursive practices constructing the political. Ideologies are shared beliefs and representations of social reality that inform how individuals both make sense of and act in the world. It is a form of practical reasoning people use to make sense of their worlds and their place in it. Ideologies are, therefore, the basis of discourse, but it is through discursive practice that ideologies are constructed and reproduced. Ideology informs how individuals and groups talk about and act in the world, and it is the ways in which individuals and groups talk about and act in the world, their discursive practice, that inform their taken-for-granted assumptions about the nature of social reality, for example, ideology (Hall, 1986). More importantly, an articulated social formation is animated by an ensemble or constellation of *ideological discourses* structuring the economic, political, and cultural domains.

Second, Laclau demonstrates the contingency and fragility of an articulated formation. There is no necessary relationship among the heterogeneous groups constituting a hegemonic historical bloc nor any inherent, *a priori* meaning attached to the signifiers around which it is organized. Laclau offers a discursive model for theorizing how a hegemonic order can be articulated out of the heterogeneous social demands of a constellation of groups and movements and how a hegemonic order can be disarticulated and re-articulated into a new hegemonic bloc.

Third, and related to the previous point, Laclau offers a way of theorizing the emergent crisis of the present and gestures toward a path out of the crisis. One way to theorize this historical moment of conjunctural crisis is as a period of accumulating, unmet social demands. The populist rupture of the 1970s constructed a new articulated formation, but four decades of proliferating antagonisms and dislocatory effects have led to a crisis of representation and created a space for a new populist rupture. The task for the Left is to construct a new counter-hegemonic historical bloc articulating the unmet social demands of heterogeneous groups around empty signifiers at work in the contemporary formation establishing a new "frontier" between "the people" and power. In short, the path out of the emergent crisis is through a new left-wing populism.

Laclau provides us with powerful tools for theorizing the emergent crisis of the present as well as a potential path out of the contemporary conjuncture. He reminds us that the stories that we collectively tell matter. However, the tools he provides do suffer from some important limitations.

First, the empty signifiers Laclau envisions are not nearly as empty as he would have us believe. Laclau is correct that there is no necessary relation between various ideological elements at work in a discourse nor between discourses and the social forces to which they are attached. There is no necessary meaning attached to the signifiers around which a formation is articulated. However, the various ideological elements, or signifiers, at work in a discourse have a history, often histories that reflect significant affective, cultural, and political investments or what Stuart Hall terms "lines of tendential force" (Grossberg, 1986b, p. 53). Laclau's move to evade the mechanical structuralism of classical Marxist theorizing of ideology erases the structural altogether.

Second, and related to the previous point, the discursive focus of Laclau's theorizing erases the ensemble of forces at work in an articulated formation. The accumulating unmet social demands that mark a populist rupture in Laclau's model seem to spontaneously emerge outside of any structuring effects. Laclau is correct that one way that we can think about the crisis of the 1970s is as a crisis of representation. However, as the preceding analysis demonstrates, the unmet social demands defining the populist rupture of the 1970s did not emerge spontaneously from a "no place" outside of the relations of force at work in that moment of conjunctural crisis. A wide array of elite forces mobilized complex networks and institutional frameworks to shape those social demands. Or, put another way, there was a constellation of forces working to re-articulate the New Deal formation into a new articulated formation.

What Laclau's theorizing erases, or at the very least backgrounds, is the complex networks of actors, movements, and institutional frameworks working in complex patterns of cooperation, competition, and contradiction within the post-1970s formation. The social demands of any group are always already situated within fields of power, both discursive and material. What is missing from Laclau's analysis is the ensemble of forces both structuring and being structured by discursive practice. What Laclau offers us is a discursive theory without materiality. Laclau offers us some important tools to understand this historical moment of emergent crisis, but we will have to look elsewhere for a way of theorizing the contemporary conjuncture that does justice to the structures and fields of power at work in the post-1970s formation.

NEOLIBERAL FASCISM

One place to look is in the recent work of Henry Giroux (2020a, 2020b). Giroux is a preeminent scholar of critical pedagogy with an expansive body of work. Critical pedagogy is most closely associated with the Freirean tradition, and the work of Paulo Freire clearly informs Giroux's thinking. However, I want to argue that what makes Giroux's approach to critical pedagogy distinctive, and indeed one of its primary strengths, is that he firmly situates critical pedagogy within a cultural studies framework.

Critical pedagogy is defined by the problem-posing, dialogic approach to pedagogical practice first developed by Freire in the 1950s. It is an approach to teaching that rejects a banking model of education in which a teacher deposits knowledge into passive students. Critical pedagogues engage learners in authentic dialogue and employ a problem-posing method as a practice of radical critique that seeks to blur the distinction between teacher and student, opting for the categories of teacher-student and student-teacher.

Giroux's work is certainly informed by this pedagogical tradition. However, his work is also informed by cultural studies (Giroux, 1994), and this influence is evidenced by how he describes critical pedagogy.

> Critical pedagogy is not about an *a priori* method that simply can be applied regardless of context. It is the outcome of particular struggles and is always related to the specificity of particular contexts, students, communities, and available resources. It draws attention to the ways in which knowledge, power, desire, and experience are produced under specific basic conditions of learning and illuminates the role that pedagogy plays as part of a struggle over assigned meanings, modes of expression, and directions of desire, particularly as these bear on the formation of the multiple and contradictory versions of the "self" and its relationship to the larger society. (Giroux, 2020a, p. 2)

Two points stand out. First, Giroux encourages us to take seriously the ideological and discursive terrain upon which students do their identity work and upon which power relations are actively (re)produced in a Gramscian sense. Second, Giroux encourages us to take seriously the structures, institutions, relations of force, and societal contexts structuring and being structured by the ideological and discursive. Put simply, Giroux's approach to critical pedagogy takes seriously that which is often absent in the work of critical pedagogues: context (Ellison, 2009).

Whereas Laclau privileges discourse Giroux takes a holistic approach to critique and critical practice that attends not just to the ideological and discursive but to the structures and relations of forces at work in a social formation. Giroux's critical pedagogy is a contextual practice in two senses. First, he sees critical pedagogy not as a set of practices that can be neatly and unproblematically transposed into any pedagogical space. It is defined by the "specificity of particular contexts, students, communities, and available resources." Second, Giroux's critical pedagogy takes seriously the social formation within which specific pedagogical spaces are situated. This requires theorizing the societal context of pedagogical and political struggle.

Giroux's recent work has made an important contribution to theorizing the contemporary formation and the political demands of this historical moment. It is theoretical work that parallels the present project in many ways and that can contribute to the theorizing of the emergent crisis of the present. Giroux argues that the contemporary formation is defined by what he terms *neoliberal fascism.*

Giroux defines neoliberal fascism as the conjoining of neoliberalism and fascism into a "comfortable and mutually compatible project" and movement "that connects the exploitative values and cruel austerity policies of 'casino capitalism' with fascist ideals" (Giroux, 2020a, p. 197). Neoliberal fascism is, in Giroux's formulation, a sociopolitical formation that has emerged out of the historical development of neoliberalism and fascist politics in the United States since the 1970s. To better understand this formation it is helpful to examine how Giroux conceptualizes its component elements.

Giroux describes neoliberalism as an extreme form of capitalism and economic policy. He describes neoliberalism as "casino capitalism" marked by financialization and globalization of capitalist economies and as a politics of austerity and a hollowing out of the state.

As an economic policy, neoliberalism creates an all-encompassing market guided by the principles of privatization, deregulation, commodification, and the free flow of capital. Advancing these agendas, it weakens unions, radically downsizes the welfare state, and wages an assault on public services such as education, libraries, parks, energy, water, prisons, and public transportation. As the state is hollowed out, big corporations take on the functions of government, imposing severe austerity measures, redistributing wealth upward to the rich and powerful, and reinforcing a notion of society as one of winners and losers. (Giroux, 2020b, p. 44)

What unifies these elements of "casino capitalism" and the politics of austerity and retrenchment in Giroux's theorizing is his conceptualization of neoliberalism as an ideological discourse or "narrative."

> [N]eoliberalism cannot be separated from its attempt to impose a new narrative in which the logic of the market is more important than the ideals that define a substantive democracy. . . . In this narrative, capital is the subject of history, everything is for sale, the rich get what they deserve, and those who fail to accumulate wealth and power are dismissed as losers, making it easier to refigure massive inequality as virtuous and responsibility as an individual choice. . . . It has produced with a kind of fraudulent weight an all-consuming narrative that treats human misery as normal and its fictional portrayals of those it considers disposable as the apogee of common sense. (Giroux, 2020b, pp. 44–45)

Thus, Giroux employs Gramscian tools to think about neoliberalism as a public pedagogy, or to borrow a turn of phrase from Raymond Williams, a permanent education working to advance not only casino capitalism but new subjectivities defined by capitalist rationality and hostility to the social. It is a public pedagogy advanced by media and networked computer technologies, what he terms "disimagination machinery" (Giroux, 2020b, p. 26). More importantly, for Giroux, neoliberalism has created the conditions for the emergence of fascist politics.

Giroux describes fascism as authoritarian ideology and forms of political behavior defined by the hatred of democracy, the celebration of violence, Social Darwinism, militarism, toxic masculinity, white supremacy, and dreams of racial and social cleansing. The fascism he describes is a form of American-style authoritarianism built on a long history of white nationalism and settler colonialism, the revanchist politics of the long southern strategy, and the Social Darwinism of neoliberal ideology. This last point is especially significant because it demonstrates that Giroux sees neoliberalism as not only creating the conditions for this new form of American authoritarianism but that it is inherently fascist (Giroux, 2020a, p. 190). It is for this reason that Giroux insists that we think about neoliberalism and fascism together as the defining characteristic of the contemporary conjuncture, a perspective that mirrors that of Wendy Brown (2006).

Giroux urges us to think about neoliberal fascism as a totality, "a single integrated system whose shared roots extend from class and racial injustices under financial capitalism to ecological problems and the increasing expansion of the carceral state and the military-industrial-academic complex"

(Giroux, 2020a, p. 213). Theorizing the contemporary formation as being defined by neoliberal fascism does justice to the complexity of this historical moment in ways that the theoretical tools Laclau offers fall short. It speaks to the articulated structures of the formation, including not only the economic but the history of white supremacy, educational apparatuses, media, and technology, as well as the ideological discourses at work in the formation that naturalize hierarchy and inequality, undermine democracy, celebrate ignorance, and subsumes the social under the rubric of capitalist reason. What Giroux offers is a way of theorizing the contemporary conjuncture that does justice to not only the ideological and discursive but also the structures and fields of power that define the post-1970s formation.

The path out of the contemporary conjuncture that Giroux attempts to chart will sound familiar to those versed in critical pedagogy. He argues that scholars and activists must develop a new discourse of critique to challenge systems of domination, a new language of radical hope with which to imagine new futures and to construct new communities of social movements into a liberatory force, and a discourse that rejects radical individualism and links liberatory ideas to concrete practice. The political and pedagogical challenge he sees in this time of neoliberal fascism is to create the "tools and tactics necessary to rethink and create the conditions for a new kind of subjectivity as the basis for a new kind of democratic socialist politics" (Giroux, 2020b, p. 178).

What I find intriguing about Giroux's recent work on neoliberal fascism is that he offers us tools for thinking about the post-1970s social formation and the period emergent conjunctural crisis into which it is entering in ways that do justice to the complexity of this historical moment. He does not privilege one element, whether economic or discursive, in his analysis but understands that a social formation is a contingent articulation of structures, ideologies, discursive practices, complex relations of force, and so on. It is a totality and must be approached from that perspective. More importantly, I am drawn to his theorizing of hegemony and political struggle as pedagogical. Giroux encourages us to think about this historical moment of potential rupture and the political struggle to construct a new liberatory social formation as a pedagogical problem.

That said, the analysis presented in the preceding chapters does complicate Giroux's theorizing in important ways. First, Giroux conceptualizes neoliberalism as being primarily economic and relatively stable. He does speak of neoliberalism as a political project. However, he frequently invokes the "hollowing out" of the state implying that it is in retreat in both size and scope. Neoliberalism, as we have seen, works to restructure and repurpose the state apparatus but does not limit or constrain the state in any meaningful way. Even in areas of neoliberal retrenchment, such as welfare reform, the actual policies pursued often expand state power into new arenas of human life. Neoliberal policies do not denote a retreat of the state from the economic nor turning over state functions to the free market so much as the blurring of distinctions between the two spheres. Likewise, Giroux conceptualizes neoliberalism as an ideological discourse, or narrative, working to produce a politics and subjectivity that is primarily economic in character. Doing so obscures the complex patterns of exchange among and between an array of ideological discourses circulating in the contemporary conjuncture as well as the multiplicity of subjectivities they work to produce. Thus, Giroux conceptualizes neoliberalism as a relatively stable economic ideological discourse as opposed to the field of mutating ideological discourses and subjectivities identified in the preceding analysis.

Second, and relatedly, Giroux's foregrounding of neoliberalism and fascism backgrounds the complexity of the contemporary formation. Giroux does an excellent job of connecting neoliberalism with the authoritarianism of the modern conservative movement, and he also wisely historicizes their co-emergence from the crisis of the 1970s to hegemonic dominance. However, what is missing is neoclassical economics and the tensions and complex patterns of exchange between it and the neoliberal project and the modern conservative movement. Similarly, Giroux takes seriously media and technology as public pedagogy, but he does not rigorously unpack the complexity of popular cultural forms as both a material and ideological force nor does he flesh out the complex patterns of exchange between and among popular cultural forms and neoclassical economics, the modern conservative movement, and the neoliberal project. The post-1970s social formation is a dynamic field of mutating material and ideological-discursive forces working in complex patterns of cooperation, competition, and contradiction. Giroux's theorizing of the contemporary formation, while laudable, simply does not capture the complexity of the post-1970s social formation.

To be clear, I do not offer these comments as damning critique nor as an effort to expose a fatal flaw in Giroux's recent work. Arguing that he did not write the book that I would have written is not a valid criticism. I find his work to be instructive, and I see my own project as extending his work. Giroux "tells a better story" about right-wing populism as neoliberal fascism, and this goes a long way toward understanding the political and, as Giroux correctly notes, pedagogical struggles of this historical moment. What I ask is for the reader to pull back her perspective on this period of potential rupture beyond an analysis of the interplay between neoliberalism and the authoritarianism of the modern conservative movement. If we pull back our analytic perspective further how can we theorize this historical moment? How can we make sense of the analysis presented in the preceding chapters? How can we tell a better story about right-wing populism that does justice to the complexity of the contemporary formation and the emergent crisis of the present, to the discipline of the conjuncture?

A BETTER STORY

Telling a better story about right-wing populism requires that we take into account the complexity of this initial problem. It requires contextualization of this simple problem within the relations of force at work in the contemporary social formation and the emergent crisis into which it is entering. A better story is this: Right-wing populism is embedded within a constellation of agents, political movements, and ideological discourses at work in the contemporary formation. Its most direct lineage can be located in the modern conservative movement, as Giroux argues, but it also draws upon an array of political ideologies and grammars employed by the dominant forces at work across the various domains of the contemporary conjuncture.

The dominant forces operating within the economic domain are neoclassical economics and the neoliberal political project. Neoclassical economics is a school of economic thought that informed an intellectual counter-revolution against Keynesian political economy during the crisis of the 1970s. The ensuing decades has seen the expansion of neoclassical economics in an imperial turn toward other disciplinary fields, such as education, health care, and law, and it has become the dominant model of social scientific research informing policymaking by governmental bodies.

It was the neoliberal political project that facilitated the expansion of neoclassical logics not only throughout the academy but beyond the university to become a governmental practice. The neoliberal project developed the techniques of power to operationalize neoclassical logics and constructed a constellation of networks made up of intellectuals, businesses, philanthropies, and so on, to achieve ideological leadership within the economic domain. The founding elites at Mont Pelèrin may have had a complicated relationship with the scientism of econometrics and neoclassical theory, but the exoteric discourse of the neoliberal project propagated a crude narrative drawn from the neoclassical imaginary.

The dominant force at work in the economic domain is, therefore, a mutation of neoclassical economics and the neoliberal political project, and this mutation has fundamentally restructured this domain at all levels of human experience. It is a mutation that re-purposed and expanded the footprint of the Bretton Woods institutions to facilitate global capital flows and the development of a global labor market while establishing constitutional constraints to the autonomy of individual nations and to the democratic ambitions of their populations. National economies were transformed through free trade agreements that exposed certain sectors of the economy to global competition and crippled organized industrial labor; financial deregulation that transformed Wall Street and other financial capitals into a global casino; tax policies that lowered taxes on the wealthy, shifted the tax burden down the economic ladder, and created new tax arbitrage opportunities for wealthy individuals and corporations; privatization of state services that created whole new markets; and retrenchment of the welfare state to ensure a reserve army of the under-employed to both keep labor costs in check and to further weaken organized labor. Corporations were transformed into entities solely focused on producing value for shareholders while benefiting from governmental largess in times of economic crisis through bailouts and monetary policy. Individual subjects, on the other hand, experience a labor market defined by precarity and ever-expanding forces of responsibilization at work and in their private lives.

The restructuring of the economic domain successfully restored capital accumulation in a period of secular stagnation and opened the world system to this most recent iteration of globalization. However, this restructuring has increased the fragility of the global economy. The contemporary formation is marked by a seemingly endless series of financial crises and government bailouts that effectively transfer losses to the public sphere, increasing public debt that must be "payed for" by austerity policies while protecting and back-stopping private profits. This restructuring has fueled the polarization of wealth and income and the dramatic growth in poverty and precarity among workers. As a result, these transformations are fueling economic antagonisms, anti-elite sentiment and resentment, and deaths of despair that are lowering life-expectancy rates among the middle and working classes.

These are the economic transformations that have created an opening for right-wing populism to achieve political salience in the contemporary conjuncture. The right-wing populists are achieving electoral success with promises to bring back jobs from overseas and to punish perceived global competitors, such as China or even immigrant labor, for taking jobs from American workers. The signature policies of the Trump administration, for example, were his trade wars with China, Canada, and Mexico, curtailing immigration from developing nations (specifically those from Latin America and Muslim majority nations), and immigration raids and deportations. Right-wing populists have achieved power with the promise to resolve the growing precarity of the working and middle classes that is framed by xenophobia and racism directed against economic competitors.

However, despite its rhetoric of restoration and bringing back jobs, it is notable that the actual economic policies implemented by right-wing populists work to deepen the very economic transformations they condemn. The Trump administration may have employed populist rhetoric to frame its trade war with China or the renegotiation of the North American Free Trade Agreement (NAFTA), but the policies they pursued were a continuation of the dominant economic policy framework of the post-1970s formation. The political goal of the trade war with China was to further open the Chinese market to global free trade (financial, services, and industrial) and to protect that most iconic of neoliberal fetishes: intellectual property. Likewise, the renegotiation of NAFTA was pursued to further open Canadian and Mexican markets to American products. What is notable about the right-wing populism of the contemporary conjuncture is that it is working to deepen and expand the economic transformations that are fueling both an emergent crisis in the economic domain and its rise to political power.

The dominant forces at work in the political domain are the modern conservative movement and the neoliberal political project. The modern conservative movement is made up of a contradictory coalition of traditionalists and religious conservatives, neoconservatives, business lobbies, and conservative economists, a category encompassing both neoclassical economists and neoliberal intellectuals. The "fusionism" credited to William F. Buckley produced a mutation of conservatism and neoliberalism that rose to hegemonic dominance in the post-1970s formation. It is a mutation that has produced a relatively stable and coherent political project that has transformed the political domain.

This mutation has constructed a complex network of think tanks, policy institutes, religious organizations, and advocacy groups to shape governmental policy and to shape public opinion. The policies and ideas generated in these networks are propagated through a sophisticated network of media outlets from traditional print media to online publications. And, it has developed a sophisticated electoral strategy through the discursive production of a new elite in government and universities; a toxic mix of nationalism, militarism, patriarchy, homophobia, and misogyny; and a long southern strategy of white supremacy and xenophobia. It is a mutant political movement that has risen to power on a politics of "us" and "them" that fundamentally restructured the political domain. It is a political transformation that achieved the economic restructuring sought by neoclassical economists and the revanchist aims of the neoliberal project, but it also fundamentally restructured the political domain in ways that made the rise of right-wing populism not just possible but a fait accompli.

These mutant politics has moved the political center significantly to the Right over the past four decades. The radicalization and political success of this mutant politics has shifted the horizon of the possible to the Right to such a degree that even historically liberal social democratic policies, such as those advanced by former presidential candidates Bernie Sanders and Elizabeth Warren, are now considered radical. The New Democrats that emerged in the 1990s, for example, are frequently described as being neoliberal, but this framing erases the conservative rhetoric employed by prominent New Democratic leaders, such as the racialized language employed by Bill Clinton and Joe Biden to justify criminal reform and welfare reform legislation. The rightward shift of the political center was propelled by the electoral successes of an increasingly radical and polarizing discourse of "us" and "them" on the Right that framed the political domain as a site of existential conflict in which dialogue and comprise becomes the equivalent of surrender to a hostile force.

The right-wing populism rising to power in the contemporary conjuncture is a direct outgrowth of this mutant politics, and it is the rise of this mutant politics that is fueling the emergent crisis in the political domain. Right-wing populism is a neofascist politics propelled to power through a politics of "us" and "them," a Schmittian formation of herrenvolk democracy framed by a politics of blood and soil. It is a mutant politics that has constructed a sophisticated framework of policy networks, media outlets, and electoral strategies that has allowed it to capitalize on the emergent crisis in the economic domain and that positions it to continue to advance in the future.

The radical right is working to solidify the power of its geographically distributed electoral base through voter suppression and immigration policies that seek to shape the electorate and through the stacking of the federal court system with reactionary judges who can both eclipse progressive changes and advance reactionary goals when the Right is out of power. Right-wing populists are also working to construct new global networks to advance their political goals, such as Steve Bannon's new American and European nonprofit organization The Movement and the growing collaboration between American think tanks such as the Heartland Institute and right-wing European parties such as AfD. The right-wing populists are building on an already formidable network of institutions and media outlets to continue to propagandize and spin conspiracy theories at a dizzying rate and to make political gains through disinformation and propaganda.

The right-wing populism at work in the post-1970s formation is a mutant political movement comprising the neoliberal political project, neoclassical economics, and the modern conservative movement that has risen to power through a dangerous neofascist politics of "us" and "them." It is a mutant politics that fundamentally restructured the economic sphere and then capitalized on the economic dislocation it produced to further advance the project. In so doing, it transformed not only the economic domain but the political domain as well and is fueling emerging crises in both.

The dominant force in the cultural domain is the cyber-utopianism of the technology industry centered around Silicon Valley. Cyber-utopianism forms one of the outer shells of the neoliberal project, but this observation also obscures the complexity of this formation. Cyber-utopianism emerged from the strange co-mingling of the military-industrial research complex in American universities during the Cold War, the New Left communitarianism of the counter-culture, and the business culture of Silicon Valley. The cyber-utopians wrapped the free market ideologies promoted by neoclassical economics and the corporate lobbies of the modern conservative movement in the language of left progressive liberalism and anti-capitalist rhetoric. It is perhaps the strangest of political mutations identified in the preceding analysis, but it has had a significant impact on the political culture of the United States.

Cyber-utopianism is an ideological discourse informing the design of networked computer technologies that have had a powerful structuring effect on the collective conversation of American political culture. New media forms have proliferated in the post-1970s formation, but it is the introduction of networked computer technologies that have had the most powerful impact. It is not just that networked computers have created new media outlets; it is that they have fundamentally transformed older forms of media. For example, print media have had to transition to an online format and the computationalism this entails to survive. Those outlets that failed to make this change have and continue to disappear.

The new media landscape made possible by networked computer technologies has fragmented information media in complex ways that is fueling an emergent crisis in the cultural domain. Users of networked computer technologies are increasingly inhabiting relatively closed epistemic communities and echo chambers in which they are exposed to ideas and information that closely align with their preexisting beliefs and world views. It has produced a media landscape in which misinformation and propaganda thrive and that polarizes and radicalizes the political culture writ large.

Right-wing populism has thrived in the political culture structured by this new media landscape. Right-wing populism has its political roots in the modern conservative movement. The conservative movement rose to hegemonic dominance in the political domain in concert with the neoliberal political project by constructing a sophisticated network of media outlets to popularize a political discourse of "us" and "them," and right-wing populists have proven to be quite adept at utilizing this networked media formation to achieve political power. The targeted messaging pioneered by the early conservative movement has become increasingly sophisticated with the introduction of networked computer technologies. Right-wing populists are using networked computer technologies to target messages to specific demographic groupings, to propagandize misinformation and conspiracy, and to shape the ideological terrain of the contemporary formation to gain political power.

Cyber-utopianism is itself a mutant political formation encompassing the neoliberal political project, neoclassical economics, and elements of the modern conservative movement. It is an articulation of dominant discourses in the economic and political domains into an anti-elite narrative that appeals to actors across the political spectrum. It is one element within an articulation that has fundamentally restructured the political culture of the post-1970s formation.

It is this political constellation of mutating forces at work within and across the economic, political, and cultural domains that has constructed the post-1970s social formation. It is a mutating political ensemble that was able to construct a relatively stable articulated formation, but the internal contradictions and emergent crises that it has produced now threaten its stability, an emergent crisis in which right-wing populism is just as much a symptom of larger forces at work in the formation as it is a driving or animating force. This is the context, or problem space, in which the simple problem of right-wing populism is situated. It is both an animating force and product of accumulating antagonisms and contradictions across the economic, political, and cultural domains that are conjoining in this period of rupture and conjunctural crisis.

It would, however, be a mistake to believe that the political opportunities created by emergent crises in the economic, political, and cultural spheres will necessarily lead to a progressive future in which the political Left will come to ascendancy. The right-wing populism of the contemporary conjuncture is symptomatic of a mutant political formation that is well positioned to capitalize on the emergent crisis of the present and to lead the world system into a dangerous new era of neofascist politics that mirror those of the interwar period. The lesson to be learned here is that the categories of political analysis are not fixed but are defined by mutation and patterns of exchange among and between an ensemble of political actors, movements, and ideological discourses operating in complex patterns of cooperation, competition, and contradiction.

Telling a better story about the contemporary social formation and this historical moment of potential rupture requires that we eschew easy formulations that conceptualize the emergent crisis of the present as a problem of right-wing populism or even a more sophisticated conceptualization of neoliberal fascism. Telling a better story requires that we attend to the complexity of the conjuncture. The post-1970s social formation is structured by a mutating ensemble of political forces made up of the neoliberal political project, neoclassical economics, the modern conservative movement, and cyber-utopianism. *This is the problem space of the contemporary conjuncture.* It is a problem space of mutating politics and emergent crises. It is a problem space defined by fragmentation.

FRAGMENTATION

The task for this chapter was to take what Stuart Hall called a necessary detour through theory to make sense of the preceding conjunctural analysis. Hall cautions us against the easy answers that theory can provide and the ways in which it can prefigure the outcome of analysis before it even begins. Yet, theory remains indispensable in that it provides the necessary level of abstraction to make sense of analysis in ways that are meaningful and that can connect to political practice. Hall famously remarked that to wrestle with theory is to take a detour toward somewhere more important (Hall, 1991).

Laclau was an obvious place to begin making sense of an analysis that began with right-wing populism as its simple problem. Laclau offers us the tools to think about the right-wing populism of this current historical moment as one element within a contingent articulation of groups organized around empty signifiers, such as liberty, nationalism or, to use a specific example made popular by Donald Trump, making America great again. Laclau provides a discursive model to think through political struggle as the contested terrain of hegemonic struggle. His project complicates the category of right-wing populism in that populism is not a variant of the political but is, in fact, its foundation. What is important is that the simple problem with which this analysis began, right-wing populism, is a manifestation of a radical right political formation that achieved hegemonic dominance in a post-1970s social formation and that is now entering into a period of emergent conjunctural crisis. However, a key limitation of Laclau's discursive model is that it backgrounds the material and structural forces at work in the contemporary social formation and the emergent crisis of the present.

Giroux's theorizing of the contemporary formation as being defined by neoliberal fascism goes a long way toward rectifying this absence. Giroux powerfully argues that a defining characteristic of this historical moment is the dangerous conjoining of neoliberalism and a peculiar form of American-style authoritarianism he correctly identifies as being fascist. His model takes seriously the dynamic interplay between the material and the discursive as well as the institutional structures mediating this dynamic. Giroux's recent work goes a long way toward mapping the terrain of political struggle in the contemporary conjuncture, but I would argue that my analysis demonstrates that his conceptualization of neoliberal fascism fails to capture the complexity of the post-1970s social formation and the emergent crisis into which it is entering. This is not to say that Giroux's work is flawed. In fact, I would say that both Giroux and Laclau have much to contribute to our understanding of this moment of conjunctural crisis. However, my concern here is to map the terrain of political struggle in a manner that does justice to the complexity of this dynamic field, not complexity for its own sake but for informing scholarly and pedagogical work.

I want to argue that meeting the political challenges posed by the emergent crisis of the present requires that we broaden the horizon of theoretical reflection to the holistic, synthetic mapping of the terrain of political and pedagogical struggle. One of the challenges for doing critical work in this historical moment is to map the problem space, or context, of the contemporary conjuncture. Or, put more simply, the challenge is to tell better stories about this historical moment to inform contemporary struggle. The political challenge of this historical moment cannot be located in any one phenomenon or category of thought but within a context or problem space.

I want to argue that the preceding conjunctural analysis points toward a problem space defined by *fragmentation*. A simple and rather straightforward read of the preceding analysis is that the post-1970s social formation is fracturing and fragmenting. This is certainly the case, but I want to think about fragmentation in a more expansive way.

Fragmentation can be conceptualized in both a sociological and epistemological sense (Gouldner, 1985). As a sociological concept, fragmentation posits a social formation as an articulated structure of mutating social forces and ideological discourses working in complex patterns of cooperation, competition, and contradiction constituting a hegemonic order that is necessarily fragile and contested by counter-hegemonic forces made up themselves of mutating social and ideological forces operating in complex patterns of cooperation, competition, and contradiction. The contemporary societal context of the United States can be understood as a fragmented social field of agents, institutions, movements, ideological discourses, mediating structures, and so on, situated and operating in complex patterns of exchange and political struggle.

This is not to say that this is a necessarily new development. Fragmentation is, in fact, a defining feature of the modern era. What is new, as Laclau notes, is the acceleration and expansion of dislocatory apparatuses from the 1970s forward. Stuart Hall echoes Laclau by arguing that "processes of diversity and fragmentation, which modernism first tried to name, have gone further, are technologically underpinned in new ways, and have penetrated more deeply into mass consciousness" such that fragmentation demarcates the specificity of this period of political struggle (Grossberg, 1986b, p. 50). It is not simply that the contemporary social formation is fragmented into various class, racial, ethnic, gender, and heteronormative hierarchies, although that is certainly the case, but that it is fragmenting and increasingly complex. Thus, as a sociological concept, fragmentation speaks to an ontological perspective on the conditions of existence within late-capitalist societies that has important implications for the ways we come to know and understand social reality.

As an epistemological concept, fragmentation points toward the discursive and material forces distorting knowledge. The fragmentation of knowledge can be understood in two ways, which Alvin Gouldner describes as two types of forgetting. The first type of forgetting refers to the fundamental complexity of our societal contexts. To focus on any one narrowly defined problem is to distract ones attention away from an array of societal processes at work in a formation working in parallel with or influencing and being influenced by the object of analysis. This is a "forgetting induced by 'problem-distraction'" (Gouldner, 1985, p. 248). The second type of forgetting speaks to the limits of ordinary language. This type of forgetting is "induced by the structural and lexical features of a specific language which may not enable persons to fix a particular thought or object in view, thus causing it to be forgotten readily" (Gouldner, 1985, p. 248).

As the preceding analysis demonstrated, it is not simply that the contemporary social formation is complex, dynamic, and fragmented but that the agents, movements, and ideological discourses that constructed the post-1970s formation as an articulated structure are actively distorting knowledge of the social and society in the active production and reproduction of power. Thus, fragmentation refers to the "social forces distorting knowledge as well as of the distortion of knowledge itself" (Gouldner, 1985, p. 248). Again, it is not simply that knowledge about contemporary society is fragmented but that there are forces actively distorting and fragmenting knowledge to advance political goals, whether that be shoring up the crumbling edifice of the post-1970s formation or constructing a new more dangerous articulation. Fragmentation speaks to the "plurality of signification" (Grossberg, 1986b, p. 50). The contemporary societal context of the United States can be understood as a fragmented social field of agents, institutions, movements, ideological discourses, mediating structures, and so on, situated and operating in complex patterns of exchange and ideological struggle.

Fragmentation is *one* way to theorize the field of political struggle upon which the emergent crisis of the present will play out. It is on this fragmented, or perhaps it is more accurate to say fragmenting, political field that hegemonic and counter-hegemonic forces will organize, build movements and institutions, construct ideological discourses, and work to mobilize the masses in a war of position. I do not mean to minimize the dangers of the radical right-wing politics advancing in the United States and across the globe. My intention is to broaden the focus of political theorizing and activism to meet the challenges posed by the emergent conjunctural crisis of the present. The preceding analysis demonstrated that this radical right politics is a manifestation of the movement of forces within the post-1970s formation, one element of an articulated structure entering a period of conjunctural crisis.

I want to argue that meeting the challenges posed by the dangerous politics of this historical moment and charting a liberatory path out of the emergent crisis *begins* with mapping the terrain of political struggle, a task that is too often displaced by technocratic logics focused on solving narrow problems in ways that ultimately recuperate larger systems of domination or utopian logics that seek to transcend the messy complexity of the political toward ultimate ends. Meeting the political challenges posed by the contemporary conjuncture requires that we reject both the technocratic positivism of progressive liberalism as well as utopian radicalism, a strain of political thinking that plagues critical work in the field of education. Meeting the political challenges of the emergent crisis requires that we attend to the complexity, dynamics, and movement of forces at work in the fragmented social reality of this historical moment.

Theorizing the problem space of the conjuncture as being defined by fragmentation does not denote a preexisting whole or a politics of restoration of some imagined past. The forces of fragmentation identified by conjunctural analysis are not necessarily new. The axioms of neoclassical economic science date back to the nineteenth century, conservatism has been a reactionary force since the dawn of the European Enlightenment project, and media have played a central role in constructing commonsense understandings of the world and in disseminating propaganda since the invention of the printing press. These are, in many ways, the forces of fragmentation that define modernity.

What is qualitatively new is the imperialism of economics in the production of academic knowledge and in informing the development of public policy; the complex institutional framework, sophisticated political strategies, and media outlets of the modern conservative movement; the increasing sophistication and ubiquity of networked computer technologies that both collect an enormous amount of granular data on individuals and use that data to influence and manipulate human behavior; and the emergence of global networks of intellectuals and institutions working within and across the economic, political, and cultural domains to advance an elite, reactionary political project with planetary ambitions. The post-1970s social formation is defined by the rapid acceleration, expansion, and penetration of dislocatory apparatuses, both material and discursive, into every domain of human experience. It is defined by fragmentation.

Charting a liberatory path out of the emergent crisis of the present requires a radical engagement with the complex, dynamic, and fragmented political terrain of this historical moment. It requires a radical engagement with the society that history has delivered to the present and not one imagined by technocratic or speculative logics. This requires that we take up specific political problems, whether that be the rise of a radical right-wing populism, systemic failures revealed by the COVID-19 pandemic or police violence against communities of color, not as isolated (or isolable) problems to be "fixed" or transcended but as elements of an articulated formation bound up with the movement of an array of social forces, movements, ideological discourses, and so on, that are often not readily apparent using the concepts at work in popular discourse. It requires that we construct contexts around specific political problems to map the field of struggle and to inform political work.

The conjunctural analysis presented in preceding chapters demonstrated, as we have seen, that the post-1970s formation and the emergent crisis of the present is an articulated structure that is not necessary or cemented but is defined by the complex movement of forces, both material and discursive, and patterns of exchange among an array of elements. No one element or combination of two elements determines the movement of forces within this articulated structure nor can an analysis of any one element adequately capture the complexity of the terrain of political struggle to inform scholarly and pedagogical work. The task for doing critical political work in the contemporary conjuncture is not to understand and directly challenge right-wing populism or even neoliberal fascism but to wrestle with a problem space of dynamic, mutating, and contingent material, ideological, and discursive elements working in complex patterns of cooperation, competition, and contradiction structuring and being structured by the articulated social formation of the contemporary conjuncture. The task is to understand the context within which and through which so-called right-wing populists are rising to power. Our task is to struggle against a problem space defined by fragmentation.

I set out to tell a better story about right-wing populism in this book, not as a purely academic exercise but to map the terrain of political struggle and establish the necessary preconditions for charting a liberatory path out of this historical moment of conjunctural crisis. In this chapter, I took a necessary detour through theory to think through this problem space as being defined by fragmentation. In the two chapters that follow, I will expand on this detour to think through the implications of this analysis for scholarly and pedagogical practice.

Chapter 7

Inquiry and Scholarship

I began this project with the simple problem of right-wing populism. I then made an analytic move from this abstract concept toward the concrete through a conjunctural analysis of the social formation in which right-wing populism is an operative social force. From there, I retraced my steps back toward the abstract through a necessary detour through theory to make sense of the problem space of contemporary political and pedagogical struggle.

I now want to move again back toward the concrete but doing so will require that I tarry with the theoretical. I must first retrace some of the concepts and theories developed in the preceding chapter as well as introduce some new voices and ideas. My goal for this chapter is to extend the theoretical work presented in the preceding chapter to think through the implications of the conjunctural analysis of the contemporary formation and the emergent crisis I have developed here for scholarly inquiry and public pedagogy. This will require three preliminary tasks.

First, I will consider the politics of inquiry. Doing meaningful inquiry in the contemporary conjuncture requires rejecting the liberal fiction of objective, apolitical research based on "social facts" established from neutral data sets. The fragmented social formation now entering into a period of conjunctural crisis is, as we have seen, constituted by struggle. To do inquiry in this historical moment is to wade into the stream of ideological and discursive struggle.

Second, I want to sketch out a methodology for doing inquiry within the problem space I developed in the preceding chapter, one defined by fragmentation. The method of inquiry I will develop here rejects problem-centered, technical inquiry informed by a positivist epistemology. I will sketch out a methodology for the mapping of contexts and the terrain of political struggle through a radical, re-contextualizing analysis informed by a politics of disarticulation and re-articulation.

Third, I must think through the implications of the politics of inquiry and the methodology I sketch here for the positionality of the inquirer. If inquiry is necessarily political then does this mean that it is incumbent for the inquirer to chart a path forward? Should mapping the terrain of political struggle include directions on how to articulate a new liberatory formation? The answer I offer is: no. My goal here is to eschew technocratic logics of liberal ideology and its fetishism of expertise in favor intellectual humility and the deepening of democratic processes. The methodology I develop in this chapter is not oriented toward giving political actors answers but to map the terrain of *collective* political struggle.

My goal here is to work through these three tasks to develop a methodological approach to doing educational inquiry in this historical moment of emergent crisis. To do so, I will draw upon select studies from my own scholarship to give the reader some perspective on how to employ this methodology in educational inquiry, but I would like to offer some words of caution first. My intent here is not to develop specific methods for the reader to unproblematically transpose to her own research agenda. I present these studies as examples so that the reader can see how I have attempted to operationalize this methodology. My hope is that other scholars can build on, advance, and even trouble the model of inquiry that I develop.

More importantly, I am looking back on these studies through the lens of the present project, and I must admit that I do not always like what I see. For example, my thinking about the neoliberal political project has shifted dramatically as a result of doing this project which makes it difficult to look back on how I have discussed neoliberalism in the past. My point is that I do not want the reader to think that I am holding up these examples as exemplary case studies to be replicated. I am merely trying to demonstrate how I attempt to operationalize this method of inquiry in doing educational research.

The task for this chapter is to sketch out a methodology of radical, re-contextualizing analysis as ideological struggle. It is a methodology that is necessarily political without being prescriptive. And, importantly, it will inform the pedagogical practice that I will discuss in the chapter that follows.

POLITICS OF SIGNIFICATION

Stuart Hall reminds us that the political is, at its root, ideological struggle over competing definitions of social reality. It is a struggle to win the majority of the people to a set of commonsensical ideas that are the impetus for political practice.

[Ideology] provides the frameworks within which people define and interpret social existence. Not necessarily in a very learned or systematic way, but in terms of everyday, practical social reasoning, practical consciousness. Events and their consequences can always be interpreted in more than one ideological framework. That is why there is always a struggle over ideology: a struggle as to which definition of the situation will prevail. This is a struggle over a particular kind of power—cultural power: the power to define, to "make things mean." The politics of signification. What matters is which frameworks are in play, which definitions fill out and articulate the "common sense" of a conjuncture, which have become so naturalized and consensual that they are identical with common sense, with the taken-for-granted, and represent the point of origin from which all political calculation begins. (Hall, 1988a, p. 188)

Hall's reading of Gramsci and Marx led him to the conclusion that "in this day and age, in our kind of society, politics is either ideological, or not at all" (Hall, 1988b, p. 274).

The politics of the emergent crisis of the present, the conjunctural crisis of the post-1970s formation, will be defined by ideological struggle between and among competing conceptualizations of the crisis itself. The post-1970s formation was constructed through ideological struggle, and it is through ideological struggle that a new formation will be constructed. The political battles to come that will define this period of emergent crisis and the formation that will ultimately emerge from it will be ideological "and every other kind of struggle has a stake in it" (Hall, 1988a, p. 177). I argue that this is the problem space to which scholars, practitioners, cultural workers, and activists must attend. This is the ground that must be contested, but I anticipate that some readers may well protest at this way of conceptualizing the terrain of contemporary political struggle.

As Hall notes, terms like ideology and popular consciousness are very much out of fashion within intellectual circles. It conjures up images of a crude, vulgar Marxism; a mechanical model of ideology as superstructure determined by the economic base. In the crude structuralism of vulgar Marxism, there is one dominant ideology borne of the economic base that is unitary and relatively stable.

However, the Marxian orientation of cultural studies offers a more compelling model of ideology than the crude structuralism of vulgar Marxism. Following Gramsci, Hall's cultural studies model conceptualizes a social formation as a hegemonic order made up of a constellation of agents, political movements, and ideological discourses operating in complex patterns of cooperation, competition, and contradiction. A hegemonic order is not the domain of an unitary dominant ideology; it is a political terrain structured by dominant ideologies with enough overlap and shared political grammars to constitute a relatively stable formation that is always already contingent and more fragile that it readily appears.

There are also counter-hegemonic discourses offering competing definitions of social reality at work in any social formation. Counter-hegemonic politics are marginalized by definition, but they share features of the dominant order. They are comprised of a constellation of agents, political movements, and ideological discourses operating in complex patterns of cooperation, competition, and contradiction, but counter-hegemonic ideologies lack the political salience of dominant ideological discourses and are open to cooptation by dominant agents and movements into their own ideological and discursive practices. A hegemonic order is structured by dominant ideologies that have won out on the contested terrain of ideological struggle, but their victory is never total nor uncontested.

The key to understanding Hall's read of Gramsci and Marx is his engagement with Laclau and Mouffe and his theorizing of articulation. As we have seen, articulation refers to the joining together of the contradictory, disjointed, and fragmented into a temporary, contingent unity born of struggle, "the complex set of historical practices by which we struggle to produce identity or structural unity out of, on top of, complexity, difference, contradiction" (Grossberg, 1986a, p. 63).

> Articulation is a continuous struggle to reposition practices within a shifting field of forces, to redefine the possibilities of life by redefining the field of relations—the context—within which a practice is located. . . . Articulation is both the practice of history and its critical reconstruction, displacement and renewal. Analyzing an event then involves (re)constructing or, in Foucault's terms, fabricating the network of relationships in which and within which it is articulated, as well as the possibilities of different articulations. (Grossberg, 1992, p. 54)

The economic, political, and cultural domains of a social formation are relatively autonomous terrains or social fields made up of agents, movements, and ideological discourses operating according to their own goals, practices, and logics in ideological struggle. A constellation of agents, movements, and ideological discourses that achieves hegemonic leadership within, between, and across the various domains can construct or articulate a contingent unity that is not structurally necessary but is borne of struggle; it can achieve hegemonic dominance through ideological struggle. A social formation is structured or articulated by a temporary unity of ideological discourses that can join together various elements into a relatively stable hegemonic order.

Hall's work on articulation sought to construct a bridge between structuralism, post-Marxism, and postmodern deconstruction.

> Hall's fundamental commitment is to a structuring principle of struggle, not as an abstract possibility, but as a recognition that human activity at all levels always takes place within and over "contested terrain." Hall occupies the middle ground between those who emphasize the determination of human life by social structures and processes, and those who, emphasizing the freedom and creativity of human activity, fail to recognize its historical limits. (Grossberg, 1986a, p. 63)

It is an understanding of the political as ideological struggle that acknowledges that humans make their own history but not under self-selecting circumstances (Marx, 1978). Hall's focus on ideological struggle does not displace the economic or political. His work re-centers the ideological and cultural and locates it within the larger context of struggle across the various domains of a social formation.

The post-1970s social formation and the emergent crisis into which it is entering is the product of historical processes that define the terrain of the conjuncture. An ensemble of forces on the political right achieved a position of leadership, in Gramscian terms, in defining popular understandings of the crisis of the 1970s. The political right developed compelling stories around which to build alliances and animate the popular imagination of a new historic bloc to construct a temporary unity out of a constellation of agents, movements, and ideological discourses operating according to their own logics and practices in complex relations of cooperation, competition, and contradiction.

Hall implores us to take the political right seriously. The constellation of forces that rose to dominance in the 1970s constructed compelling stories that touched "people's understanding of how they live and work" and that made "a new kind of sense about what's wrong with society and what to do about it" (Hall, 1988a, p. 188). The ensemble of forces on the right that rose to dominance in the 1970s did not sing with one voice or tell one story. It drew upon a diverse set of ideological discourses and mutating political grammars, but there was enough overlap and patterns of exchange between these discursive practices to construct a coherent, relatively stable hegemonic order through which individuals made sense of their social existence. Put simply, the Right succeeded in contextualizing the crisis of the 1970s in ways that spoke to the lived experiences of individuals in meaningful ways, and it was through this storytelling that it constructed, or articulated, a relatively stable social formation.

The terrain of ideological struggle in the contemporary conjuncture is, accordingly, a struggle to *contextualize* the emergent crisis of the present. This is the terrain of political struggle. There is no escape hatch, no utopic leaps to take.

The radical right is well-positioned to define the crisis in popular imagination. They have access to and work through the political networks, media outlets, think tanks, ideological discourses, and so on, structuring the contemporary formation, the elements of the formation that are already in a position of hegemonic dominance. The radical right has the institutional and political capacity to contextualize the emergent crisis of the present in ways that can either work to recuperate and transform the contemporary formation or construct a darker, more dangerous formation.

The lesson to be learned from this detour through theory is now becoming clear. The emergent crisis of this historical moment presents a moment of opportunity for scholars and activists doing left-liberatory work but only if they attend to the task at hand.

> When a conjuncture unrolls, there is no "going back." History shifts gears. The terrain changes. You are in a new moment. You have to attend, "violently," with all the "pessimism of the intellect" at your command, to the "discipline of the conjuncture." (Hall, 1988c, p. 162)

The task for activists and scholars doing left-liberatory work is to *re-contextualize* or *re-articulate* the contemporary social formation and the emergent crisis into which it is entering. The task is to re-contextualize the emergent crisis of the present in ways that speak to the lived experiences of situated individuals within the contemporary conjuncture. It is a politics without guarantees, a politics of ideological struggle, a politics of signification. It is a politics of telling better stories.

The implication of these observations for education scholars is that educational problems are bound up with the relations of force at work in the contemporary social formation and the period of emergent crisis into which it is entering. Hotly debated topics in education from racial inequality and the achievement gap to STEM education and the integration of one-to-one technology in classrooms to the issues of school choice, standards, testing, and accountability are all bound up with the movement of forces that I worked to identify in the preceding conjunctural analysis. To wade into the politics of education is to wade into the larger political struggles at work in the contemporary conjuncture. There are no objective, apolitical spaces to inhabit. Educational inquiry in a period of conjunctural crisis is always already situated within a fragmented, articulated formation constituted by ideological struggle. The question that I wish to ask is: How can educational inquiry contribute toward a transformative path out of this period of emergent conjunctural crisis?

RE-CONTEXTUALIZATION AND SYNTHESIS

The argument that I am making in this project is that the United States and the world system are entering a period of emergent conjunctural crisis and that the path out of the crisis will be defined by the stories we collectively tell, by ideological struggle. My analysis began with the problem of right-wing populism. I set out to demonstrate that right-wing populism is a manifestation of the relations of force at work in the post-1970s formation and the emergent crisis of the present. The problem space I constructed through this analysis is, therefore, not right-wing populism itself but the constellation of agents, political movements, and ideological discourses structuring the post-1970s formation and the emergent crisis into which it is entering. It is a problem space defined by the dynamic movement of relations of force, dislocatory apparatuses, and fragmentation. I want to argue that constructing a new left-liberatory formation out of this period of emergent crisis will require a mode of ideological struggle oriented around the radical re-contextualization of the contemporary conjuncture.

I will argue that telling better stories is a politics of ideological struggle. It is a politics of radical re-contextualization, of re-articulation. It is a critical political orientation informed by ontological and epistemological assumptions that can be located in Marxian theory.

Alvin Gouldner (1985) argues that radical, re-contextualizing analysis constitutes the "deep structure" of Marx's critical project. In his posthumously published manuscript *Against Fragmentation*, Gouldner reads Marx's critical project as a struggle against a social totality fragmented and fractured by unequal power relations and social forces that distort knowledge and the tools of inquiry with which we come to understand the social totality and ourselves. I will quote Gouldner here at length and then unpack its implications.

> Marx's critique here is kin to his central objection to idealism; his insistence that "consciousness" cannot be understood in isolation; his conviction that rationality is part of a larger array of human talents no one of which can be understood in isolation from the others, and that reason is a partner in, not master over, the human enterprise. Most basically, Marx's views of consciousness, rationality, and interpretation are a critique of any tendency to substitute part for whole; they are an affirmation of the whole, of "social being," of sensuous praxis. Marx's project of emancipation, then, is at bottom a critique of and drive to overcome fragmentation. The most fundamental character of his project is to make the world whole, to connect the disconnected, to integrate the isolated, to remember the forgotten and the repressed, and to overcome old contradictions. The deep structure of Marx's project moves toward a vision of a new human

unity overcoming the divisiveness of competitive, possessive individualism of a civil society where the common interest is no one's business. At this level Marx's macroscopic sociology and his epistemology share a common structure, the sociology seeking to reconstruct the class-riven society into a solidary human community, and the epistemology aiming at the reconstruction of discourse, in which meaning is established by the joining of hitherto disconnected fragments, by a *re-contextualizing analysis*. (Gouldner, 1985, pp. 265–266)

For Gouldner, the analytic orientation of critical scholarship from Marx to the present day is defined by radical, re-contextualizing analysis that transgresses disciplinary and theoretical barriers in pursuit of new generative holistic understandings of social reality. It speaks to an intellectual practice oriented toward re-contextualizing, holistic analyses that navigate the dialectical tensions of "an effort to encompass the larger whole, to provide a picture of the social whole in its complexity, on the one side, and to rescue fugitive elements of cognitively underprivileged social reality, on the other" (Gouldner, 1985, p. 288).

Gouldner argues that the Marxian project inhabits the dialectical space between holistic analysis and recovery. Holistic analysis situates societal phenomenon/a within the totality of forces and relations that make up and animate it. It seeks to establish connections, map the movement of forces, and unpack the "rich totality of many determinations and relations" at work in an object of analysis (Marx, 1973, p. 100). Recovery captures and brings to the surface a neglected aspect of social reality in service to understanding the larger totality, to make visible reified concepts, ideologies, and discursive practices that animate, structure, and (de)stabilize a social formation. Recovery analytically centers holistic analysis toward naturalized ways of thinking and being and the underlying movement of social forces they animate that work to either stabilize, challenge, or displace a social formation. "The task, here, is thus not to find a solution to this or that partial 'social problem' in different spheres of life but to overcome the sheer disconnectedness of the several spheres" (Gouldner, 1985, p. 273). The Marxian project is marked by a theoretical commitment to re-contextualizing a fragmented social totality. It is, in a word, synthetic.

Importantly, this mode of radical re-contextualizing analysis is necessarily inter-disciplinary or even perhaps trans-disciplinary. Gouldner identifies the originality of Marx's critical project as a transgression of the theoretical borders of multiple traditions, a transgression "that is systematically generative of intellectual novelty and creativity . . . a multilinguality that facilitates an incongruous perspective and distances the theorist from the paradigms dominant within an intellectual specialization" (Gouldner, 1985, p. 204). The theories and disciplinary perspectives employed in this mode of synthetic, re-contextualizing analysis are determined by the object of analysis itself and not the theoretical commitments of the inquirer. Put simply, it is the questions that we ask that should determine the theoretical, methodological, or disciplinary tools we employ in inquiry.

What I find compelling in Gouldner's read of Marx and the critical project more generally is the theoretical tension in his commitments. He is clearly sympathetic to Marx's project and locates within it the analytic orientation, or "deep structure," of critical inquiry. Gouldner takes up Marx's social ontology of capitalist modernity as a dynamic totality fractured by unequal power relations, ideology, and class divisions and Marx's epistemological concern for the "social forces distorting knowledge [of the social totality] as well as of the distortion in the knowledge itself" (Gouldner, 1985, p. 248), and he ends the manuscript with a call "for the development of an effective community of theorists committed to the understanding of the social totality" as "one of the central tasks of social theory" (Gouldner, 1985, p. 299). Nevertheless, throughout *Against Fragmentation*, Gouldner offers a careful analysis that brings into focus the internal contradictions inherent in a radical theory that fails to explore and take seriously its own social origins and, more importantly, that clearly articulates the significant barriers to the realization of the task he envisions for critical social theory as both an intellectual project and as a politics.

What Gouldner leaves us with is theoretical tension in place of utopic resolution. He points toward a critical orientation, a mode of relating to social reality: critical inquiry in search of not restoration of a preexisting whole but struggle against a fragmented social reality, not totalizing claims of a "new truth" but radical re-contextualization as an intellectual project and as a politics. A critical Marxian orientation denotes not the restoration of an imagined whole but a struggle against fragmentation that transgresses theoretical and disciplinary boundaries.

The translation of cultural studies into the intellectual culture of the United States largely erased, or at least marginalized, the Marxian roots of British cultural studies (Nelson, 1991). Something important was lost in translation. I want to argue that reinvigorating cultural studies within the intellectual and political culture of the United States requires a re-engagement with the foundational Marxian-critical theorists who informed much of the early work at the Centre in Birmingham. Early cultural studies took from Marx a "conception of a social formation as a combination of relations or levels of abstraction . . . as historically specific articulations of concrete social forces. . . . From Gramsci, the notions of hegemony, articulation and ideology as . . . a process by which a hegemonic class articulates (or co-ordinates) the interests of social groups such that those groups actively 'consent' to their subordinate status . . . [and] from Althusser, the conception of a complex totality structured in dominance" (Slack, 1996, pp. 118–119). I argue that a common thread linking these theorists is the "deep structure" Gouldner identifies and that this analytic orientation is one of the animating forces within cultural studies.

What I take from the Marxian contribution to the cultural studies project is the centrality of struggle as a politics and as an intellectual practice. A social formation is constructed, or articulated, through ideological struggle over competing definitions of reality propagated by various social forces. To do intellectual work in this fragmented ontology is to accept that knowledge of a dynamic, complex totality is always already contested and that inquiry is itself a form of political struggle that requires a transdisciplinary approach to scholarship. The Marxian roots of the cultural studies project informs an intellectual practice committed to transdisciplinary, re-contextualizing analysis understood as a radical politics.

This radical, re-contextualizing analysis does not, however, entail simply situating an object of analysis within a context before moving on to a technical analysis. Cultural studies inquiry seeks to map a context understood as a structured ensemble of forces. Context is itself the end point of analysis.

> [A] structured assemblage is a force-field encompassing different forms of objects, facts, practices, events, whatever can be found along the way. . . . [C]ultural studies attempts to construct a contour map measuring the effects of underlying processes over time. The map describes a configuration of practices which is constantly working on itself, deconstructing and reconstructing, reproducing and changing, extending and drawing back. Its history will not be coherent and linear but will follow the discontinuous and often serendipitous histories and relations of a number of contiguous maps. The "truth" of the result is not hidden below the surface of the real, but rather obscured by its very visibility on the surface; cultural analysis seeks to discern a pattern dispersed on the surfaces that have to be traversed. The maps of cultural studies fabricate the real in an attempt, not to represent or mimic it, but to strategically open up its possibilities, to intervene into its present in order to remake its future. (Grossberg, 1992, p. 64)

In contrast to traditional modes of inquiry that *begin* with contextualizing an object of analysis or specific social problem, often in a deeply reductive manner, cultural studies inquiry seeks to map networks of relationships among the agents, movements, and ideological discourses articulating and re-articulating a social formation. "The apparent unity needs to be prised apart, disarticulated, challenged by looking at how the articulation was itself accomplished" (Grossberg, 1992, p. 60).

To tell a better story is to struggle against a fragmented social reality through a radical, re-contextualizing analysis. The goal is not to produce a singularity or restore an imagined whole but to construct the context of struggle. The goal is to develop a holistic perspective that recovers the complex patterns of exchange among the various forces of a structured assemblage. It is to map the terrain of ideological struggle as a *necessary precondition* for left-liberatory politics.

The story that I attempted to tell in the preceding pages is not neat or tidy. The story I offer is messy and complex. It is a story of the assemblage of agents, movements, and ideological discourses that constructed and continuously re-constructed, articulated and re-articulated, the post-1970s social formation, a dynamic and fragile unity borne of struggle. The story cannot be summed up in academic jargon nor a catchy turn of phrase. It is a story that is messy, complex, and contradictory. What I have attempted to do is to map the terrain of the contemporary conjuncture, to map the terrain of political struggle.

This was not a sequential, linear mapping that presents the object of analysis as a product of evolutionary processes with a clearly defined genesis. The mapping presented in preceding chapters involved the tracing and retracing of processes over time with an eye toward identifying patterns of exchange and tracing the movement of forces. It was a telling of the present history of the post-1970s formation as a differentiated unity (Hall, 1973).

The task I envision for educational inquiry is to demonstrate how specific struggles in the politics of education are bound up with larger struggles at work in the contemporary conjuncture. This involves mapping the terrain of political struggle surrounding specific educational policies and practices using a radical, re-contextualizing analysis. The task is to disarticulate and re-articulate specific educational problems, to construct a present history of contemporary political struggle in the field of education and the larger social formation. The goal is to tell a better story about specific educational problems that can inform the work of practitioners, activists, cultural workers, and scholars in collective struggle in this period of emergent conjunctural crisis. The goal is to tell better stories to, hopefully, inform better educational politics. This positions the educational researcher not as an expert, or that most empty of signifiers "policy wonk," but as one who contributes to collective struggle through negative critique of the taken-for-granted through radical, re-contextualizing analysis.

DESPAIR AS A DIALECTICAL PASSION

My project is to tell a better story about the contemporary social formation and the emergent crisis into which it is entering and to then think through the implications of this analysis for educational inquiry and practice. I began with the problem of right-wing populism and set about a radical, re-contextualizing analysis not to situate right-wing populism within a context but to map the context through which and within which it is an operative social force. I set out to map the contemporary formation and the emergent crisis of the present through conjunctural analysis.

The goal was to map the terrain of ideological struggle, to tell a better story about the contemporary conjuncture than the stories currently at work in political discourse. My hope is that telling a better story can inform better politics and a liberatory path out of the emergent crisis of the present. The reader might, with some justification, anticipate that I will offer her directions or point toward a positive path out of this historical moment of potential rupture, but such a reader will be disappointed.

I want to argue that the role of politically engaged scholarship is not to construct utopic visions toward which to strive nor to provide answers to technical problems. It is to map the terrain of collective struggle. It would be a performative contradiction for a scholar committed to deepening democratic life and collective struggle to proclaim "this is what must be done." More importantly, it is imperative to remember that a commitment to democratic collectivities demands that scholars remain intellectually humble. Scholars have a role to play in the struggle over the emergent crisis, but we do not inhabit a privileged epistemic position.

I have attempted to tell a better story, but the story I have told is by no means the final word on the nature of the present crisis. Others have stories to tell that can contribute to our understanding of this historical moment. I want to argue that one path for politically engaged scholarship can be located in the logic of negative critique within cultural studies, an approach to scholarship informed by Marxian theory. In other words, the radical potential of inquiry is not to be located in the "answers" it provides but in its ability to tease out or clarify the field of political struggle itself.

In an open letter to Arnold Ruge, Marx (1978b, p. 14) articulated a critical political project that does not seek to construct utopic visions toward which to strive but a politics that seeks "to find the new world only through criticism of the old," what Fraser (1989, p. 97) termed a critical project of "self-clarification." Marx's revolutionary project was one defined by a commitment to negative critique that was grounded in Hegelian thought.

Marx was a revolutionary thinker who was steadfastly anti-utopian. The goals toward which to strive are not to be found beyond the horizon but in the everyday struggles of concrete, material reality. Accordingly, Marxian inquiry dwells in the negative not as a purely intellectual pursuit, what he derided as critical criticism, but to find hope where there is no rational basis for it.

Robyn Marasco (2015) argues that critical theory after Hegel is grounded in locating hope in the face of catastrophe and despair. Marx was inspired not just by the inhumanity of capitalist development but also the failures of the Enlightenment project. Gramsci's work was driven by the collapse of the revolutionary moment into fascism and by his growing disillusionment with Stalinism and the Comintern. Theodor Adorno was driven by the catastrophe of fascism and the Holocaust, the rational development of increasingly sophisticated technologies of death, and the collapse of culture into capitalist consumerism. And, the touchstone for the cultural studies projects at Birmingham was the re-emergence of authoritarian populism and Thatcherism. What unites these projects (which I categorize here under a broad definition of critical) is not just that they persist in the face of catastrophe and failure but that they dwell in the negative seeking radical potential in the ruins of the present.

Marasco identifies despair as a political category animating the critical project, as "a distinctive—and enduring—feature of the dialectic that survives the ruins of [Hegel's] speculative system" (Marasco, 2015, p. 28). Despair in Hegel is not to be mistaken for pessimism or a turn toward nihilism nor is it a psychological conceptualization, such as melancholia or depression. It is, instead, a dialectical passion, the somatic experience of loss and deferral, that propels us forward against all rational hope.

> [D]espair is at odds with itself. It militates against itself. It conserves and preserves the possibility of what it also denies. If, in etymological terms, despair indicates the absence of hope, this is no simple absence. Despair can never let go of its familiar and estranged other. . . . [It anticipates] how dreams get deferred, projects derailed, and causes lost. And how these deferrals, derailments, and losses always carry with them a new constellation of possibilities and foreclosures. (Marasco, 2015, pp. 5–6)

Despair speaks to the somatic experience of loss and catastrophe in a concrete social reality that seemingly extinguishes any hope of radical transformation even as it implies, or carries with it, that which it denies.

Marasco takes her cue from the recurring figure of natural consciousness in the drama depicted in Hegel's *Phenomenology of Spirit*. Put simply, the journey of natural consciousness depicts the somatic experience of learning and acting in the world, in "thinking on one's feet." Natural consciousness is a naive consciousness holding concepts that sets out on a journey of learning, an imminent dialectic, through a process of conceptual failure and re-conceptualization. Hegel depicts the journey of natural consciousness this way:

> Natural consciousness will prove itself to be only knowledge in principle or not real knowledge. Since, however, it immediately takes itself to be the real and

genuine knowledge, this pathway has a negative significance for it; what is a realization of the notion of knowledge means for it rather the ruin and overthrow of itself; for on this road it loses its own truth. Because of that, the road can be looked on as the path of doubt, or more properly a highway of despair. (Hegel, 2003, p. 47)

Hegel depicts a process philosophy of worldly revelation that challenges the conceit of theory that begins with the "truth" of the matter. Natural consciousness sets out on a journey of inquiry in which:

> its flawed and narrow truths will be systematically disrupted and its attachments continuously loosened by the acquisition of knowledge, by the encounter with others, and by an objective world that it erroneously sees as separate from its subjectivity. . . . [T]he text reads as a philosophical *passion play*, a staging of the somatic suffering and spiritual torment that natural consciousness suffers so that we—author and reader—may be free. (Marasco, 2015, pp. 50–51)

Conceptual failure is experienced by natural consciousness as not simply a tear or split in consciousness but as a radical fragmentation or dismemberment of the self. It is a journey of passion and torment in which natural consciousness must not only re-conceptualize its knowledge of the world but its own subjectivity.

Truth in the Hegelian system is an educative process borne of conceptual failure in the face of a concrete, material reality that militates against the pretense of knowledge. Knowing is doing for Hegel. It is an educative process that is experienced as the loss of self on the highway of despair. It is a journey with no predetermined course nor endpoint. It is the path itself that defines the journey. It is true that there is a logic of reconciliation and resolution in Hegel's speculative system (Hutchings, 2003). However, as Marasco convincingly argues, this turn toward positivity is notably absent in the work of critical theorists influenced in various ways by Hegel's work, and this embrace of the negative, this embrace of despair as a political category, provides the kinetic energy propelling the project forward.

Critical theory dwells in the negative. It takes from Hegel a cultivated misrelation to social reality but without the guarantee of ultimate resolution or absolute freedom proposed by the speculative system. It is, as Stuart Hall notes, a politics without guarantees.

Critical theory lingers and tarries in the catastrophe of late capitalist modernity. Like natural consciousness, critical consciousness is compelled to "think on its feet" as it journeys through a fragmented ontological and epistemological landscape that it experiences as a loss of self, as despair. Yet, this loss of self is not the impetus for a retreat into nihilist resignation but is itself the dialectical energy that provides hope in spite of a concrete reality that militates against the possibility of it.

> Critique has everything to do with despair. . . . [It] persists in the ruthless critique of everything existing, while persevering in the impossible task of changing the world. The challenge for contemporary critical theory is to inhabit this no-man's-land between the prevailing order of things and a more just and humane world. This position is drawn from the limits of reason and faith, from the aporias of knowledge, and from the forceful determination of our passions. What is needed is the cultivated misrelation to the present that comes with the work of the negative. That is to say, what lives in the gay science is nourished by our despair. (Marasco, 2015, pp. 182–183)

What I take away from Marasco's embrace of despair as a political category is a commitment to struggle. Critical work entails a commitment to struggle against a fragmented social reality of unequal power relations, the dynamic movement of forces, and systems of domination that systematically distorts knowledge of concrete social existence. It entails a commitment to forms of critique that assumes "there is no end to or exit from conditions of existence, and no *rational* hope that a brighter future will repay patient struggle in the present" (Marasco, 2015, p. 1).

Despair is the somatic, lived experience of struggle against all odds. It is a political category that speaks to a misrelation to the present that presupposes one is already struggling against the conditions of social existence. Critical theory and activism after Hegel is, therefore, a mode of political struggle fueled by our despair.

The conjunctural analysis presented in these pages is fueled by my despair over our contemporary conditions of existence. The impetus for this inquiry was my despair over the rise to power of so-called right-wing populism, but mapping the context of the contemporary social formation and the emergent crisis demonstrates that this initial problem is bound up with larger societal forces. The complex, messy, and (hopefully) better story that I am telling about the contemporary conjuncture provides insight into the landscape of political struggle but one that is also hostile to any hope for radical transformation.

Right-wing populism is a manifestation of an assemblage of agents, political movements, and ideological discourses that achieved dominance in the post-1970s formation. The terrain of struggle in the contemporary conjuncture is defined by ideological struggle over contextualizing the emergent crisis, and these dominant forces inhabit, by definition, a privileged position in delineating the nature of the crisis and in charting a path out of it, whether that means some form of recuperation or the construction of a more dangerous formation. It is difficult to not look on in despair at the story I have attempted to tell, but the telling of the story itself speaks to a misrelation to the present fueled by hope in the face of conditions of existence that militate against it. The story I have attempted to tell offers no rescue to the reader; it only attempts to map the terrain of struggle.

I argue that the commitment of cultural studies to telling better stories is rooted in a critical project seeking to cultivate a misrelation to the present by mapping the terrain of struggle. It is a politics of inquiry and activism that is, as Hall went to great lengths to demonstrate, *without guarantees* (Hall, 1986). Telling better stories speaks to inquiry and activism as political struggle that is, like the journey of natural consciousness, an educative process defined by negative critique. To tell a better story is to cultivate a misrelation to the present, to establish the necessary preconditions for left-liberatory struggle. It is fueled by despair over the conditions of existence and the radical hope it presupposes.

To be clear, it is not my intention to subsume cultural studies under critical theory. British cultural studies and its many manifestations around the world are informed by many different theoretical and methodological approaches to inquiry and activism. My goal is to recover the critical Marxian foundations of cultural studies that originated in Birmingham and that is often absent from cultural studies in the United States. I want to recover this critical orientation so as to reinvigorate cultural studies in American intellectual and political culture and to think through its implications for doing inquiry and activism in the field of educational foundations and education studies.

Telling better stories about educational problems requires situating them within the catastrophe of the present through a radical, re-contextualizing analysis. It denotes an educational politics without guarantees. It is an educational politics that finds radical hope through a ruthless criticism of a social formation and emergent crisis that militates against it.

PUBLIC PEDAGOGY

The radical, re-contextualizing analysis I envision is a materialist analysis focused on the dominant political actors, movements, and ideological discourses at work in the economic, political, and cultural domains of the contemporary formation. Constructing a context around specific educational topics, issues, controversies, policies, and so on, involves the mapping of the relations of force and the terrain of struggle surrounding these simple educational problems. Put another way, the construction of a problem space involves the disarticulation of a simple educational problem through a negative critique that opens up new possibilities for re-articulation, understood as a re-articulation of an educational problem impacting both the field of education and the larger social formation. Radical, re-contextualizing analyses seek to map the terrain of ideological struggle surrounding simple educational problems that scholars, practitioners, cultural workers, and activists doing left-liberatory work must traverse toward transformative change. It is an approach to educational inquiry that involves two interrelated forms of analysis.

A hegemonic order is not, as we have seen, a rigid formation structured by one hegemonic power organized around a singular ideological discourse. It is an articulated structure made up of networks of political actors, movements, and ideological discourses operating within, between, and across the economic, political, and cultural domains in complex patterns of exchange, cooperation, competition, and contradiction. Untangling this Gordian knot begins with the mapping of the political actors and movements at work in the conjuncture that are relevant to the simple problem.

One of the more exciting lines of educational inquiry over the past decade has been the adoption of tools from social network analysis to map policy networks at work in the field of education (Au & Ferrare, 2015). Stephen Ball (2012) has done pioneering work in critical policy sociology using network ethnography (Hogan, 2016; Howard, 2002) to map education policy networks operating at the local, national, and global levels. His "non-linear policy cycle approach" (Lingard & Seller, 2013) to educational inquiry provides a "topological perspective to the opaque web of relations and influence among government, think tanks, policy institutes, philanthropic organizations, and edu-business driving contemporary trends in education reform around the globe" (Ellison & Allen, 2018, p. 270). Network analysis is a powerful tool for mapping the movement of forces on the education field, and it can offer some insight into the construction and continual re-construction of power relations not only within the field of education policy and practice but also the larger social formation. However, unpacking the patterns of exchange and mutations between, among, and across the networks at work in education policy and practice requires a second mode of analysis that untangles the means by which political actors and movements work to construct and continually re-construct power through ideological struggle.

One way to gain insight into the relations of force and patterns of exchange among, between, and across the political actors and movements at work in the field of education is through critical analyses of the ideological discourses that form the terrain of struggle. I envision critical analyses that, following Laclau and Hall, disarticulate the empty signifiers at work in an articulated formation. Such critical analyses begin with the ideological; the common sense, taken-for-granted ideas and concepts informing education policy and practice. The goal is to employ a variety of tools ranging from qualitative content analysis (Schreier, 2012) to critical discourse analysis (Dijk, 1993) to tease out the interplay of ideological discourses at work in an articulated formation operating in complex patterns of exchange, competition, cooperation, and contradiction; to trace patterns of exchange between, among, and across the various discourses at work in the education field; and to both untangle and anticipate discursive and ideological mutations and new articulations.

Thus, constructing a problem space around simple educational problems involves the mapping of the political actors and movements working to construct and re-construct educational formations and the discursive practices that constitute the field of ideological struggle over the maintenance or potential transformation of educational formations. I would add that the radical, re-contextualizing analysis I am describing here is necessarily bound up with the political actors, movements, and ideological discourses constituting the hegemonic bloc structuring the post-1970s formation and is, therefore, necessarily bound up with the emergent crisis of the present developed in the preceding analysis. The particular and the universal are necessarily bound up each with the other. What I am attempting to describe here is a methodology for critical analyses that move beyond instrumental, positivist research by connecting political struggle in the field of education to the larger field of ideological struggle at work in the conjuncture. To borrow a turn of phrase from Stuart Hall (1990), it is a way of thinking about educational inquiry as a tiny piece of ideological struggle.

What does this approach to educational inquiry look like? I want to offer the reader some examples from my own research agenda. However, to be clear, my goal is not to offer a prescriptive "how-to" manual. What I offer here is a narrative description of an approach to radical, re-contextualizing inquiry that draws upon examples from my own work.

The elevation of Betsy DeVos to Secretary of Education in 2017 created a relatively minor political scandal in the early days of the Trump administration. Her disastrous performance during Senate hearings over her confirmation demonstrated that DeVos did not possess even rudimentary knowledge about the federal department she was nominated to lead. The ensuing scandal over her qualifications for the position raised important questions that, for a few fleeting moments, brought public attention to the power of elite actors to influence education policy and practice. DeVos' elevation to federal office was a function of her work through advocacy organizations that she and her family fund with their vast wealth, specifically the American Federation for Children (AFC). The controversy over DeVos brought public attention to the philanthropic and advocacy organizations funded by elite actors that work to achieve their political goals outside of formal democratic processes. It was a scandal that was easily connected to larger public debate over the plutocratic politics of the twenty-first century, and it offers an important simple educational problem around which to construct a problem space.

Constructing a problem space around this scandal involves two modes of analysis: mapping the networks of political actors and movements surrounding this simple problem and untangling the ideological discourses employed by these actors to achieve their political goals (Ellison et al., 2019). To map the networks surrounding the AFC, my colleagues and I employed tools from network ethnography to carry out two tasks. First, we conducted a careful search of publicly available tax records filed by the AFC between 2010 and 2015 (U.S. Internal Revenue Service Form 990). This part of the analysis identified a wide range of advocacy organizations, think tanks, political lobbying organizations, and so on, receiving funding from the AFC. Many of the organizations identified in this initial phase are also nonprofit organizations required to file Form 990 tax documents. A search of publicly available tax forms filed by these organizations over the same time period identified political actors who both fund and receive funding from organizations identified in the initial search of tax documents and expanded the number of actors working with and alongside the AFC. This expanded network also identified new cohesive networks that work alongside and with the AFC, such as the Walton Family Foundation network. Second, we carried out a careful web search using search engines, such as Google and LexisNexis, to identify affiliations and connections to both actors identified in the search of tax documents as well as actors and organizations not previously identified. All of the data collected during these procedures were recorded in an adjacency matrix and maps were generated using social network analysis software.

Mapping the AFC network revealed a number of important insights. First, the AFC is one piece of a larger network of organizations, such as the AFC Growth Fund, AFC Action Fund and the Alliance for School Choice, created and funded by the DeVos family. Second, the AFC is one node of a larger network of elite economic actors, such as the New Schools Venture Fund; influential organizations in the conservative movement, such as the Walton Family Foundation and Alliance for Catholic Education; political actors associated with the technology industry, such as the Silicon Valley Community Foundation; and boundary blurring neoliberal actors, such as Democrats for Education Reform (DFER), the Bill and Melinda Gates Foundation, and EdChoice (formerly the Friedman Foundation for Educational Choice). Third, the network of elite actors that include the AFC are affiliated with and provide funding to a vast array of political actors operating at the state and local levels, such as think tanks, advocacy and community organizations and single-issue political action committees. This means that the education policy field is made up of multiple, cohesive networks connected to one another in complex patterns of cooperation, competition, and contradiction.

What the maps demonstrate is that there is a hierarchical ordering to the networks of actors at work on the education policy field. AFC and other elite organizations make up a complex network of political actors operating at all levels of education policy development, from the national to the local. National organizations such as the AFC and the Bill and Melinda Gates Foundation fund and collaborate with a large and shifting array of political actors at work on the education policy field. This involves patterns of exchange between, among, and across these elite network actors as well as more complex patterns of exchange between, among, and across the organizations and groups working at the state and local levels. More importantly, the various nodes that make up these complex networks make for some interesting and contradictory bed fellows. The DeVos family are members of the Republican party and have given lavishly to the campaigns of Republican politicians, yet the AFC works with an organization closely tied to the opposition Democratic Party, DFER. Likewise, it is difficult to see at first glance how the evangelical Christian DeVos family can work with an organization that has dedicated millions of dollars of funding for family planning and contraceptive services around the globe, the Bill and Melinda Gates Foundation. What the maps reveal is a hierarchical ordering of the education policy field, but, more importantly, they hint at the polyvocality of the political actors involved and indicate that they work on this field in complex patterns of cooperation, competition, and contradiction.

Untangling the patterns of exchange among these network actors requires an analysis of the ideological discourses advanced by these network actors. To accomplish this task, my colleagues and I carried out a critical analysis of the discursive strategies employed by actors in the AFC network to influence the policy cycle. Data for this analysis were gathered through exhaustive internet searches of the actors receiving funding from and affiliated with AFC. Textual data gathered included: organizational mission statements, official statements on political events and legislation, news and blog posts, parent testimonials featured on organizational websites, policy briefs, and research summaries. We analyzed the data using tools from qualitative content analysis to tease out the ways in which the actors at work in the AFC network seek to influence the policy cycle, from defining problems to the diagnosis of causes to the making of moral judgment to the development of problem solutions.

The analysis demonstrated that the AFC network employs the time-worn category of an educational crisis to define the policy problem. The discursive strategies they employ frame public education as a failing institution plagued by bureaucracy and low achievement that fails to prepare future generations for the twenty-first century technologically driven knowledge economy. Interestingly, this educational crisis is framed by concerns over inequality. Public education is described as being defined by systemic inequality that denies opportunity for students "trapped" in the failing institutions available to working-class families and communities of color. The discursive strategies employed by these network actors take up the familiar frame of educational failure as it adopts and reformulates the categories and concepts employed by activists working toward racial and economic justice in the education system.

The cause of educational crisis and inequality is identified as being driven by an elitist establishment of self-interested political actors. The discursive strategies employed by the AFC network seek to construct an education establishment made up of bureaucratic officials, teachers' unions, and political groups who engage in dishonest attacks on advocates for change and, by proxy, the families and students served by this failing institution. This education establishment is described as being made up of self-interested actors working in schools, elite political actors who think they know what is best for children and families, and outside political groups that use dishonest tactics to attack educational reformers working toward racial and economic equality.

The policy solutions advanced by the AFC network involve various market-based, "school choice" strategies, such as voucher school programs, charter schools, tax credits, and so on. More importantly, these policy solutions are described as being proven strategies to increase student achievement and alleviate racial and economic inequality that are being pursued by a growing grassroots movement working to challenge the elite power of the education establishment. It is a discourse that positions the actors of the AFC network as fighting alongside advocates for social justice in education against entrenched bureaucratic elites who work inside and outside public education. Tellingly, the research used to bolster claims that market-based solutions are effective policy tools to resolve historic inequalities come from other network actors, such as EdChoice, and the "grassroots" movements they reference are all organizations within the AFC network or other elite networks with which the AFC is affiliated. What we see in the discursive strategies employed by the AFC network is an ideological discourse of anti-elite populism rising up to challenge the unaccountable power of a distant elite.

The analysis of the discursive strategies employed by the AFC network point toward three important findings. First, the hierarchical ordering of the AFC network identified in the network maps discussed previously are borne out by this discursive analysis. The political actors in the AFC network often use the same text in their promotional and advocacy materials, highlight the same research reports and policy documents, and even elevate the same "grassroots" voices working to change the education system. For example, the parent testimonials posted to various websites were all very similar and followed a similar template. What this demonstrates is that the AFC distributes a wide variety of resources to the various actors in the network beyond funding, including marketing material and advocacy research.

Second, while the various actors in the network employed similar discursive strategies and categories, they are not univocal. The political actors in the AFC network may be singing from the same hymn book, but they are not singing the same songs with one voice. The discursive strategies employed by these network actors are mutable and opportunistic. The overall policy goal of the network is to advance market-based "school choice" policies, but the specific policies pursued and the means by which individual actors advocate for them reflect the state and local contexts in which these actors operate. Just as the network maps demonstrated the divergent and often contradictory actors at work in the education policy field the discursive analysis demonstrates a polyvocality within the AFC network and suggests that such polyvocality is characteristic of other policy networks at work on the policy field.

Third, what this analysis demonstrates is a sophisticated political practice. The actors at work in the AFC network employ sophisticated discursive strategies to influence policymakers and public opinion. They employ malleable discursive strategies that are contextually specific and, more importantly, that contest oppositional discourses. The AFC network works to adopt and reframe the political categories and grammars employed by social justice activists working toward racial and economic equity to further its own political goals. Put simply, the actors at work in the AFC network employ a sophisticated political practice of ideological struggle. The AFC network demonstrates the ways in which elite political actors in the education policy field work to appropriate the "needs discourses" of subaltern groups working toward racial and economic justice (Swalwell & Apple, 2011) by linking their policy goals with broader notions of political empowerment (Scott, 2013). Or, as Laclau might observe, these elite actors are working to hegemonize the concepts and categories employed by nondominant, counter-hegemonic political actors.

Stephen Ball offers us one way to make sense of the analysis I am describing here. Ball has come to conceptualize the education policy field as being heterarchical, which he describes this way:

> Heterarchy is an organisational form somewhere between hierarchy and network which draws upon diverse horizontal and vertical links that permit different elements of the policy process to cooperate (and/or compete) while individually optimising different success criteria. That is, it replaces or com-bines bureaucracy and administrative structures and relationships with a system

of organisation replete with overlap, multiplicity, mixed ascendacy and/or divergent-but-coexistent patters of relation, which operates at and across "levels" (local, sub-national, national and international). (Ball, 2009, p. 689)

The analysis I described above lends credence to this perspective. "The AFC is one network among many others linked to one another in complex relations of reciprocal interdependence and varying degrees of independence and autonomy" (Ellison et al., 2019, p. 16). The education policy field is, on the one hand, a somewhat chaotic space inhabited by a diverse array of dominant and nondominant political actors vying for influence that is, on the other hand, a structured space that is "collectively orchestrated without being the production of the orchestrating action of a conductor" (Bourdieu, 1977, p. 72).

Situating the example of radical, re-contextualizing analysis I am describing here within the conjunctural analysis developed in preceding chapters offers important insight into what it means to do left-liberatory work in the field of education at this moment of emergent crisis. The discursive strategies employed by the AFC network mirror the dominant ideological discourses at work in the post-1970s formation. These strategies are informed by the market logics of neoclassical economics; the anti-elite, "us" versus "them" rhetoric of the modern conservative movement; and the cyber-utopian logics of the technology industry that are all unified by the reactionary logics of the neoliberal political project. The field of education policy is embedded in the hegemonic logics of the contemporary formation, and the discursive strategies employed by political actors on this field are necessarily bound up with the ideological discourses at work in the economic, political, and cultural domains of the conjuncture. Ideological struggle on this field is therefore bound up with the ideological struggles of the emergent crisis.

To tell a better story is to interrogate a simple educational problem through a materialist analysis of the movement of forces on the field of education policy and practice and a discursive analysis of the ideological work of dominant forces at work on this field to achieve their political goals. Telling a better story means moving between these two analytic moments to construct a context, or problem space, around specific educational phenomena. However, to be clear, the methodology I have attempted to construct in this chapter is not exhaustive nor the only way to tell better stories.

Qualitative analyses that explore the lived experiences of situated actors who must negotiate, make sense of, and (sometimes) challenge the ideological discourses structuring the education field are vital and necessary. This can include a wide variety of approaches to qualitative research, from descriptive studies that seek to elevate the policy knowledge of urban school teachers into policy debates from which they are presently excluded (Ellison et al.,

2018) to more expansive cultural studies projects that juxtapose the lived experiences of teachers working in a model STEM school against a network analysis of the elite forces at work in STEM education and a discursive analysis of the ideological work they employ to achieve their political goals (Ellison & Allen, 2018). The argument that I want to make is that qualitative work can be a vital part of telling better stories but only if it is situated within a critical framework of radical contextualism. So, for example, critical qualitative analyses of the "no excuses" charter school model targeted toward working-class students of color (Ellison & Iqtadar, 2020) must be situated within a synthetic analysis of the materialist and ideological work bound up in this school model (Ellison, 2012). The point that I am trying to make is that the radical, re-contextualizing analysis that I describe here is not exhaustive or even sufficient, but it is *necessary*.

To do critical work in education policy and practice, to tell better stories, is to construct contexts around simple phenomena. It challenges traditional, positivist educational scholarship by conceptualizing an object of analysis not as a point of departure from which inquiry is to proceed but as a point of arrival that must be constructed through synthetic, radical, re-contextualizing analysis. It constructs contexts around education problems to map the terrain of ideological struggle on the field of education policy and practice and to situate educational problems with the larger terrain of struggle structuring the contemporary conjuncture.

CONCLUSION

To do educational inquiry in the contemporary conjuncture is to engage in ideological struggle. The examples from my own scholarship demonstrate that educational policy and practice in the contemporary conjuncture is bound up with the hegemonic bloc structuring and being structured by the post-1970s formation. The policies and practices that have defined education reform from 1980 to the present are informed by a toxic mix of neoclassical economic theory; the white nationalist, neo-fascist politics of the modern conservative movement; the cyber-utopian discourse of Silicon Valley; and the elite social engineering of the neoliberal political project. The human capital theory of neoclassical economics informs both the normative ideals of education policy and the curricula and pedagogical practices employed in schools. The modern conservative movement draws upon the language of neoclassical market theory to advance "school choice" policies that direct public funding toward religious institutions and that work to maintain school segregation, and it has been the driving force behind the "curriculum wars" that frame everything from literacy instruction to social studies and science curricula as examples of leftist indoctrination. The ideological discourse of cyber-utopianism draws upon the human capital discourse of neoclassical economics to advance the introduction of networked computer technologies into schools and classrooms, narrow school curricula to STEM subjects, and create new market opportunities for the technology sector. The neoliberal political project works within and across these domains to advance the marketization of public education, encourage the development of a productive and compliant workforce, and centralize authority within elite networks that eclipse democratic possibilities that can interfere with the global market society they envision.

There is no neutral ground outside of the power dynamics of a fragmented, articulated social formation constituted through ideological struggle. Technocratic research oriented around resolving narrowly defined problems operate within and draw upon the dominant political grammars of the social formation and are, therefore, reproductive. This is not to say that quantitative analyses or descriptive qualitative studies, for example, are without merit, only that they must be informed by critical conceptual and theoretical frameworks that take seriously the movement of forces at work in the contemporary social formation. I argue that scholars who wish to contribute to transformative, progressive societal change must commit to forms of inquiry that re-contextualize, or disarticulate and re-articulate, contemporary educational policies and practices to inform political struggle in not only the field of schooling and education but also to larger struggles around the emergent crisis of the present.

The mapping of the terrain of struggle surrounding the AFC network and the education policy field described in this chapter does not offer solutions to technical problems. Instead, it works to cultivate a misrelation to the cemented ways in which we collectively talk about and contest education policy and practice; tease out the complex network of actors working in complex patterns of cooperation, competition, and competition on the policy field; and map the terrain of ideological struggle that activists, practitioners, cultural workers, and so on, must navigate to do left-liberatory work in education. Radical, re-contextualizing analysis troubles the crude binaries that structure political discourse in the United States (Democratic vs. Republican, conservative vs. liberal) by teasing out both the dominant political actors at work on this social field and the complex patterns of exchange and mutation among and between them. This mapping of the relations of force among the dominant actors on the education policy field identifies the elite actors whose power must be directly challenged by counter-hegemonic movements and actors. More importantly, this mapping identifies both the empty signifiers around which dominant actors orient their ideological and discursive practice and the ways in which they work to appropriate and hegemonize

counter-hegemonic discourses. It identifies the taken-for-granted and contested concepts, categories, and ideologies that constitute the field of ideological struggle in education policy and practice.

To do critical inquiry in education is to take up a politics of ideological
struggle. The task is to hegemonize the categories, concepts, and ideological
discourses at work on this social field through a new political grammar
informed by left-liberatory logics. The approach to inquiry that I am
describing here seeks to establish the necessary preconditions for a politics
of ideological struggle that connects the everyday, taken-for-granted ideas,
issues, controversies, and so on, at work in the field of education to a
transformational politics.

What I have attempted to do with this project and in previous research
projects is to develop a radical, re-contextualizing analysis that can contribute
to these necessary tasks. It involves a transdisciplinary practice that
transgresses theoretical and disciplinary boundaries to produce holistic
analyses that situate objects of analysis within the movement of forces
(material, ideological, and discursive) at work in the contemporary formation
and to recover reified concepts, ideologies, and discursive practices structuring
and being structured by the social formation. I have attempted to develop
tools for a radical, re-contextualizing analysis that constructs problem spaces
around simple educational problems to inform collective political struggle.

The task I envision for educational inquiry is to struggle against a
fragmented social reality through a "ruthless criticism" that identifies the
movement of forces and patterns of exchange at work in the contemporary
conjuncture and that connects them to the everyday and taken-for-granted
ways in which we collectively talk about schooling, education, and society.
I envision a mode of inquiry that draws energy from the catastrophe of our
present circumstance and that seeks to cultivate a misrelation to the present so
as to open up the horizon of collective political struggle. This kind of negative
critique does not preclude radical hope but seeks to establish the necessary
preconditions for collective, democratic struggle and the building of a new
articulated formation out of the ashes of the contemporary conjuncture.

The role I envision for education scholars is to be participants in collective
political struggle. We must work to tell better stories about the contemporary
conjuncture to inform better politics. This does not mean offering technocratic
solutions to narrowly defined problems nor constructing utopian visions that
attempt to transcend the catastrophe of the present. It means contributing
to the work of activists, cultural workers, practitioners, scholars, and so on,
through the production of knowledge.

The work of educational scholars is, of course, not confined to ideological
struggle in the public sphere or the scholarly community. In the next chapter,
I want to explore the implications of this approach to inquiry for pedagogical

practice. Scholars can and often do engage in direct action, but it is in the educational spaces that they inhabit that they can most readily operationalize radical inquiry. They can work within their classrooms and institutions to tell better stories about schooling, education, and the emergent conjunctural crisis of the present.

Chapter 8

Pedagogical Practice

This project began with the initial problem of right-wing populism as a dangerous political force gaining power across the globe. I set about making sense of this phenomenon through a conjunctural analysis of the contemporary social formation. The analysis traced the development of emergent crises in the economic, political, and cultural domains driven by the rise to dominance of neoclassical economics, the modern conservative movement, and cyber-utopianism, and it recovered the neoliberal political project as a material force working within and across these domains and as a driving force behind the emergent crises within each.

I argued that right-wing populism is a manifestation of a constellation of mutating political forces that achieved hegemonic dominance in the wake of the crisis of the 1970s and the emergent crisis of the present into which this social formation is now entering. I told the story of how an assemblage of agents, political movements, and ideological discourses articulated a fragile, contested unity and how it set into motion forces animating the rise of right-wing populism. Telling a better story about right-wing populism involved constructing a problem space, or context, surrounding this complex and dynamic phenomenon.

The project then took a necessary detour through theory to think through the implications of the analysis for politically engaged scholarship. I argued that scholars and activists must attend to the specificity and political dynamics of this historical moment; they must attend to the discipline of the conjuncture. Specifically, I argued that the path out of the emergent crisis of the present will be determined by ideological struggle over the nature of the crisis itself. The task for scholars and activists doing left-liberatory work is to map the terrain of ideological struggle through radical, re-contextualizing analysis, a mode of negative critique that speaks to a politics of disarticulation as a necessary precondition for societal transformation (i.e., re-articulation).

Right-wing populism presents a clear and present danger to the possibility of a more just, humane, and equitable society. I will argue in this chapter that educational practice has an important role to play in forging a transformative path out of the emergent crisis of the present and in challenging the dangerous politics of this historical moment. I now turn to the task of conceptualizing right-wing populism as a pedagogical problem or as a pedagogical problem space.

The conjunctural analysis in the preceding pages contextualized right-wing populism within the ensemble of forces that constitute and are constituted by it. The conjunctural analysis constructed a context, or problem space, around the simple problem of right-wing populism. The analysis demonstrated that the political challenge of this historical moment is not so much right-wing populism as much as it is the context surrounding it, making it possible, and to which it is contributing as a concrete material force. What is important is the sociological and epistemological terrain upon which right-wing populism is an operative social force alongside and in competition with a constellation of competing forces and the emergent conjunctural crisis into which this social formation is entering. In other words, the problem space I have constructed is the contemporary social formation and the emergent crisis of the present.

Gouldner's concept of fragmentation provides an interesting starting point for constructing a pedagogy appropriate to this problem space. Fragmentation serves as a conceptual tool to think about a social reality fragmented along multiple, intersecting lines of unequal power relations and domination, such as social class, ethnicity, gender, race, sexuality, and so on. It also speaks to a social structure made up of a constellation of social forces operating on a dynamic social field in complex relations of cooperation, competition, and contradiction. It is a conceptual tool to think about the hierarchical ordering of society and the (re)production of power that cannot be reduced to mechanical theories of social reproduction. It is a sociological concept that speaks to a fragmented and dynamic social ontology.

Embedded within this sociological concept are specific epistemological assumptions. Put simply, knowledge production within a fragmented social totality will necessarily produce fragmented knowledge about the nature of social reality. However, following Marx, fragmentation does not simply speak to a social totality that is fragmented in a static or fixed way but one that is *fragmenting*. Fragmentation denotes a dynamic epistemological field bound up with the larger social processes and power relations within and through which knowledge of the social totality is produced, reproduced, and potentially challenged. It speaks to a social formation constructed through ideological struggle.

It is on this fragmented epistemological field that educators construct their pedagogical practice. Rising to the challenge of an emergent conjunctural crisis in ways that can eclipse the rise of a dangerous right-wing politics and that can chart a transformative path out of the crisis will require that educators ask important questions about the nature of their work. What pedagogical questions are raised by this problem space? What are their implications for classroom practice and curricula? How can educators construct a pedagogical practice that tells better stories about this historical moment? What does a pedagogy against fragmentation look like?

I will argue that one place to look for answers to these questions is toward the eccentric way cultural studies scholars approach inquiry. Cultural studies offers a pedagogical model oriented toward constructing contexts around simple pedagogical problems through radical, re-contextualizing analysis. Cultural studies points toward a pedagogy of telling better stories about the social totality and students' experiences within it. I want to argue that a pedagogy appropriate to this historical moment of emergent conjunctural crisis must seek to cultivate in students a misrelation to the present through a pedagogical practice of re-contextualizing analysis. It is a pedagogy of ideological struggle that seeks to disariculate the dominant ideological discourses structuring the contemporary social formation through a negative critique, a ruthless criticism. It is a pedagogy of telling better stories.

In this chapter, I will begin with a discussion on the possibility of a cultural studies of education and its potential to create a common ground for critical pedagogical projects, broadly defined. I will then turn to theorizing a pedagogy of telling better stories as ideological struggle and delineating some of the features of what such a pedagogical approach might look like. I will then attempt to give readers some insight into how I attempt to tell a better story in my classroom space. What I offer here is not a "how-to" model for others to copy. I want to give readers some insight into my practice and invite them to build on, advance, or develop their own pedagogy of telling better stories.

CULTURAL STUDIES OF EDUCATION

One of the more common stories told about the founding of the Centre in Birmingham is that early cultural studies scholars were motivated by a crisis in the humanities. This should not be mistaken, of course, for the crisis envisioned by E. D. Hirsch. The Centre set out to construct an intellectual project that took seriously the Gramscian concept of the national popular and the ways in which a hegemonic order is constituted and challenged. They sought "to conduct an ideological critique of the way the humanities and the arts presented themselves as parts of disinterested knowledge . . . a work of demystification to bring into the open the regulative nature and role the humanities were playing in relation to the national culture" (Hall, 1990, p. 15). The scholars that founded the Centre entered the academy from the margins of scholarly practice, working in adult education, and, they set about de-centering disciplinary fields in the humanities and the social sciences through the lens of their political commitments and their educational practice.

Indeed, education and pedagogy were important themes in the early work of the Centre, but its impact on cultural studies remains under-appreciated (Wright & Maton, 2004). Richard Hoggart, Raymond Williams, E. P. Thompson, and Stuart Hall began their careers working in adult education, and the topic of education was central to some of their foundational texts, such as the *Uses of Literacy* (Hoggart, 1957) and *Learning to Labour* (Willis, 1981). Hall (1990) notes that questions of pedagogy were especially important in the early days of the Centre, because they were essentially making it up as they went. There were no preexisting bodies of knowledge nor formal curricula in cultural studies. The approach they took was to form working groups organized around various topics. The Education Working Group was one of the more active at the Centre publishing collaborative research examining educational change during the Thatcher era, and it created a model for a cultural studies of education that would take root across the globe (Centre for Contemporary Cultural Studies Education Group, 1981, 1991).

Cultural studies made inroads into Colleges of Education in the United States in the 1990s, but the relationship between the two was always strained. An intellectual project informed by an explicitly leftist politics was not always welcome in a practice-based and often deeply conservative institution. Today, cultural studies has a presence in Colleges of Education and Social Foundations of Education programs at Miami University, the University of North Carolina at Greensboro, the University of Kansas, the University of Tennessee, and Washington State University to name a few, but it is clear that the project remains on the margins of scholarly work in the field. It is also clear that, despite its importance to early work at the Centre, questions of education and pedagogy are equally marginalized in contemporary cultural studies work.

Handel Wright (2003) points toward the intersection of education and cultural studies as an important site for cultural praxis and argues that cultural studies and education have much to contribute to one another. He specifically points toward three forms of praxis: policy, performative acts, and empirical research. I took up the topics of educational policy research in the preceding chapter. In this chapter, I want to focus on pedagogical practice as a form of performative, cultural studies praxis.

Kathy Hytten (2011) argues that, as an applied field, education offers cultural studies scholars a site for the political engagement and activism that is often missing from a discipline rooted in leftist politics. Social and cultural foundations of education scholars often work with a large number of pre-service teachers who will, in turn, work with an even larger number of students over the course of their careers. Pedagogical practice within the university, as well as primary and secondary schooling, is an important and under-appreciated site for a Gramscian project of cultural politics and for educators to come to think of themselves "as a tiny piece of a hegemonic struggle" (Hall, 1990, p. 18).

The interdisciplinarity of cultural studies and the theoretical and methodological "openness" of cultural studies praxis holds a great deal of unrealized potential for the field of education, in general, and the social foundations of education, in particular. Critical work in education is a fragmented field informed by differing theoretical approaches to inquiry and activism, such as critical race theory, critical disability studies, decoloniality, feminist theory, and queer theory. Hytten argues that cultural studies can provide a common ground to bring these different approaches into conversation with one another and to work toward transformative change.

> [L]eftist educational scholars of all stripes . . . need to do a better job of working together to speak back to so many problematic trends in education and society, especially the ways conservative, competitive, individualistic, capitalist visions for education have captured the public imagination. In these efforts, cultural studies may indeed be a symbolically efficient way to bring a variety of progressive discourses together so that they may share the visions, resources, and energy needed to act on the passionate commitments to social justice. (Hytten, 2011, p. 217)

I would argue that Hytten's call to collaborative praxis remains all the more urgent in this historical moment of a radical right politics and emergent conjunctural crisis. It is imperative to bring the various critical projects in education and the social foundations of education into conversation and to organize pedagogical responses appropriate to the discipline of the conjuncture. My goal for this chapter is to think through what a pedagogy of telling better stories might look like and to use my own pedagogical practice as an example of how to operationalize it in a classroom space.

TELLING BETTER STORIES IN THE CLASSROOM

A pedagogy of telling better stories begins with the observation that a classroom space is situated within a social totality fragmented along multiple intersecting lines of power relations and dominations. Classrooms are a product and are productive of the relations of force operative within a hegemonic order that is necessarily contingent and more fragile than it readily appears. It is an approach to pedagogy that seeks to intervene at the level of ideology and knowledge production.

The pedagogical implications of this observation can be found in a Gramsican perspective on the relations of force constituting a social formation. Gramsci points educators toward the importance of knowledge production and ideology as a structuring force. His important observations about the necessary relationship between base and superstructure in Marx's work point educators toward the hegemonic field of ideology as an important site of political struggle. Ideology is here a material force reflecting and (re) producing concrete social relations operating on a contested epistemological terrain of hegemonic and counter-hegemonic struggle.

Marx conceptualized ideology as the dominant ideas of the age that reflect the interests of dominant groups in modern capitalist societies, a formulation that was far more complex than the classical Marxist formulation that was to follow him (Hall, 1986). Gouldner extends Marx's work by arguing that a fragmented social reality necessarily fragments our collective knowledge of the social totality, and Gramsci extends this further by arguing that it is on the epistemological field of ideological struggle where a social formation, or hegemonic order, is actively constructed, reconstructed, and contested. It is on this epistemological field that educators doing left-liberatory work can challenge the dangerous politics of this historical moment.

Classrooms, as well as the schools, colleges, and universities in which they are situated, are always already sites of ideological struggle. The logics and practices of dominant ideologies structuring a social formation inform educational and institutional practices. This means that the logics and practices of neoclassical economics, the modern conservative movement, cyber-libertarian discourse, and the neoliberal political project structure educational practice in the contemporary formation. These dynamic, mutating forces work in complex patterns of exchange, cooperation, competition, and contradiction to structure educational institutions, curricula, and instructional practices which means that they are, in turn, reproductive. Students also bring these ideological discourses and practices with them into classroom spaces in various mutating forms and then interact with institutional spaces working to reproduce these dominant ideologies. Classrooms are specific locations within the social field of ideological struggle, and it is on this field and in these specific locations that educators must seek to challenge the dangerous politics of the contemporary conjuncture.

A pedagogy of telling better stories is informed by a pedagogical politics of ideological struggle. It is a pedagogy of disarticulation that constructs contexts around objects of study to both map the terrain of ideological strug-gle and to demonstrate the contingency of articulated formations. It mirrors the eccentric approach to inquiry of cultural studies in that it begins with a simple problem and works to construct a problem space around it through a radical, re-contextualizing analysis. It is a pedagogy that seeks to cultivate in students a misrelation to the contemporary social formation through negative critique, a ruthless criticism, that begins with simple problems linked to the everyday practices and ideologies of human life and constructs around these chaotic conceptions a problem space, "a rich totality of many determinations and relations" (Marx, p. 100).

Hall's theory of articulation gestures toward pedagogical methods that educators can employ to take up a pedagogy of ideological struggle understood as the wellspring of the political. Hall points toward the necessary fragility of an articulated social formation and the ideological field of commonsense understandings of the social totality as a contested political space of articulation, disarticulation, and re-articulation.

> The theory of articulation then is about recognizing the social construction of reality. Such social constructions bring things into relations with each other, and they also render human identities complex, through multiple possible inter-sections between different types of identities, even within the same individual. These forms of social constructions and relations are not necessary. They are contingent. They are also in a complex interplay which has no necessary belong-ingness, and as much as they interplay in such non-necessary way to construct, they can be deconstructed and changed. (Carrim, 2017, p. 31)

Articulation speaks to a relational and intersectional pedagogy that works to disarticulate the ideological, hegemonic order structuring a social formation to demonstrate its contingency and fragility. A pedagogy of disarticulation seeks to demonstrate that the social totality that students experience is neither fixed nor necessary, and it seeks to open up new spaces for an educational politics of hegemonic struggle, that is, an educational politics of disarticulation and re-articulation. What I am describing here is a pedagogy of radical, re-contextualizing analysis that disarticulates simple pedagogical problems into dynamic contexts. It is a pedagogical practice that disarticulates a simple problem into a complex pedagogical problem space.

This pedagogical problem space, following Marasco, is defined by a pedagogy of negative critique. It is an approach to pedagogy that seeks to cultivate in students a misrelation to the present through the disarticulation of the dominant ideologies structuring the contemporary social formation. It is a pedagogy of counter-hegemonic struggle defined by a radical, re-contextualizing analysis, what Gouldner termed holistic analysis and recovery. Or, to put it more simply, it is a pedagogy of telling better stories about this historical moment that de-naturalizes the present and that creates space for students to tell new stories.

It is an approach to pedagogical practice that does not seek to restore an imagined whole. Nor is it a pedagogical practice that seeks the transcendence of an utopic future toward which to strive. The pedagogical approach I am describing here is an approach to pedagogical practice that takes up negative critique, of telling better stories, as a dialectical passion that locates hope in the catastrophe of the present.

INSTRUCTIONAL PRACTICE

Constructing a pedagogical problem space around the simple problem of right-wing populism means that right-wing populism itself is not what is important. It is the context surrounding this problem, the problem space, that is important. It is a pedagogical approach that seeks to disarticulate a social totality fragmented along multiple lines of asymmetrical power and domination. It is a pedagogy that works to disarticulate the relations of force at work on the ideological field of hegemonic struggle and to understand right-wing populism as an articulated formation situated within the dynamic totality of an articulated social formation.

Understanding right-wing populism as a pedagogical problem space focuses attention on the dynamic and contested epistemological field on which knowledge of the social totality is produced and contested. In other words, a pedagogy of disarticulation attempts to intervene and challenge an articulated social formation at the level of ideological struggle over common sense understandings about the nature of social reality. It works to disarticulate the dominant ideologies structuring a formation to both demonstrate their contingency and fragility and to open up new spaces to begin re-articulating a more socially just formation.

The curricula for a pedagogy of telling better stories is oriented around simple problems that are relevant to the context of the learning space, such as the disciplinary field in which the class is situated, and that are relevant to the everyday practices and commonsense assumptions that students bring with them to the classroom space. The curricula for the kind of radical, re-contextualizing analysis I am describing is necessarily inter- or even trans-disciplinary.

The conjunctural analysis presented in the preceding pages is instructive here. Constructing a context around right-wing populism required that I draw upon a wide range of disciplinary knowledge including economics, history, political science, philosophy, sociology, communication and media studies, and so on. As Gouldner observed, it is the generative transgression of disciplinary boundaries that is a defining characteristic of critical intellectual practice.

The bodies of knowledge and methods of inquiry employed in a pedagogy of telling better stories is determined by the simple problem with which inquiry begins, the questions being asked by teacher and students, and the new directions and questions that emerge from the process of inquiry. The end goal of classroom inquiry and dialogue cannot be neatly mapped or prefigured, nor can student learning be precisely measured and quantified. The products or, to employ the reductive language of the contemporary academy, "learning outcomes" are contextual representations of the problem spaces surrounding the simple problems with which inquiry began.

To tell better stories is to take a clear pedagogical stance that acknowledges the politics of thinking and learning. It denotes a pedagogical practice connecting the everyday ideas and practices at work in a field of study to unequal power relations, hierarchy, and domination. This requires that educators lead their students through a radical, re-contextualizing analysis that begins with the taken-for-granted ideas that students bring with them, both in terms of what they've learned in other classes and their ideological beliefs about social reality. It requires an educator to create intentional learning experiences that build contexts around objects of study to cultivate a misrelation to the common sense ideas students bring with them to the classroom; model techniques for conducting radical, re-contextualizing analysis; and open up spaces for students do their own re-contextualizing analyses in collaboration with one another.

To tell better stories in the classroom is to adopt a clear political stance that seeks to challenge what students take for granted. An educator cannot assume that students hold critical ideas about their social worlds. A critical misrelation to a social formation must be cultivated through intentional learning experiences. This means that a teacher must construct an intentional classroom practice that models forms of inquiry that will challenge what students hold dear. This step cannot be bypassed through dialogics or a utopic turn toward another imagined world. It begins with instructor-led inquiry, ruthless criticism, and authentic classroom discussion and debate. Over time, an educator can begin to de-center the classroom by creating space for students to do their own re-contextualizing analyses and tell their own stories, but it begins with an educator who sets out to deconstruct students' social worlds and that challenges what they often hold dear.

Students enter the classroom space embedded within a fragmented and fragmenting social reality, and the commonsense assumptions they bring with them will necessarily reflect their lived experiences within it. The social formation structuring their daily lives constitutes the largely unquestioned, reified, and naturalized worlds in and through which they have constructed and continually reconstruct their identities in complex and divergent ways. Students are not monolithic nor do they suffer from a crude false consciousness. Young people and adults alike actively construct their identity as a bricolage artist creates new work using artifacts of material culture. Young people do their identity work within a fragmenting social totality by drawing upon the ideas, concepts, and ideologies at work in their social worlds in creative and generative ways.

You can think of their identity work as a process of (re)articulation. This (re)articulation takes place within a fragmented social reality and will therefore necessarily reflect both the dominant ideologies structuring the social forma-tion and the complexity of the epistemological field in which those dominant ideologies are operative. This means that an educator practicing a pedagogy of telling better stories seeks to cultivate in students a misrelation not only to the social formation in which they live but the identities that they have constructed within it. This is a potential source for conflict within a classroom space that can only be mitigated through relational work between teacher and students.

A pedagogical practice of telling better stories is, at its root, relational. The importance of relationship building in the classroom is, of course, not a revolutionary idea. It is commonly referenced in the often mechanical language of "best practices" that dominate the field of education. As such, it is often thought of as a way to begin a lesson plan using some form of prompt and within a clearly defined period of time.

I am arguing instead that educators must take the time to build authentic relationships between teacher and students, as well as between students, to the greatest extent possible within an institutional space. This begins with teachers bringing their authentic selves to the classroom. It requires that educators create a space in which they share their lives with students and in which students share theirs with educators and other students. In short, educators must work to create community.

An educator can never erase the power relations between teacher and students within an institutional space. It is, at best, possible to mitigate those relations by being vulnerable in class, by creating space to engage your students on their own terms about their beliefs and concerns, and by being intellectually humble. No story told about the social totality is ever final or complete, and every inquirer is limited by their own positionality and situ-atedness. Telling better stories requires an educator to be transparent about the limits of her/his knowledge and to use those limitations as a tool to spark new inquiry and analysis. To tell a better story is to challenge what students bring with them to the classroom space, to construct a pedagogical space of inquiry and dialogue between teacher and students, and to invite students to begin telling their own stories as they grow and learn.

I argue that challenging the dangerous politics of this historical moment begins with a pedagogical practice that seeks to cultivate in students a misrelation to the contemporary conjuncture. A pedagogy of telling better stories seeks to create instructional spaces of negative critique in which teachers and students carry out a ruthless criticism of the dominant ideological discourses and practices at work in their disciplinary fields and connect them to the larger problem spaces surrounding them. There are two necessary processes at work here. First, classrooms and the students who inhabit them are situated within the larger social totality, and the asymmetrical power relations and systems of domination structuring a social formation are always already at work in those spaces. This means that what students bring with them to the classroom must be disarticulated through intentional learning experiences as a necessary preconditon for transformative change. Second, students must learn how to disarticulate the dominant ideologies at work in their daily lives to tell their own stories. Learning to tell their own stories is a necessary skill that young people will need for re-articulating a new social formation out of the wreckage of the emergent crisis of the contemporary conjuncture.

CONTEXT

Understanding how I operationalize this approach to pedagogy begins with understanding the context of my practice. I work in a relatively large teacher education program at a historical institution in the upper Midwest. The university began as a normal school in the nineteenth century preparing teachers for the common school. It transitioned into a teachers' college as public education began to expand in the twentieth century and became a university in the 1960s. The state in which I work has a long and storied reputation as a leader in education, and my institution has an equally storied reputation for producing excellent teachers.

The university where I work has a large teacher education program relative to the size of the university. In fact, the College of Education is the largest college on campus even though it does not include secondary education majors. And, while the university is experiencing enrollment declines, the teacher education program continues to graduate approximately four hundred new teachers annually who are highly sought after across the state, region, nation, and even internationally.

The state in which I work is a rural and largely homogeneous state, although it is more diverse than is commonly assumed. The students who enter my classroom are primarily from suburban and rural communities and, like teacher education more generally, are predominantly white, female, and middle class. The young people in my classrooms are "good" students in the conventional sense of the term. They are diligent about doing course readings for example, and they show up prepared to participate in classroom activities, despite the fact that the overwhelming majority hold jobs and often work long hours to help pay for the outrageous tuition fees that are common in the United States. The students in my classroom come out of a public education system defined by federal education reforms oriented around standards, assessment, accountability, and marketization. For them, instruction and curricula informed by state assessments and the taken-for-grantedness of human capital theory are understood as simply "what schools do."

Students take my course toward the end of their program of study. They come in with experience in curriculum development and instructional methods, and they have had field experiences in which to practice what they have learned in their methods courses under supervision. They have also taken two courses in educational psychology from a department heavily influenced by positive psychology, one course on classroom assessment, and at least one course dealing specifically with issues of diversity and inclusion.

I teach only one core course in the teacher education program which is not unusual for a marginalized field such as educational foundations. The course is entitled "Schools and American Society," and it introduces students to the history, sociology, political economy, and philosophical foundations of K-12 education. The course focuses on the societal issues that impact student learning and classroom practice and the political processes that impact public education and the teaching profession. My students enter class well-versed in topics such as the achievement gap, but they generally possess only rudimentary knowledge about the organizational structure of public schooling, such as governance, sources of funding, and so on, and know even less about the larger political and sociological dynamics surrounding public education.

Social justice issues are discussed in the course work students take prior to mine, but these issues are frequently framed as technical ones. The implicit message is that issues of inequality, racism, ableism, and so on, can be overcome with better lesson plans, curricula, assessments, and classroom management techniques. Students are taught that they can be hero teachers who can overcome these issues with the right skills and professional dispositions.

I say this not to disparage my colleagues; they are introducing systemic and structural perspectives to social justice issues in education. However, teacher education is a practice-based field of study, and the majority of the courses in the teacher education program are geared toward "practical" questions of lesson planning, curriculum, assessment, and "managing" a classroom. Further, our teacher education program has strong ties to local school districts which encourages an institutional focus on the "practical issues" teachers face in classrooms and developing "best practices" in how to resolve those issues.

The students who enter my classroom at the beginning of an academic term generally think about schools and education in an uncritical way. Students come to class inculcated with broadly held notions that American schools are falling behind other nations and about the persistence of achievement gaps between White students and students of color, but the structures and practices of schooling remain largely unquestioned. Students may have had some negative experiences along their journey through the education system, but there is a general attitude of "It worked for me." They see schools as being mostly meritocratic institutions that offer equal opportunity and reward hard work, and the problems facing marginalized students are ones that can be resolved through technical fixes.

Their relation to the larger social formation is similarly uncritical. My students are very clear from the outset that they are not interested in political issues and are not at all confident in their political knowledge. This is not to say that my students are completely apolitical. Many of my students are interested in activism and are active on campus. However, for the majority, my students understand economics and economic policy through the lens of neoclassical logics, discuss politics using the languages of the modern conservative movement and the neoliberal political project, and enter into the collective conversation of American political culture through the mediations of networked computer technologies. The ideological discourses structuring the contemporary social formation and the emergent crisis are ever-present in my classroom. They constitute the background radiation of my students' lives; they are the building-blocks my students use to construct and continually reconstruct their identities.

The reason that I am taking the time to describe the institutional context of my pedagogical practice and the students that I teach is to give the reader some insight into the context in which I try to operationalize a pedagogy of telling better stories. I do not want to give the reader the impression that I hold a negative attitude toward my students. In fact, I hold my students in high regard, and their course evaluations indicate that they value my course. I would also not say that they are uniquely different from students in other parts of the country. They are similar in many ways to students I worked with at a research university and a community college in the Southeastern United States. My goal here is to give the reader insight into what students bring with them to a class run by a professor who seeks to problematize what they take for granted as natural or as "just the way things work."

I use my classroom practice to denaturalize the schools, education system, and social formation through which my students have come to know the world and themselves. The organizing framework for my course is to cultivate a misrelation between students and the larger social formation, schools, and education system, and, ultimately, their own subjectivities through a radical, re-contextualizing analysis that begins with what they bring with them to the classroom. I am, therefore, not positioning myself as what critical pedagogues might term a teacher-student or a co-participant with my students.

I am making a *pedagogical intervention* into the identity work of my students as teachers and as political actors. I attempt to tell a better story about the contemporary conjuncture using the practices and policies of schooling as a heuristic device. I do this not simply as an intellectual pursuit for my own gratification. As Gramsci notes, critical analysis maps the context of struggle to inform political activity, to inform a war of position. This means that I must not only tell a better story but that I must help my students develop their own sense of political agency, and I must do this within the context of an institution that privileges instrumental logics and in the space of *one sixteen-week course.*

Needless to say, this is an ambitious project, and I am sure that I often fall short in execution. My intent here is to demonstrate how I go about operationalizing a pedagogy of telling better stories. I am not offering the reader a clear ten-step plan on how to implement this approach to pedagogy nor am I developing "best practices." My goal is to demonstrate how I work to implement this pedagogical approach in a specific context and to invite readers to think about how they might implement it in their own contexts. So, with that said, I will now offer the reader a narrative description of how I approached my "Schools and American Society" course the academic term I completed just before sitting down to write this chapter. It is the most current iteration of what is an ongoing struggle to tell a better story in my classroom through an iterative process of critique and reflection informed by the method of inquiry I developed in the preceding chapter.

MY PRACTICE

I start the semester by introducing a simple problem and a conceptual framework to analyze its discursive structure. The simple problem is education reform. I introduce this to students through a series of readings from elite policy actors in conservative and neoliberal think tanks, such as the Thomas B. Fordham Institute, the Hoover Institution, the Brookings Institution, and so on (what I term the dominant discourse of education reform), and we use the frame theory of Robert Entman (1993) to analyze the discursive structure these actors employ to advance education reform policies. Entman argues that frames focus attention on specific ideas or practices associated with a topic of public communication or debate to establish salience. Frames do this by carrying out three basic tasks: frames define problems, make causal diagnoses, and offer problem solutions.

This first foray into disarticulation is often revelatory for my students. They are usually familiar with some of the terms of debate used by these elite policy actors, but they are surprised by the ways teachers and schools are discussed in these texts and, more importantly, how all of the pieces of this discursive structure work together. It is both familiar and strange, and it makes for some lively classrooms discussions. I tell my students that my goal for the semester is to tell a better story about education reform through a critique of the ways in which this discourse frames education, and that we will end the semester reflecting on how we might tell a different story about the problems facing schools and what to do about them.

The dominant discourse establishes three interrelated problems. First, American schools are "falling behind" their global competitors in academic achievement, and this educational failure both explains contemporary economic issues facing the United States and constitutes a dire threat to the nation's future prosperity. Second, and related to previous problem, growing inequality and wealth polarization are the result of schools not providing graduates with the necessary job skills for success in a new economy defined by technology and automation. Third, schools are failing historically marginalized student populations, in particular, producing large achievement gaps between White majority students and students of color. The cause of these educational failures is attributed to the bureaucracy of public institutions and teachers' unions. The institution of public education is described as a byzantine bureaucracy of self-interested actors resistant to the interests of the students and communities they serve. Insulated from accountability by public sector unions and bureaucratic politics, teachers and administrators have little incentive to innovate, make needed changes, or even respond to the wishes of parents.

Two solutions are offered by the dominant discourse. First, fix incentives for teachers and school administrators through the introduction of managerial policies that set performance metrics (curricular standards), measure performance (standardized assessment), and accountability and through the introduction of market competition in the form of charter schools or voucher school programs. Second, teach students the content and skills they will need to succeed in the modern job market by focusing on science, technology, engineering, and mathematics (STEM) curriculum and the so-called non-cognitive skills labeled social-emotional learning.

This initial move toward disarticulation is followed by a move toward reflection. I use small group and classroom discussions to give my students space to connect these initial readings to their experiences in previous classwork and their field experiences in schools. Students frequently make sophisticated connections between the dominant discourse of education reform and their experiences in teacher education, for example, detailed lesson plan assignments requiring them to develop specific learning objectives from state standards, performance outcomes, and assessment techniques or field experiences in which they witnessed instruction being eclipsed by testing drills in preparation for state assessments. What usually dominates the discussion in these early reflections, however, is the way in which teachers and schools are singled out as the loci of failure. Overall, what this early reflection does is that it creates space for students to make connections between the dominant discourse of education reform and their own experiences as students and teachers or, to borrow a turn of phrase from C. Wright Mills, to begin to grasp the relations between biography and history.

This reflection is followed by a disarticulation of the problems identified by the dominant discourse. I begin by introducing the work of Gary Becker and the historical development of human capital theory. We discuss how the logics of neoclassical economics frame investments in education, both public and individual, as economic inputs or investments made with the promise of economic growth for the economy as a whole and for the income potential of individuals. I introduce news pieces and material from popular culture to demonstrate how the collective conversation around public education and schooling is defined by the language of job training and how this shift toward human capital is accompanied by the erasure of democratic possibilities and the potential for thinking about education as means of liberation and human flourishing.

I then turn attention to the problem of economic inequality and wealth polarization. I use data and information presented in chapter 2 to give students some perspective on these issues. However, as I did in the preceding analysis, I also use that data to offer an alternative explanation. We discuss free trade policies, deindustrialization, financialization, and changes in tax policies to demonstrate that wealth and income inequality are the necessary and entirely predictable outcome of economic policies implemented over the past four decades.

We then turn our focus to the achievement gap and issues of racial and ethnic inequality. I introduce data from national and international assessments to demonstrate that the achievement gap is a real phenomenon, but I then turn to offering an alternative explanation. I begin by first troubling racial and ethnic categories through an exploration of the history of colonization, slavery, Social Darwinism, and eugenics as well as the contemporary biological racism promoted by public intellectuals, such as Charles Murray.

We then turn to an analysis of structural and systemic racism as well as the White racial politics of the long southern strategy discussed in chapter 3. I present students with examples of racial and ethnic injustice across a variety of social fields using research on labor market discrimination, the criminal justice system, housing discrimination, and so on, before then discussing educational issues related to inequalities in school funding, school segregation, the school-to-prison pipeline, and the carceral logics of urban schools. In short, I demonstrate to students that racial and ethnic inequality are the necessary and predictable outcome of systemic racism and educational policy.

We follow this work of disarticulation by reflecting on the way in which the dominant discourse of education reform frames the problems facing public education and schooling. We reflect on how the logics of neoclassical economics have colonized education and appropriated the language of social justice. The ultimate aim of education and schooling is to prepare young people for capitalist economies, and educational inequality is transformed into a problem of average assessment scores and a failure of human capital development. More importantly, we reflect on how this process of colonization and appropriation erases structural and historical issues. In the dominant discourse of education reform, economic, racial, and ethnic inequality are the result of educational failure, and only managerial and market-based education reforms can resolve these issues. There is no need for radical change to the larger social structure. Fix schooling and everything will fall into place. And, I conclude this period of reflection by encouraging students to make connections between the dominant discourse and the ways in which these issues are discussed in their teacher education coursework and popular culture more generally.

This period of reflection is followed by an analysis of the causal diagnosis offered by the dominant discourse. I begin by introducing representations of the bureaucratic nature of public institutions from popular culture, using common examples such as long lines at post offices and departments of motor vehicle, and then turn to a discussion of bureaucratic institutions in the private sector, using examples from the health care and technologies industries. We then turn to discussions on how, from a neoclassical perspective, public institutions exist outside of the price signaling system and the discipline of market logics and, further, how public institutions can "distort" markets, for example how the differential quality of schooling impacts the price of housing. I then introduce the public choice theory of James Buchanan to demonstrate how, from an economic perspective, the idea of public service is an impossibility. Public choice theory argues that public officials, like all economic agents in the neoclassical model, are self-interested actors seeking to optimize their own utility instead of serving the greater good of the communities they supposedly serve. I use these texts to demonstrate how neoclassical economics attempts to explain macro-level phenomena through micro-level logics that position individuals as crudely economic agents maximizing a utility function and how this conceptualization, if accepted, leads to an inevitably dark conclusion about the possibility of not just the idea of public service but the possibility of altruism and selfless acts of kindness.

I follow this analysis of causal diagnosis by asking my students to reflect on the connections between public choice theory and the problem definition offered by the dominant discourse. We discuss how defining macro-level problems in education as having micro-level explanations positions teachers as the primary problem facing our schools and how this narrow framing lends itself to technical fixes. Fix the incentives governing economic agents (i.e., teachers), and you will fix larger educational issues. And, I close this period of reflection by asking my students to think through the connections between the dim view of humanity offered by public choice theory and their course work in teacher education and the trope of the hero teacher.

It is at this point in the semester that I turn to a critical analysis of the solutions offered by the dominant discourse beginning with standards, testing, and accountability. I begin by introducing students to the history of technocratic management in education from the progressive era through the Keynesian era and into the present. We discuss the dominant paradigm of educational research operating under the positivist rubric of "what works" and how this narrow framing of educational problems erases the structural in pursuit of technical fixes. We then analyze curricular standards as performance metrics and investigate the complex network of policy actors in politics, universities, textbook publishers, and testing companies that crafted the Common Core standards. This analysis leads us to explore the markets created for textbooks, assessments, curricular programs, and supplementary services, including the growing army of consultants who run professional development programs for individual schools and school districts, and we discuss how many of the actors who participated in the crafting of these standards now profit off of them.

I then shift the class discussion toward different forms of assessment and how they compare to standardized assessment. We discuss how standardized assessment scores are used to evaluate the quality of schools and how they are used to justify often draconian accountability policies, such as school turnaround policies, school closings and privatization, and teacher evaluation. We examine evidence demonstrating that out-of-school variables, such as family income or parental education, are the best predictors of student performance on standardized assessment and that highly variable and unstable teacher ratings based on assessment scores say more about student characteristics than teacher quality. From this, I make the argument that standards, testing, and accountability systems are not simply a reflection of structural inequality but work to reproduce them. I argue that assessment and accountability systems identify schools serving subaltern populations as failing and then apply institutional pressure on those schools to narrow the curriculum and employ reductive teaching techniques to mechanically raise assessment scores.

I conclude our analysis of standards, testing, and accountability by introducing classic works in social reproduction theory, such as Jean Anyon and Pierre Bourdieu, and asking my students to reflect on the problem definition offered by the dominant discourse and their own experiences with these policies. We discuss the relationship between assessment-focused accountability systems and the scientism of neoclassical economics; how the policy solutions offered can work to reproduce the racial, ethnic, and economic inequality they are said to resolve; and how the focus on teachers and schools as being the loci of failure erases larger structural concerns. And, we conclude this period of reflection by examining connections between the networks of policy actors advancing the dominant discourse of education reform and the networks of actors who created the Common Core standards and who produce curricula, instructional material, and assessments aligned with those standards.

We follow this reflection by turning to market incentives in education. We begin by discussing different mechanisms for introducing market competition, such as voucher school programs, educational saving accounts, charter schools, and tax credits, and then examine the geographic distribution and demographic trends associated with these various schemes in the United States. We examine international examples of school marketization including Chile and the history of the "Chicago Boys," the United Kingdom, and Sweden. I introduce evidence from research studies demonstrating the limited impact of marketization schemes on assessment scores and the more disturbing outcomes related to social segregation. From here, we examine several case studies including the radical marketization of schools in New Orleans following Hurricane Katrina and the instructional, curricular, and disciplinary practices employed in widely celebrated "no excuses" charter school models serving primarily working-class students of color. I conclude the analysis by introducing qualitative studies on how differently positioned parents and care-givers navigate school choice policies and demonstrate that it is the families with the most cultural and social capital who benefit from "school choice."

I then ask my students to reflect on the problems identified by the dominant discourse, and we discuss how, by its own standards, marketization fails to raise overall achievement or narrow the achievement gap. Students generally have limited experience with educational markets, but we do work to connect these topics to their coursework and to our previous discussions. We discuss how, in the name of equity, marketization contributes to social segregation and how it "incentivizes" reductive teaching and strict disciplinary techniques for dis-empowered student populations in pursuit of higher test scores. We think through the connections between market incentives and the managerial incentives associated with standards, testing, and accountability. We consider the relations between market actors in education and the policy actors promoting education reform policies, and we discuss the emergence of new bureaucratic systems in the form of distributed governance across a range of networked policy actors in the public and private spheres.

We move on from there to analyze STEM and educational technology. I begin by dissecting the idea of a STEM crisis. I present data from the Bureau of Labor Statistics on long-term compensation trends in STEM fields to demonstrate that there is no contemporary STEM crisis as well as near term projections demonstrating the fields adding the most jobs over the next decade are primarily low wage, low skill jobs in the service and health care sectors. I use this data as a jumping-off point to discuss the history of STEM discourse in education from the Sputnik panic of the 1950s to the publication of *A Nation at Risk* in the 1980s to the present day to demonstrate that this is a very old conversation and one that was always more rhetoric than reality. We then discuss the growing pressure to focus learning on STEM fields and how it impacts their experiences in teacher education. A common tale students tell deals with pressure to link non-STEM areas, like art and social studies, to the "real" curriculum.

We begin our analysis of educational technology by exploring some of the persistent myths associated with youth and technology, such as the idea of "digital natives" and the idea that technology can "personalize" instruction. We discuss their experiences using technology in classrooms and think through how they differ from more traditional classroom practices. It is revelatory for students to realize that, while there are genuine activities made possible by technology that would not be practical otherwise, technology is often used for activities that could be accomplished using older and much less expensive forms of technology such as dry erase boards, books, pens, and so on. We then examine evidence from international comparative assessment data and case studies, such as Kansas' experiments with technology, that demonstrate the limited impact and controversies surrounding classroom technology.

We then begin to reflect on human capital theory and the problematic ways in which STEM and technology is taken up in both popular culture and my students course work. One of the most lively discussions of the term involve student experiences with classroom technology in their field experiences and their experiences taking online courses at university. I am always amazed at the disconnect between how we collectively talk about the dominant age group in my classroom (so-called Gen Z) and their perspectives and experiences. Online courses and blended courses, in particular, are unpopular with my students. This discussion leads us to reflect on how the dominant discourse constructs linkages between STEM and educational technologies and issues of social justice, and we conclude our reflection by thinking through the connections between actors promoting STEM and technology and the policy actors working to advance accountability and marketization policies. And, I conclude by discussing the Waldorf schools preferred by the elite of Silicon Valley and how the low technology instruction in these schools differ from that being advanced by policy actors in the technology industry.

I conclude the analysis of policy recommendations made by the dominant discourse by examining social-emotional learning. I trace the history of positive psychology and character education focusing specifically on concepts like "grit" and the Western appropriation of mindfulness. We examine the dark history of population sorting in psychology and how character education was employed in American Indian boarding schools and the industrial schools for African Americans after the Civil War. We examine how social-emotional learning and character education are employed in classrooms through analyses of "no excuses" pedagogies and school-wide leadership programs, and we explore classroom management applications that surveil students and attempt to influence their behavior through rewards and punishments.

We conclude our analysis by reflecting on the ways in which social-emotional learning curricula individualizes student success and failure. Low-performing students, a category in which subaltern populations are over-represented, are low performers, because they lack social-emotional learning or grit. We discuss how these psychological categories compliment economic categories, such as human capital, and how they erase structural issues associated with racial, ethnic, and class inequalities. Moreover, we examine how social-emotional learning informs disciplinary practices that are dis-proportionally focused on disciplining the bodies of subaltern student populations.

It is toward the end of the semester that we then take a necessary detour into theory to make sense of our analysis of the dominant discourse of education reform and to reflect on what it might mean to deviate from the policies and subjectivities it seeks to construct. I introduce readings on neoliberalism and work to connect the neoliberal political project to the ways in which the dominant discourse constructs problems, diagnoses causes, and proposes solutions. We examine the complex networks of policy actors advancing education reform policies and discuss the distributed model of governance defining the landscape of education policy. We discuss how the neoliberal project works to appropriate the language of social justice to cultivate a sense of crisis in education and to use the perception of crisis to advance a radical program of educational change that works to cement structural inequalities.

We conclude by thinking through the relations of force at work in the field of education and discuss how we might go about re-framing education, that is, define problems, diagnose causes, and construct solutions.

We conclude the course by reflecting on how we began with a simple problem grounded in my students experiences in teacher education and then worked to construct a context around it. We discuss how the everyday, taken-for-granted practices of teaching and teacher education are connected to the relations of force that structure the field and, therefore, their careers as future educators. And, we examine recent teacher strikes and research literature examining teachers' perspectives on schooling and education reform to think about how they might tell a different, better story about education.

This lengthy narrative describes in broad strokes the way in which I attempt to operationalize a pedagogy of telling better stories in my teacher education course. I work to cultivate in students a misrelation to the everyday practices of teaching and learning in schools. I work to disarticulate what my students take for granted through a radical, re-contextualizing analysis that constructs a context, or problem space, around their experiences in teacher education and their field experiences in schools. I try to tell a better story about the relations of force that structure the field of education, and I attempt to equip my students with the knowledge, perspectives, and skills to tell their own stories.

I work to map the terrain of political struggle surrounding teaching, schooling, and education. I attempt to map the movement of forces, ideologies, and discursive practices at work in the field of education through a radical, re-contextualizing analysis. I work to construct a problem space around specific educational problems and connect that problem space to the common sense logics my students bring with them to class and to their previous course work in teacher education. More importantly, I work to connect these struggles to the movement of forces, ideologies, and discursive practices at work in the contemporary conjuncture. I work to connect educational problems to societal problems and the emergent crisis of the present. I work to map the terrain of political struggle in the contemporary conjuncture. My goal is to both cultivate in my students a misrelation to the present and help them develop the tools that they will need to engage in collective political struggle in the field of education and to contribute to the charting of a transformative path out of this historical moment of conjunctural crisis.

There are, of course, important limitations that must be acknowledged. I would begin by reminding the reader that I cover all of the above in one sixteen-week course. This means that we cannot always dive into specific topics with the level of sophistication that I would like, nor do students get extensive opportunities to engage in long-term research projects. Student learning is driven by course readings and classroom dialogue. I would prefer to spread this course work out over multiple courses to allow more time for in-depth discussion and student-led inquiry, but I have limited control over how much contact I have with teacher-candidates at my institution.

I also worry that the linear way in which I constructed the preceding narrative conceals the messiness of how the class actually operates. I do take a clear pedagogical stance, and I do structure both the pace and content of readings and classroom discussion. However, students are not passive actors in my classroom. Every class period involves small group and class discussion, and students often make insightful connections in ways that shift the overall tone of our analyses and discussions in novel and unpredictable ways. One of the consistent themes in student feedback is that they appreciate my willingness to take a clear stand, how they have room to engage in dialogue with their peers, and how they are encouraged to challenge the story that I tell.

Finally, there is a certain conceit in describing one's own teaching practice as a model for other educators. I am uncomfortable positioning myself in the role of expert as I am continually tweaking and refining my own practice. I feel that I still have much to learn as a teacher, and I do not want to give the impression that I have it all worked out. I certainly do not want the reader to see the preceding narrative as a "how-to" that can be neatly copied or emulated. I offer this narrative description of my practice as an example, and I invite the reader to translate, advance, and refine the pedagogical approach I develop here into their own context. Much like this book more generally, I see my project here as inviting the reader to engage in a conversation with the text. Take what I have to offer, such as it is, and do something with it. I have had the privilege of working with many excellent educators, and I trust that someone more skillful than myself could expand upon and improve on the work that I have done. This is my invitation to the reader.

CONCLUSION

I have attempted to construct a pedagogical approach appropriate to this historical moment of conjunctural crisis and to give the reader an example of what such a practice might look like in a classroom. I have described my approach, following Grossberg, as telling better stories about teaching, schooling, and education. I do this by disarticulating taken-for-granted ideas, practices, and policies in education through a radical, re-contextualizing analysis. I have argued that doing critical education work in this historical moment requires that educators take a clear pedagogical stance in their classrooms.

It must be acknowledged that a critical educational practice offers no guarantees in terms of political outcomes. I have relied heavily on Marxian theory in the preceding pages, but I would caution the reader against reading into this the teleological politics of vulgar Marxism. Doing critical work in education is not about lifting the veil of false consciousness from students who then unproblematically take up a left politics, that is, what critical pedagogues term critical consciousness. No matter how carefully and thoroughly an educator encodes meaning into a classroom discourse there are no guarantees how this discourse will be decoded by students. Doing critical work in the classroom requires intellectual humility; it requires thinking deeply about the institutional contexts of our practice, technical constraints, and the situatedness of human life.

The students who enter a classroom are situated beings who navigate a range of social and ideological fields, and they will bring the logics and discursive tools they developed on, across, and within those fields with them. How they interpret, operationalize, or challenge the stories I tell in the classroom will be informed, in many ways, by what they bring with them. However, acknowledging the limitations of critical practice is not a retreat from the political so much as an invitation to do politics differently.

Taking a clear pedagogical stance in the classroom is a politics of intervention without guarantees. We can think of intervention in two senses. First, to take up a pedagogy of telling better stories is to intervene in the institutional logics regulating schools, colleges, and universities. In my context, I seek to intervene in the instrumental logics of a practice-based field by disarticulating the dominant ideas and practices of schooling and teacher education. Second, to take up a pedagogy of telling better stories is to intervene in the political identity work of students. Individuals negotiate multiple subject positions over the course of their lives. A political identity is not fixed but is an ongoing process of identity work in which an individual continually reconstructs a political identity as s/he moves within, through, and across the hegemonic and counter-hegemonic discursive practices at work in a social formation. A pedagogy of telling better stories seeks to intervene in this process by de-naturalizing and critiquing dominant discourses. In my context, I seek to intervene in the identity work of my students as they continually construct and reconstruct both their political identities and their professional identities as teachers. My students bring the dominant discourses at work in the conjuncture as well as the technical discourses of teacher education into my classroom space, and my approach to pedagogy seeks to intervene in their political and professional identity work as they creatively and generatively navigate these various discursive practices.

I argue that the pedagogical approach that I have developed here is not about the transmission of a body of knowledge but about cultivating a way of relating to and being in the world. Telling better stories is a way of talking about the world and a social practice of inquiry. My goal is not to construct measurable student outcomes and measure their performance but to cultivate a misrelation to the present in terms of their political and professional identity work and to model a social practice of holistic inquiry. It is about teaching students how to "think on their feet."

The cultural studies influenced pedagogy I constructed in the preceding pages is what I would term an inclusive critical practice that creates space for a number of different theoretical and methodological approaches to educational practice. The radical re-contextualizing analysis I described in this chapter drew upon a wide range of disciplinary fields, such as history, economics, and sociology, and social theories, such as critical race theory, post-structuralism, and critical theory, that are often represented in academic discourse in antagonistic terms. One of the important lessons to be learned from the success of the Right over the past five decades is the way in which it was able to articulate a unity out of difference. The Right did not construct a relatively stable formation in spite of the often profound differences among the actors, movements, and ideological discourses that make up the hegemonic bloc of the post-1970s formation but through an ongoing process of re-articulation. The Right was able to advance a relatively stable program of political change while maintaining space for disagreement and debate among its constituent groups. In fact, it was the discursive tensions within the political right that made possible a reflexive politics that enables the Right to respond to societal change and to advance politically during times of crisis. Scholars and activists doing left-liberatory pedagogical work must learn how to articulate a relatively stable political agenda that draws upon the diversity of political commitments, theoretical frameworks, and methodological approaches at work on the Left. "In these efforts, cultural studies may indeed be a symbolically efficient way to bring a variety of progressive discourse together so that they may share the visions, resources, and energy needed to act on the passionate commitments to social justice that cut across all of their unique approaches and concerns" (Hytten, 2011, p. 217).

Chapter 9

Concluding Remarks

We live in a time of dangerous politics. A set of crises are conjoining in this historical moment of conjunctural crisis, and the evidence for this crisis is readily apparent. The rise to power of a radical, right-wing populism oriented around white supremacy, virulent nationalism, and xenophobia; the violence of the carceral state; the acceleration of wealth and income polarization; the flourishing of dangerous misinformation and propaganda online; and the preventable devastation associated with the novel coronavirus are all bound up with an emergent crisis of the present. It is a historical moment, to adapt a turn of phrase from Gramsci, in which an old social formation is dying and the new cannot be born. The "morbid symptoms" that make up our present circumstance are the terrain of struggle; they are the conjunctural terrain upon which the emergent crisis will be worked through.

The post-1970s formation was constructed by an ensemble of reactionary forces on the political right, and the right-wing populism of this historical moment is a product of that construction. The emergent conjunctural crisis of the present constitutes a direct challenge to this hegemonic order, but the lines of political struggle are not confined to a simple Right-Left dualism. The various actors and movements at work within this articulated hegemonic order are struggling with one another for dominance. The conjunctural analysis developed here demonstrates that the actors, movements, and networks on the Right command sophisticated structural frameworks and apparatuses to advance their goals both against the Left and their competitors on the Right while also retaining the mutability to adapt to societal change.

The focus for my analysis was the movement of forces in the United States, but important work by Melinda Cooper, Quinn Slobodian, and Dieter Plehwe on the movement of forces in Europe point toward two possible lines of development on the political right from the contemporary conjuncture. Cooper (2020) traces the way in which radical right parties, such as Lega and Popular Front, are effectively adopting heterodox economic policies associated with the center-left and socialist parties as a means of appropriating anti-neoliberal sentiment to advance a radical right project. In a similar vein, Slobodian and Plebwe (2020) trace the patterns of exchange and growing cooperation between prominent neoliberal actors and the anti-European Union ethno-nationalists on the Right. What both of these analyses demonstrate is the mutability of ideological discourses at work on the political right and the ways in which reactionary political actors work to appropriate counter-hegemonic discourses. This points toward the possibility of a recuperation or mutation of the post-1970s social formation or the possibility of a more dangerous political order resembling those of the interwar period, that is, fascism.

The question for those doing work on the political left is a familiar one: What is to be done? This project offers no simple answer to this question. I develop no political program in these pages. No manifesto is on offer.

What this project does offer is a mapping of the terrain of political struggle. It maps the movement of forces that constructed the post-1970s social formation and teases out the emergent crises at work in the economic, political, and cultural domains conjoining in this historical moment of potential rupture. This mapping was not a purely academic exercise. The goal was to construct a problem space around the right-wing populism rising to power in the United States and beyond so as to inform left-liberatory work in the contemporary conjuncture. So, what does this project have to offer activists, practitioners, and cultural workers?

First, it demonstrates that the post-1970s social formation is an articulated structure. There is not a singular dominant force structuring the contemporary formation. Left-liberatory work does not challenge a singular Right, so often simplified to neoliberalism or populism, but a contingent formation made up of competing interests. The contemporary formation was constructed by a hegemonic bloc of actors, political movements, and ideological discourses operating in complex patterns of cooperation, competition, and contradiction that successfully *hegemonized* the crisis of the 1970s. These political actors constructed ideological discourses that told better stories about the conjunctural crisis of the 1970s, and they constructed a complex political infrastructure to propagate these ideological discourses to capture the popular imagination and cultivate political power. Put simply, they constructed a new historical bloc through ideological struggle.

Second, this project demonstrates that the ideological discourses at work in the contemporary formation are not univocal nor fixed. Analysis reveals that the dominant forces of the post-1970s social formation employ a sophisticated political practice that shifts with the movement of historical time. Political actors and movements continually adopt and hegemonize competing discourses at work within this hegemonic order, and, as we have seen, they work to hegemonize counter-hegemonic discourses at work on the Left. The relations of force and patterns of exchange within this hegemonic bloc is defined by mutation, and it is this mutability that both made it possible to construct a new hegemonic order from the wreckage of the 1970s and continually reconstruct it over the ensuing decades.

Third, the conjunctural analysis demonstrates that the restructuring of the economic, political, and cultural domains of the contemporary formation have set into motion forces that are animating a series of crises conjoining in this moment of potential rupture. There is, therefore, not one battle to be won but many. Activists and cultural workers on the Left must learn from the successes of the Right. Attending to the discipline of the conjuncture entails constructing a counter-hegemonic bloc of diverse actors, political movements, and ideological discourses that have many different stories to tell about the present crisis. Telling a better story about the emergent crisis of the present requires the telling of better *stories* about the emergent crises at work in the various domains of the present conjuncture that connect to the lived experiences and practical reasoning of individuals. This does not, of course, mean adopting the white supremacy of the modern conservative movement, for example. It means a politics of contesting, appropriating, re-conceptualizing, and so on, the ideological discourses at work in the various domains of the conjuncture that is informed by left-liberatory logics of deep democratic practice, human equality, and the elimination of scarcity.

I began this project by asking: What are the educational questions posed by right-wing populism? How can educational research and pedagogy respond to the questions posed by right-wing populism? Or, more fundamentally, what does it mean to do educational work in this time and in this place?

Answering these questions required that I analyze right-wing populism as a social phenomenon bound up with the ensemble of forces and structures that define this historical moment. I argued that thinking through the educational questions raised by this social phenomenon required that I contextualize right-wing populism within the ensemble of forces that constitute and are constituted by it. It required that I first construct a problem space around this simple problem. It required that I first tell a better story about right-wing populism.

The analysis presented here constructed a problem space defined by fragmentation. I attempted to tell a better story about the ensemble of forces at work in the post-1970s formation and the conjunctural crisis into which it is entering. I told a story about an articulated structure that is fragmenting and fracturing across multiple lines of development within the economic, political, and cultural domains. In this telling, right-wing populism is bound up with a growing array of economic, political, and cultural antagonisms that threaten the stability of the contemporary formation. I told a story of an articulated structure of mutating social forces and ideological discourses and the accelerating dislocatory apparatuses fragmenting political identities, fostering epistemic closure and radicalization, and fueling political antagonism. I argued that the contemporary societal context of the United States can be understood as a fragmented social field of agents, institutions, movements, ideological discourses, mediating structures, and so on, situated and operating within complex patterns of exchange and ideological struggle.

One set of questions raised by this analysis relate to educational scholarship. What does it mean to do educational inquiry within a problem space defined by fragmentation? How can educational inquiry contribute to political struggle in this time of emergent conjunctural crisis? I argue that educational inquiry that attends to the discipline of the conjuncture must tell better stories about this historical moment through radical, re-contextualizing analysis. I argue for a mode of synthetic analysis that constructs problem spaces around simple educational problems. Synthetic analysis disarticulates and re-articulates the movement of forces and structures surrounding simple problems so as to denaturalize taken-for-granted issues and problems in education and to map the terrain of political and ideological struggle surrounding them. The task for this mode of re-contextualizing analysis is to map the terrain of struggle not just on the social field of educational policy and practice but the movement of forces at work in the contemporary conjuncture that both structure and are structured by educational practices.

Another set of questions raised by this analysis relate to pedagogical practice. What might a pedagogy against fragmentation look like? How can pedagogical practice contribute to political struggle in this time of emergent conjunctural crisis? I argue for a pedagogy of telling better stories oriented around radical, re-contextualizing analyses of specific curricular content. The approach to pedagogy I describe seeks to disarticulate and re-articulate simple problems to both cultivate in students a misrelation to their present circumstance and to map the terrain of political and ideological struggle surrounding curricular content. The goal is to cultivate a misrelation to the present by constructing problem spaces around disciplinary subjects and curricula. In short, I argue for a pedagogical practice that works to tell a better story about this historical moment of conjunctural crisis, that instructs students in how to connect the everyday and taken-for-granted to the ensemble of material and ideological forces at work in the conjuncture, and that helps students develop the tools they will need to tell their own stories.

Telling better stories can be understood as a critical intervention in educational inquiry and pedagogical practice. To dwell in the negative is to take up a critical politics that seeks to cultivate in others a misrelation to some aspect of social reality, whether that be disciplinary knowledge or the common sense notions that students bring to a classroom space. This project sought to develop a method of conjunctural analysis to construct a problem space around the simple problem of right-wing populism and to think through the implications of this analysis and the problem space it constructed for educational inquiry and pedagogical practice. I sought to demonstrate how a radical, re-contextualizing analysis can be operationalized in educational inquiry and how it can inform classroom practice.

Education scholars and practitioners have an important role to play in future struggle. Scholars must challenge the technocratic focus of educational research and connect educational issues and problems to the political and ideological struggles of the present conjuncture. Practitioners must take up their classrooms as sites of ideological struggle to help students connect the movement of forces within the contemporary formation to their daily lives and contextualize simple problems within a fragmented social reality. Educational scholars and educators must work to tell better stories about our present circumstance and help others to begin to tell new stories that can advance progressive, transformative change.

I have attempted to make clear that neither the method of inquiry nor the pedagogical practice that I developed in these pages are a finished project. They are both works in development. The examples I have offered are not the only way to do educational research or to teach in a time of emergent crisis. The cultural studies approach to educational inquiry and practice that I developed here is theoretically and methodologically "open" in the sense that scholars, practitioners, activists, and cultural workers with different political, theoretical, and pedagogical commitments can adapt it to their unique needs. I have had the honor of meeting talented scholars and practitioners in my career. This project is not a "how-to" manual but is my attempt to sketch out this period of emergent conjunctural crisis and to think through the implications for my work as a scholar and educator. This project is an invitation to others to take up these tools, to think about what it means to tell better stories, and to take up collective struggle as public pedagogy and classroom practice.

We have a new world to construct and the stakes could not be higher. The effects of global climate change and the Sixth Great Extinction of the Anthropocene are already being felt, and they will accelerate toward a potentially epochal crisis in the coming decades. How human society collectively responds to this will depend on the social formation that emerges from the emergent crisis, not just in the United States but across the global North and South. A new radical right formation or a mutation of the post-1970 formation are possible outcomes of contemporary struggle, and the effects of either one could prove to be truly catastrophic.

References

Abramowitz, A., & McCoy, J. (2019). United States: Racial resentment, negative partisanship, and polarization in trump's America. *The Annals of the American Academy of Political and Social Science, 681*(1), 137–156.

American Society of Civil Engineers. (2019). *2017 infrastructure report card: A comprehensive analysis of America's infrastructure*. American Society of Civil Engineers.

Amountzias, C. (2019). An investigation of the effects of income inequality on financial fragility: Evidence from organization for economic co-operation and development countries. *International Journal of Finance & Economics, 24*(1), 241–259.

Anspach, N. M. (2017). The new personal influence: How Facebook friends influence the news we read. *Political Communication, 34*(4), 590–606.

Appelbaum, B. (2019). *The economists' hour: False prophets, free markets, and the fracture of society*. Little, Brown.

Au, W., & Ferrare, J. (2015). *Mapping corporate education reform: Power and policy networks in the neoliberal state*. Routledge.

Bacon, P., Jr. (2020). Will the democratic primary remain split along racial lines? *Five Thirty Eight*. https://fivethirtyeight.com/features/will-the-democratic-primary-remain-split-along-racial-lines/.

Bail, C. A., Argyle, L. P., Brown, T. W., Bumpus, J. P., Chen, H., Hunzaker, M. B. F., . . . Volfovsky, A. (2018). Exposure to opposing views on social media can increase political polarization. *Proceedings of the National Academy of Sciences, 115*(37), 9216–9221.

Ball, S. (2009). Beyond networks? A brief response to "which networks matter in education governance?" *Political Studies, 57*(3), 688–691.

Ball, S. (2012). *Global education inc.: New policy networks and the neoliberal imaginary*. Routledge.

Barbrook, R., & Cameron, A. (1996). The Californian ideology. *Science and Culture, 6*(1), 44–72.

Barker, D. C. (2002). *Rushed to judgment: Talk radio, persuasion, and American political behavior.* Columbia University Press.

Bartels, L. M. (2016). *Unequal democracy: The political economy of the new gilded age.* Princeton University Press.

Bartels, L. M. (2020). Ethnic antagonism erodes republicans' commitment to democracy. *Proceedings of the National Academy of Sciences, 117*(37), 22752–22759.

Bartlett, B. (2015). How fox news changed American media and political dynamics. SSRN 2604679.

Bayer, P., & Charles, K. K. (2018). Divergent paths: A new perspective on earning differences between black and white men since 1940. *The Quarterly Journal of Economics, 133*(3), 1459–1501.

Benkler, Y., Faris, R., & Roberts, H. (2018). *Network propaganda: Manipulation, disinformation, and radicalization in American politics.* Oxford University Press.

Berlet, C., & Lyons, M. N. (2000). *Right-wing populism in America: Too close for comfort.* Guilford Press.

Bessi, A., & Ferrara, E. (2016). Social bots distort the 2016 US presidential election online discussion. *First Monday, 21*(11).

Bessi, A., Zollo, F., Del Vicario, M., Puliga, M., Scala, A., Caldarelli, G., . . . Quattrociocchi, W. (2016). Users polarization on Facebook and Youtube. *PLoS One, 11*(8), 1–24.

Bjerre-Poulsen, N. (2002). *Right face organizing the American conservative movement 1945–65.* Museum Tusculanum Press.

Blanchflower, D. G. (2019). *Not working: Where have all the good jobs gone?* Princeton University Press.

Bourdieu, P. (1977). *Outline of a theory of practice.* Cambridge University Press.

Boyd, J. (1970). Nixon's southern strategy: "it's all in the charts." *The New York Times.*

Bracha, A., & Burke, M. A. (2017, October). *Wage inflation and informal work.* Federal Reserve Bank of Boston.

Brandes, S. (2020). The market's people: Milton Friedman and the making of neoliberal populism. In W. Callison & Z. Manfredi (Eds.), Mutant neoliberalism: Market rule and market rupture (pp. 61–88). Fordham University Press.

Braudel, F. (1960). History and the social sciences: The long duration. *Political Research, Organization and Design, 3*(6), 3–13.

Brennan Center for Justice. (2019). *New voting restrictions in America.* Brennan Center for Justice at New York University School of Law.

Brennan Center for Justice. (2021). *State voting bills tracker 2021.* Brennan Center for Justice at New York University School of Law. https://www.brennancenter.org/our-work/research-reports/state-voting-bills-tracker-2021.

Bright, J. (2018). Explaining the emergence of political fragmentation on social media: The role of ideology and extremism. *Journal of Computer-Mediated Communication, 23*(1), 17–33.

Brown, W. (2006). American nightmare: Neoliberalism, neoconservatism, and de-democratization. *Political Theory, 34*(6), 690–714.

Brown, W. (2019). *In the ruins of neoliberalism: The rise of antidemocratic politics in the west.* Columbia University Press.

Buchanan, J. M. (1972). *Theory of public choice: Political applications of economics.* University of Michigan Press.

Buchanan, J. M. (2005). *Why I, too, am not a conservative: The normative vision of classical liberalism.* Edward Elger Publishing.

Buckley, W. F. (1955). Our mission statement. *National Review, 1*(1).

Buckley, W. F. (1968). *Up from liberalism.* Arlington House.

Buckley, W. F. (2002). *God and man at Yale: The superstitions of "academic freedom."* Regnery.

Burnham, J. (1947). *The struggle for the world.* John Day Co.

Burnham, J. (1953). *Containment or liberation? An inquiry into the aims of United States foreign policy.* John Day Co.

Burnham, J. (1964). *Suicide of the west: An essay on the meaning and destiny of liberalism.* John Day Co.

Callison, W., & Manfredi, Z. (2020). Introduction: Theorizing mutant neoliberalism. In W. Callison & Z. Manfredi (Eds.), Mutant neoliberalism: Market rule and market rupture (pp. 61–88). Fordham University Press.

Camp, J. T. (2016). *Incarcerating the crisis: Freedom struggles and the rise of the neoliberal state* (Vol. 43). University of California Press.

Carney, N. (2016). All lives matter, but so does race: Black lives matter and the evolving role of social media. *Humanity and Society, 40*(2), 180–199.

Carrim, N. (2017). Stuart Hall and education: Being critical of critical pedagogy. In R. Osman and D. J. Hornsby (Eds.), Transforming teaching and learning in higher education (pp. 15–35). Palgrave Macmillian.

Centre for Contemporary Cultural Studies Education Group. (1981). *Unpopular education: Schooling and social democracy in England since 1944.* Hutchinson.

Centre for Contemporary Cultural Studies Education Group. (1991). *Education limited: Schooling, training and the new right in England since 1979.* Unwin Hyman.

Chetty, R., Grusky, D., Hell, M., Hendren, N., Manduca, R., & Narang, J. (2017). The fading American dream: Trends in absolute income mobility since 1940. *Science, 356*(6336), 398–406.

Chomsky, N. (1957). *Syntactic structures.* Mouton & Co.

Cilluffo, A., & Fry, R. (2019, January). *An early look at the 2020 electorate.* Pew Research Center.

Clarke, J. (2004). Dissolving the public realm? The logics and limits of neoliberalism. *Journal of Social Policy, 33*(1), 27–48.

Clarke, J. (2008). Living with/in and without neo-liberalism. *Focaal, 51.*

Clarke, J. (2010). Of crises and conjunctures: The problem of the present. *Journal of Communication Inquiry, 34*(4), 337–354.

Clarke, J. (2014). Conjunctures, crises, and cultures. *Focaal, 2014*(70), 113–122.

Cohen, N. (2018, September). After years of abusive e-mails, the creator of linux steps aside. *The New Yorker.*

Conroy, M., & Bacon, P., Jr. (2020). White democrats are wary of big ideas to address racial inequality. *Five Thirty Eight.* https://fivethirtyeight.com/features/white-democrats-are-wary-of-big-ideas-to-address-racial-inequality/.

Conway, E. (2015). *The summit: J. M. Keynes and the reshaping of the global economy.* Pegasus Books.

Cooper, M. (2017). *Family values: Between neoliberalism and the new social conservatism.* Zone Books.

Cooper, M. (2020). Anti-austerity on the far right. In W. Callison & Z. Manfredi (Eds.), *Mutant neoliberalism: Market rule and political rupture* (pp. 112–145). Fordham University Press.

Cooperman, A., Smith, G., & Ritchey, K. (2015, May). *America's changing religious landscape.* Pew Research Center.

Coutinho, C. N. (2012). *Gramsci's political thought.* Brill.

Cramer, K. J. (2016). *The politics of resentment: Rural consciousness in Wisconsin and the rise of Scott Walker.* University of Chicago Press.

Crothers, L. (2019). *Rage on the right: The American militia movement from ruby ridge to the trump presidency.* Rowman & Littlefield.

Curry, B. (2019). Janus v. AFSCME on mandatory fees to public sector unions. In D. Klein & M. Marietta (Eds.), *SCOTUS 2018* (pp. 51–60). Palgrave Macmillan.

Daub, A. (2020). *What tech calls thinking.* Farrar, Straus and Giroux.

Del Vicario, M., Bessi, A., Zollo, F., Petroni, F., Scala, A., Caldarelli, G., . . . Quattrociocchi, W. (2015). Echo chambers in the age of misinformation. *arXiv*, arXiv:1509.00189.

Del Vicario, M., Vivaldo, G., Bessi, A., Zollo, F., Scala, A., Caldarelli, G., & Quattrociocchi, W. (2016). Echo chambers: Emotional contagion and group polarization on Facebook. *Scientific Reports*, 6, 1–12.

Del Vicario, M., Zollo, F., Caldarelli, G., & Scala, A. (2017). Mapping social dynamics on facebook: The brexit debate. *Social Networks*, 50, 6–16.

Delmont, M. F. (2016). *Why busing failed: Race, media, and the national resistance to school desegregation.* University of California Press.

Dettling, L., Hsu, J., & Llanes, E. (2018, September). *A wealthless recovery? Asset ownership and the uneven recovery from the great recession.* US Federal Reserve Bank.

DeVito, M. A. (2017). From editors to algorithms: A values-based approach to understanding story selection in the Facebook news feed. *Digital Journalism*, 5(6), 753–773.

Diamond, S. (1995). *Roads to dominion: Right-wing movements and political power in the United States.* Guilford Press.

Diamond, S. (1998). *Not by politics alone: The enduring influence of the Christian right.* Guilford Press.

Doherty, C., Kiley, J., & Jameson, B. (2016, April). *Partisanship and political animosity in 2016: Highly negative views of the opposing party—And its members.* Pew Research Center.

Doherty, C., Kiley, J., & Johnson, B. (2017, October). *The partisan divide on political values grows even wider.* Pew Research Center.

Doherty, C., Kiley, J., & O'Hea, O. (2018, March). *Wide gender gap, growing educational divide in VVoter' party identification.* Pew Research Center.

Duca, J. V. (2016, April). *Online retailing, self-employment disrupt inflation.* Federal Reserve Bank of Dallas.

Dyson, E. (1996). Cyberspace and the American dream: A magna carta for the knowledge age. *The Information Society*, 12(3), 295–308.

Eco, U. (1997). Ur-fascism. In A. McEwen (Trans.), *Umberto eco: Five moral pieces* (pp. 65–88). Harvest Books.

Edin, K., & Shaefer, L. (2016). *Two dollars a day: Living on almost nothing in America*. Houghton Mifflin Harcourt.

El-Erian, M. (2020). What the weakening dollar means for the global economy: The falling value of the greenback heralds a Large, gradual fragmentation of the international economic order. *The Guardian*. https://www.theguardian.com/business /2020/aug/12/what-weakening-dollar-means-for-global-economy.

Elliott, J. E. (1980). Marx and schumpeter on capitalism's creative destruction: A comparative restatement. *The Quarterly Journal of Economics, 95*(1), 45–68.

Ellison, S. (2009). On the poverty of philosophy: The metaphysics of McLaren's "revolutionary critical pedagogy." *Educational Theory, 59*(3), 327–351.

Ellison, S. (2012). It's in the name: A synthetic inquiry of the knowledge is power program [KIPP]. *Educational Studies, 48*(6), 550–575.

Ellison, S. (2014). God and man at a southern appalachian community college: Cognitive dissonance and the cultural logics of conservative news talk radio programming. *Review of Education, Pedagogy, and Cultural Studies, 36*(2), 90–108.

Ellison, S. (2019). Against fragmentation: Critical education scholarship in a time of crisis. *Educational Studies, 55*(3), 271–294.

Ellison, S., & Allen, B. (2018). Disruptive innovation, labor markets, and big valley STEM school: Network analysis in STEM education. *Cultural Studies of Science Education, 13*(1), 267–298.

Ellison, S., Aloe, A. M., & Iqtadar, S. (2019). Policy field and policy discourse: The American federation of children network. *Education Policy Analysis Archive, 27*, 1–25.

Ellison, S., Anderson, A. B., Aronson, B., & Clausen, C. (2018). From objects to subjects: Repositioning teachers as policy actors doing policy work. *Teaching and Teacher Education, 74*, 157–169.

Ellison, S., & Iqtadar, S. (2020). A qualitative research synthesis of the "no excuses" charter school model. *Educational Policy*. doi:10.1177/0895904820917362.

el Ojeili, C. (2015). Reflections on Wallerstein: The modern world-system, four decades on. *Critical Sociology, 41*(4–5), 679–700.

Entman, R. M. (1993). Framing: Toward clarification of a fractured paradigm. *Journal of Communication, 43*(4), 51–58.

Eyal, N. (2014). *Hooked*. Penguin Books.

Faris, R., Roberts, H., Etling, B., Bourassa, N., Zuckerman, E., & Benkler, Y. (2017, August). *Partisanship, propaganda, and disinformation: Online media and the 2016 U.S. Presidential election*. The Berkman Klein Center for Internet & Society Research Publication Series.

Fea, J. (2018). *Believe me: The evangelical road to Donald Trump*. William B Eerdmans Publishing Company.

Federal Reserve Bank of St. Louis. (2019a). *Federal debt: Total public debt as percent of gross domestic product*. Federal Reserve Bank of St. Louis.

Federal Reserve Bank of St. Louis. (2019b). *Federal government budget surplus or deficit (-)/real gross domestic product*. Federal Reserve Bank of St. Louis.

Federal Reserve Bank of St. Louis. (2019c). Real gross domestic product, percent change from preceding period, annual, not seasonally adjusted.

Federal Reserve Bank of St. Louis. (2019d). Shares of gross domestic income: Compensation of employees, paid: Wage and salary accruals: Disbursements: To persons, percent, annual, not seasonally adjusted.

Fingerhut, H. (2016). *Most Americans say US economic system is unfair, but high-income republicans disagree*. Pew Research Center.

Foucault, M. (2010). *The birth of biopolitics: Lectures at the collège de France 1978–1979*. Picador.

Fox, J., & Moreland, J. J. (2015). The dark side of social networking sites: An exploration of the relational and psychological stressors associated with Facebook use and affordances. *Computer in Human Behavior, 45*, 168–176.

Frank, A. G. (1983). Global crisis and transformation. *Development and Change, 14*(3), 323–346.

Fraser, N. (1989). What's critical about critical theory?: The case of Habermas and gender. In N. Fraser (Ed.), *Unruly practices: Power, discourse, and gender in contemporary social theory*. University of Minnesota Press.

Fraser, N. (2019). *The old is dying and the new cannot be born*. Verso.

Freire, P. (2004). *Pedagogy of the oppressed* (30th anniversary ed.). Continuum.

Frey, W. H. (2018). *Diversity explosion: How new racial demographics are remaking America*. The Brookings Institution.

Friedman, M. (1962). *Capitalism and freedom*. University of Chicago Press.

Friedman, M. (1963). *A monetary history of the United States, 1867–1960*. Princeton University Press.

Friedman, M. (2002). *Capitalism and freedom* (14th anniversary ed.). University of Chicago Press.

Friedman, M., & Friedman, R. (1990). *Free to choose: A personal statement*. Houghton Mifflin Harcourt.

Friedman, T. L. (2005). *The world is flat: A brief history of the twenty-first century*. Farrar, Straus and Giroux.

Frow, J., & Morris, M. (2000). Cultural studies. In N. K. Denzin & Y. S. Lincoln (Eds.), Handbook of qualitative research in education (pp. 315–346). Sage.

Funke, M., Schularick, M., & Trebesch, C. (2018, September). *The financial crisis is still empowering far-right populists*. Foreign Affairs.

Galbraith, J. K. (1958). *The affluent society*. Houghton Mifflin.

Galbraith, J. K. (1968). *The new industrial state*. New American Library.

Garimella, K., De Francisci Morales, G., Gionis, A., & Mathioudakis, M. (2018). *Proceedings of the 2018 World wide web conference* (pp. 913–922). International World Wide Web Conferences Steering Committee.

Geruso, M., Spears, D., & Talesara, I. (2019). Inversions in US presidential elections: 1936–2016. *NBER Working Paper Series*. http://www.nber.org/papers/w26247.

Gilbert, A. S. (2019). *The crisis paradigm: Description and prescription in social and political theory*. Palgrave Macmillan.

Gilliam, T., & Jones, T. (1975, April). *Monty python and the holy grail*. Python (Monty) Pictures.

Giroux, H. (1994). Doing cultural studies: Youth and the challenge of pedagogy. *Harvard Educational Review, 64*(3), 278–308.

Giroux, H. (2020a). *On critical pedagogy* (2nd ed.). Bloomsbury Publishing.

Giroux, H. (2020b). *The terror of the unforeseen.* The Los Angeles Review of Books.

Golumbia, D. (2009). *The cultural logic of computation.* Harvard University Press.

Golumbia, D. (2013, September). *Cyberlibertarianism: The extremist foundations of "digital freedom."* Clemson University Department of English. http://www.uncomputing.org.

Golumbia, D. (2016). *The politics of bitcoin: Software as right-wing extremism.* University of Minnesota Press.

Golumbia, D. (2019). Mirowski as critic of the digital. *Boundary 2: An International Journal of Literature and Culture, 46*(1), 133–156.

Gouldner, A. W. (1985). *Against fragmentation: The origins of Marxism and the sociology of intellectuals.* Oxford University Press.

Gramsci, A. (2000). *An Antonio Gramsci reader: Selected writings, 1916–1935.* New York University Press.

Greenfield, A. (2017). *Radical technologies: The design of everyday life.* Verso.

Gross, N., Medvetz, T., & Russell, R. (2011). The contemporary American conservative movement. *Annual Review of Sociology, 37,* 325–354.

Grossberg, L. (1986a). History, politics and postmodernism: Stuart hall and cultural studies. *Journal of Communication Inquiry, 10*(2), 61–77.

Grossberg, L. (1986b). On postmodernism and articulation: An interview with Stuart Hall. *Journal of Communication Inquiry, 10*(2), 45–60.

Grossberg, L. (1992). *We gotta get out of this place: Popular conservatism and postmodern culture.* Routledge.

Grossberg, L. (2010a). *Cultural studies in the future tense.* Duke University Press.

Grossberg, L. (2010b). On the political responsibilities of cultural studies. *Inter-Asia Cultural Studies, 11*(2), 241–247.

Gu, X., Tam, P. S., Zhang, Y., & Lei, C. K. (2019). Inequality, leverage and crises: Theory and evidence revisited. *The World Economy, 42*(8), 2280–2299.

Hacker, J. S., & Pierson, P. (2019). The republican devolution: Partisanship and the decline of American governance. *Foreign Affairs, 98*(4), 42–50.

Hadden, J. K. (1987). Religious broadcasting and the mobilization of the new Christian right. *Journal for the Scientific Study of Religion, 26*(1), 1–24.

Hajnal, Z., Lajevardi, N., & Nielson, L. (2017). Voter identification laws and the suppression of minority votes. *The Journal of Politics, 79*(2), 363–379.

Hall, S. (1973). *A "reading" of Marx's 1857 introduction to the Grundrisse* (Working Paper). Centre for Contemporary Cultural Studies: The University of Birmingham.

Hall, S. (1986). The problem of ideology-Marxism without guarantees. *Journal of Communication Inquiry, 10*(2), 28–44.

Hall, S. (1988a). The battle for socialist ideas in the 1980s. In S. Hall (Ed.), *The hard road of renewal: Thatcher and the crisis of the left* (pp. 177–195). Verso.

Hall, S. (1988b). Learning from Thatcher. In S. Hall (Ed.), *The hard road of renewal: Thatcher and the crisis of the left* (pp. 271–283). Verso.

Hall, S. (1988c). Gramsci and us. In S. Hall (Ed.), *The hard road of renewal: Thatcher and the crisis of the left* (pp. 161–174). Verso.

Hall, S. (1990). The emergence of cultural studies and the crisis of the humanities. *The Humanities as Social Technology, 53*, 11–23.

Hall, S. (1991). Old and new identities, old and new ethnicities. In A. D. King (Eds.), *Culture, globalization and the world system* (pp. 167–173). University of Minnesota Press.

Hall, S. (1993). Encoding, decoding. In S. During (Ed.), *The cultural studies reader* (pp. 507–517). Routledge.

Hall, S. (2011). The neoliberal revolution: Thatcher, Blair, Cameron—The long March of neoliberalism continues. *Soundings: A Journal of Politics and Culture, 48*(1), 8–26.

Hall, S. (2017a). The great moving right show. In S. Davidson, D. Featherstone, M. Rustin, & B. Schwarz (Eds.), *Selected political writings: The great moving right show and other essays* (pp. 172–186). Duke University Press.

Hall, S. (2017b). The neoliberal revolution. In S. Davidson, D. Featherstone, M. Rustin, & B. Schwarz (Eds.), *Selected political writings: The great moving right show and other essays* (pp. 317–335). Duke University Press.

Hall, S., Critcher, C., Jefferson, T., Clarke, J., & Roberts, B. (1978). *Policing the crisis: Mugging, the state and law and order.* Macmillan International Higher Education.

Hall, S., & Massey, D. (2010). Interpreting the crisis. *Soundings, 44*(44), 57–71.

Hart, J. (2007). *The making of the American conservative mind: National review and its times.* ISI Books.

Harvey, D. (2007). *A brief history of neoliberalism.* Oxford University Press.

Hayek, F. (1952). *The sensory order: An inquiry into the foundations of theoretical psychology.* The University of Chicago Press.

Hayek, F. (1956). *The road to serfdom.* University of Chicago Press.

Hayek, F. (1960). *The constitution of liberty* (pp. 397–414). University of Chicago Press.

Hayek, F. (1978). *New studies in philosophy, politics, economics and the history of ideas.* University of Chicago Press.

Hayek, F. (1979). *Law, legislation and liberty: A new statement of the liberal principles of justice and political economy.* University of Chicago Press.

Hegel, G. W. F. (2003). *Phenomenology of mind.* Dover Publications.

Heikkilä, N. (2017). Online antagonism of the alt-right in the 2016 election. *European Journal of American Studies, 12*(2), 1–22.

Himelboim, I., Sweetser, K. D., Tinkham, S. F., Cameron, K., Danelo, M., & West, K. (2014). Valence-based homophily on Twitter: Network analysis of emotions and political talk in the 2012 presidential election. *New Media & Society, 18*(7), 1382–1400.

Hochschild, A. R. (2016). *Strangers in their own land: Anger and mourning on the American right.* The New Press.

Hogan, A. (2016). Network ethnography and the cyberflâneur: Evolving policy sociology in education. *International Journal of Qualitative Studies in Education, 29*(3), 381–398.

Hoggart, R. (1957). *The uses of literacy: Aspects of working-class life with special references to publications and entertainments*. Chatto & Windus.

Hollis-Brusky, A. (2015). *Ideas with consequences: The federalist society and the conservative counterrevolution*. Oxford University Press.

Howard, P. N. (2002). Network ethnography and the hypermedia organization: New media, new organizations, new methods. *New Media & Society, 4*(4), 550–574.

Hutchings, K. (2003). *Hegel and feminist philosophy*. Polity.

Hytten, K. (2011). Cultural studies in education. In S. Tozer, B. P. Gallegos, A. M. Henry, M. B. Greiner, & P. G. Price (Eds.), *Handbook of research in the social foundations of education* (pp. 205–219). Routledge.

Jamieson, K. H., & Cappella, J. N. (2008). *Echo chamber: Rush Limbaugh and the conservative media establishment*. Oxford University Press.

Katz, A. J. (2019, April 2). Q1 2019 ratings: Fox news continues its reign as basic cable's most-watched network. AdWeek. https://www.adweek.com/tvnewser/q1-2019-ratings-fox-news-continues-its-reign-as-cables-most-watched-network/398384/.

Katz, L. F., & Krueger, A. B. (2019). The rise and nature of alternative work arrangements in the United States, 1995–2015. *ILR Review, 72*(2), 382–416.

Keynes, J. M. (1936). *The general theory of employment, interest and money*. Harcourt.

Kil, S. H. (2019). Reporting from the whites of their eyes: How whiteness as neoliberalism promotes racism in the news coverage of "all lives matter." *Communication Theory, 30*(1), 21–40.

Kirschenmann, K., Malinen, T., & Nyberg, H. (2016). The risk of financial crises: Is there a role for income inequality? *Journal of International Money and Finance, 68*, 161–180.

Kramer, A. D. L., Guillory, J. E., & Hancock, J. T. (2014). Experimental evidence of massive-scale emotional contagion through social networks. *Proceedings of the National Academy of Sciences USA, 111*(24), 8788–8790.

Kruse, K. (2015). *One nation under god: How corporate America invented Christian America*. Basic Books.

Kruse, K. M. (2013). *White flight: Atlanta and the making of modern conservatism*. Princeton University Press.

Laclau, E. (2018). *On populist reason*. Verso.

Laclau, E., & Mouffe, C. (2014). *Hegemony and socialist strategy: Toward a radical democratic politics*. Verso.

Lamis, A. P. (1999). *Southern politics in the 1990s*. Louisiana State University Press.

Lawson, T. (1997). *Economics and realty*. Routledge.

Lazear, E. P. (2000). Economic imperialism. *The Quarterly Journal of Economics, 115*(1), 99–146.

Lingard, B., & Seller, S. (2013). Globalization, edu-business and network governance: The policy sociology of Stephen J Ball and rethinking education policy analysis. *London Review of Education, 11*(3), 265–280.

Long, S. (2019). The financialization of the American elite. *American Affairs, 3*(3).

Loomis, E. (2015). *Out of sight: The long and disturbing story of corporations outsourcing catastrophe*. New Press.

Mandel, E. (1980). *Long waves of capitalist development: The Marxist interpretation.* Cambridge University Press.

Marasco, R. (2015). *The highway of despair: Critical theory after Hegel.* Columbia University Press.

Marwick, A., & Lewis, R. (2017). *Media manipulation and disinformation online.* Data and Society Research Institute.

Marx, K. (1973). *Grundrisse: Foundations of the critique of political economy.* Vintage Books.

Marx, K. (1978a). The eighteenth Brumaire of Louis Bonaparte. In R. C. Tucker (Ed.), *The Marx-Engels reader* (pp. 594–617). W. W. Norton & Company.

Marx, K. (1978b). For a ruthless criticism of everything existing. In R. C. Tucker (Ed.), *The Marx-Engels reader* (pp. 12–15). W. W. Norton & Company.

Massanari, A. (2017). #gamergate and the fappening: How reddit's algorithm, governance, and culture support toxic technocultures. *New Media & Society, 19*(3), 329–346.

Maxwell, A., & Shields, T. (2019). *The long southern strategy: How chasing white Voter in the south changed American politics.* Oxford University Press.

Mayer, J. (2017). *Dark money: The hidden history of the billionaires behind the rise of the radical right.* Anchor Books.

Mazzucato, M. (2018). *The value of everything: Making and taking in the global economy.* Allen Lane.

McGann, J. G. (2019, January 1). 2018 global go to think tank index report. Think tanks and civil societies program University of Pennsylvania. https://repository.upenn.edu/think_tanks/16/.

McKinsey Global Institute. (2017, December). *Jobs lost, jobs gained: Workforce transitions in a time of automation.* McKinsey & Company.

McLuhan, M. (1964). *Understanding media: The extensions of man.* McGraw-Hill.

Medvetz, T. (2012). *Think tanks in America.* The University of Chicago Press.

Minneapolis Federal Reserve Bank. (2019). *Consumer price index 1913–2018.*

Minsky, H. P. (1975). *John Maynard Keynes.* Columbia University Press.

Mirowski, P. (2002). *Machine dreams: Economics becomes a cyborg science.* Cambridge University Press.

Mirowski, P. (2009). Postface: Defining neoliberalism. In P. Mirowski & D. Plehwe (Eds.), *The road from Mont Pèlerin: The making of the neoliberal thought collective* (417–456). Harvard University Press.

Mirowski, P. (2011). The spontaneous methodology of orthodoxy, and other economists' afflictions in the Great Recession. In J. B. Davis & D. W. Hands (Eds.), *The Elgar companion of recent economic methodology* (pp. 473–513). Edward Elgar Publishing.

Mirowski, P. (2014a). *Never let a serious crisis got to waste: How neoliberalism survived the financial meltdown.* Verso.

Mirowski, P. (2014b). The political movement that dared not speak its own name: The neoliberal thought collective under erasure. *Institute for New Economic Thinking Working Papers* (23), 1–34.

Mises, L. V. (1944). *Omnipotent government: The rise of the total state and total war.* Yale University Press.

Mishel, L., Gould, E., & Bivens, J. (2015, January 6). Wage stagnation in nine charts. Economic Policy Institute. https://www.epi.org/publication/charting-wage-stagnation/.

Mitchell, A., & Weisel, R. (2014, October). *Political polarization and media habits: From fox news to Facebook, how liberals and conservative keep up with politics.* Pew Research Center.

Mont Pèlerin Society. (1947). *Statement of aims.* The Mont Pèlerin Society. https://www.montpelerin.org/statement-of-aims/.

Morozov, E. (2011). *The net delusion: The dark side of internet freedom.* Public Affairs.

Morozov, E. (2013). *To save everything, click here: The folly of technological solutionism.* Public Affairs.

Mouffe, C. (2018, September). Populists are on the rise but this can be a moment for progressives too. *The Guardian.*

Mudge, S. L. (2018). *Leftism reinvented: Western parties from socialism to neoliberalism.* Harvard University Press.

Nash, G. H. (1976). *The conservative intellectual movement in America, since 1945.* Basic Books.

National Commission on Excellence in Education. (1983). A nation at risk: The imperative for educational reform. *The Elementary School Journal, 84*(2), 113–130.

Negroponte, N. (1995). *Being digital.* Random House.

Nelson, C. (1991). Always already cultural studies: Two conferences and a manifesto. *The Journal of the Midwest Modern Language Association, 24*(1), 24–38.

Nielsen Media Research. (2018). *Tops of 2018: Radio.*

Norton, M. (2011). A structural hermeneutics of the O'Reilly factor. *Theory and Society, 40*(3), 315–346.

Oberhauser, A. M., Krier, D., & Kusow, A. M. (2019). Political moderation and polarization in the heartland: Economics, rurality, and social identity in the 2016 U.S. Presidential election. *The Sociological Quarterly, 60*(2), 224–244.

O'Dell, R., & Penzenstadler, N. (2019, April). You elected them to write new laws. They're letting corporations do it instead.

Page, B. I., Seawright, J., & Lacombe, M. J. (2018). *Billionaires and stealth politics.* University of Chicago Press.

Pariser, E. (2011). *The filter bubble.* The Penguin Press.

Parker, K., Horowitz, J., Brown, A., Fry, R., Cohn, D., & Igielnik, R. (2018, May). *What unites and divide urban, suburban and rural communities.* Pew Research Center.

Parker, K., Morin, R., & Horowitz, J. (2019, March). *Looking to the future, public sees an America in decline on many fronts.* Pew Research Center.

Pautz, H. (2011). Revisiting the think-tank phenomenon. *Public Policy and Administration, 26*(4), 419–435.

Peck, J. (2010). Zombie neoliberalism and the ambidextrous state. *Theoretical Criminology, 14*(1), 104–110.

Perlstein, R. (2001). *Before the storm: Barry Goldwater and the unmaking of the American consensus.* Bold Type Books.

Perlstein, R. (2008). *Nixonland: The rise of a president and the fracturing of America.* Scribner.

Perrin, A., & Anderson, M. (2019, April). *Share of US adults using social media, including Facebook, is mostly unchanged since 2018.* Pew Research Center.

Pew Research Center. (2019, April). Growing partisan divide over fairness of the nation's tax system.

Philanthropy Roundtable. (n.d.). John Olin.

Phillips, K. (1969). *The emerging republican majority.* Arlington House.

Piketty, T., & Saez, E. (2007). How progressive is the U.S. Federal tax system? A historical and international perspective. *Journal of Economic Perspectives, 21*(1), 3–24.

Pilkington, E. (2014, September). Koch brothers sought say in academic hiring in return for university donation.

Polanyi, K. (1944). *The great transformation.* Farrar; Rinehart, Inc.

Polletta, F., & Callahan, J. (2019). Deep stories, nostalgia narratives, and fake news: Storytelling in the trump era. In J. L. Mast & J. C. Alexander (Eds.), *Politics of meaning/meaning of politics* (pp. 55–73). Springer.

Ponczek, S. (2020). Stock market warns workers that they're the problem for business. *Bloomberg.* https://www.bloomberg.com/news/articles/2020-08-25/stock -market-warns-workers-that-they-re-the-problem-for-business.

Postman, N. (2006). *Amusing ourselves to death: Public discourse in the age of show business* (20th anniversary ed.). Penguin Books.

Powell, L. F. (1971). Attack on American free enterprise system.

Ransby, B. (2020, July). The white left needs to embrace black leadership. *The Nation.* https://www.thenation.com/article/activism/black-lives-white-left/.

Reich, C. A. (1970). *The greening of America: How the youth revolution is trying to make America livable.* Random House.

Rich, A. (2004). *Think tanks, public policy, and the politics of expertise.* Cambridge University Press.

Robin, C. (2011). *The reactionary mind: Conservatism from Edmund Burke to Sarah Palin.* Oxford University Press.

Roitman, J. (2014). *Anti-crisis.* Duke University Press.

Rothstein, R. (2017). *The color of law: A forgotten history of how our government segregated America.* Liveright Publishing.

Ruck, D. J., Rice, N. M., Borycz, J., & Bentley, R. A. (2019). Internet research agency Twitter activity predicted 2016 US election polls. *First Monday, 24*(7), 1–19.

Sachs, J. (2005). *The end of poverty: Economic possibilities for our time.* Penguin Press.

Salter, M. (2018). From geek masculinity to gamergate: The technological rationality of online abuse. *Crime Media Culture, 14*(2), 247–264.

Saukko, P. (2003). *Doing research in cultural studies: An introduction to classical and new methodological approaches.* SAGE.

Schaeffer, K. (2020, April). *Nearly three-in-ten Americans believe COVID-19 Was made in a lab.* Pew Research Center.

Schreier, M. (2012). *Qualitative content analysis in practice.* SAGE.

Schumpeter, J. A. (1976). *Capitalism, socialism, and democracy.* Allen and Unwin.

Scott, J. (2013). School choice and the empowerment imperative. *Peabody Journal of Education*, *88*(1), 60–73.

Sherman, G. (2014). *The loudest voice in the room: How the brilliant, bombastic Roger Ailes built fox news—And divided a country*. Random House.

Sides, J., Tesler, M., & Vavreck, L. (2018). *Identity crisis: The 2016 presidential campaign and the battle for the meaning of America*. Princeton University Press.

Slack, J. D. (1996). The theory and method of articulation in cultural studies. In D. Morley & K. Chen (Eds.), *Stuart Hall: Critical dialogues in cultural studies* (pp. 113–129). Routledge.

Slobodian, Q. (2018). *Globalists: The end of empire and the birth of neoliberalism*. Harvard University Press.

Slobodian, Q., & Plebwe, D. (2020). Neoliberals against Europe. In W. Callison & Z. Manfredi (Eds.), *Mutant neoliberalism: Market rule and political rupture* (pp. 89–111). Fordham University Press.

Smith, A., Rainei, L., & Page, D. (2018, June). *Public attitudes toward technology companies*. Pew Research Center.

Smith, G. A., Schiller, A., & Nolan, H. (2019, October). *In U.S., decline of Christianity continues at rapid pace*. Pew Research Center.

Standing, G. (2011). *The precariat the new dangerous class*. Bloomsbury Publishing.

Stanley, J. (2018). *How fascism works: The politics of us and them*. Random House.

Stiglitz, J. E. (2002). *Globalization and its discontents*. Norton.

Stiglitz, J. E. (2018). A rigged economy. *Scientific American*, *5*(5), 56–61.

Stokes, B. (2013, January). Public attitudes toward the next social contract.

Stone, C., Trisi, D., Sherman, A., & Taylor, R. (2019, August). *A guide to statistics on historical trends in income inequality*. Center on Budget and Policy Priorities.

Swalwell, K. M., & Apple, M. M. (2011). Reviewing policy: Starting the wrong conversations: The public school crisis and "Waiting for Superman." *Educational Policy*, *25*(2), 368–382.

Swint, K. C. (2008). *Dark genius: The influential career of legendary political operative and Fox News founder Roger Ailes*. Union Square Press.

Talker's Magazine. (2019). Top talk audiences.

Temin, P. (2018). *The vanishing middle class: Prejudice and power in a dual economy*. MIT Press.

Tenold, V. (2018). *Everything you love will burn: Inside the rebirth of white nationalism in America*. Bold Type Books.

Thaler, R. H., & Sunstein, C. R. (2003). Libertarian paternalism. *The American Economic Review*, *93*(2), 175–179.

Thaler, R. H., & Sunstein, C. R. (2009). *Nudge: Improving decisions about health, wealth, and happiness*. Penguin Books.

The Center for Media and Democracy. (n.d.a). *American legislative exchange council*.

The Center for Media and Democracy. (n.d.b). *American's for prosperity*.

The Center for Media and Democracy. (n.d.c). *Institute for humane studies*.

Thorson, K., & Wells, C. (2016). Curated flows: A framework for mapping media exposure in the digital age. *Communication Theory*, *26*(3), 309–328.

Tomich, D. (2012). *The order of historical time: The longue durée and micro-history* (R. E. Lee, Ed.). SUNY Press.

Tornberg, P. (2018). Echo chambers and viral misinformation: Modeling fake news as complex contagion. *PLoS One*, *13*(9), 1–21.

Tufekci, Z. (2014). Engineering the public: Big data, surveillance, and computational politics. *First Monday*, *19*(7), 1–14.

Tufekci, Z. (2017). *Twitter and tear gas: The power and fragility of network protest*. Yale University Press.

Turner, F. (2006). *From counterculture to cyberculture: Stewart Brand, the Whole Earth Network, and the rise of digital utopianism*. The University of Chicago Press.

US Bureau of Labor Statistics. (2019, January). *Union membership rate 10.5 percent in 2018, down from 20.1 percent in 1983*. US Bureau of Labor Statistics.

US Bureau of Labor Statistics. (2020, April). *Table 1.4 occupations with the most job growth, 2018 and projected 2028*. https://www.bls.gov/emp/tables/occupations-most-job-growth.htm.

US Census Bureau. (2019, April). *Table 1. Report voting and registration, by sex and single years of age: November 2018*. US Census Bureau Current Population Survey.

US Federal Reserve Bank. (2018, May). *Report on the economic well-being of U.S. Households in 2017*. Board of Governors of the Federal Reserve System.

US Government Accountability Office. (2016). *Corporate income tax: Most large profitable U.S. Corporations paid tax but effective tax rates differed significantly from the statutory rate*.

US Internal Revenue Service. (2018). *Table 24. U.S. Corporation income tax: Tax brackets and rates, 1909–2010*.

US Office of Family Assistance. (2004). *Caseload data 1994 (AFDC total)*.

US Office of Family Assistance. (2019). *TANF caseload data 2018*.

US Office of Management and Budget. (2019). *Table 2.1—Receipts by source: 1934–2024*. US Office of Management and Budget Historical Tables.

van Dijk, T. A. (1993). Principles of critical discourse analysis. *Discourse & Society*, *4*(2), 249–283.

Veblen, T. (1900). The preconceptions of economic science. *The Quarterly Journal of Economics*, *14*(2), 240–269.

Viguerie, R. A., & Franke, D. (2004). *America's right turn: How conservatives used new and alternative media to take power*. Bonus Books, Inc.

Vollgraaff, R., Torres, C., & Withers, T. (2019, July). *The world's central banks are debating whether to change their strategies*. Bloomberg.

Vosoughi, S., Roy, D., & Aral, S. (2018). The spread of true and false news online. *Science*, *359*(6380), 1146–1151.

Wagner, K., & Swisher, K. (2017, February). *Read mark Zuckerberg's full 6,000-word letter on Facebook's global ambitions*. Vox.

Walby, S. (2015). *Crisis*. Polity.

Wallerstein, I. (1974). The rise and future demise of the world capitalist system. *Comparative Studies in Society and History*, *16*(4), 387–415.

Wallerstein, I. (2004). *World-systems analysis: An introduction*. Duke University Press.

Wallerstein, I. (2010). Structural crises. *New Left Review*, *62*(2), 133–142.

Wallerstein, I. (2011). *The modern world-system I: Capitalist agriculture and the origins of the European world-economy in the sixteenth century.* University of California Press.

Wasserman, J. (2019) *The marginal revolutionaries: How Austrian economists fought the war of ideas.* Yale University Press.

Watson, J. (1997). *The Christian coalition: Dreams of restoration, demands for recognition.* St. Martin's Press.

Weaver, R. M. (1948). *Ideas have consequences.* University of Chicago Press.

Weaver, R. M. (1968). *The southern tradition at bay; a history of postbellum thought.* Arlington House.

Webster, J. G. (2005). Beneath the veneer of fragmentation: Television audience polarization in a multichannel world. *Journal of Communication, 55*(2), 366–382.

Webster, J. G. (2017). Three myths of digital media. *Convergence, 23*(4), 352–361.

West, C. (2016, November). Goodbye, American neoliberalism: A new era is here. *The Guardian.* https://www.theguardian.com/commentisfree/2016/nov/17/american-neoliberalism-cornel-west-2016-election.

Willis, P. E. (1981). *Learning to labour: How working class kids get working class jobs.* Gower.

Winner, L. (1997). Cyberlibertarian myths and the prospects for community. *ACM Sigcas Computers and Society, 27*(3), 14–19.

Wood, M. M. (2019). On "telling better stories." *Cultural Studies, 33*(1), 19–28.

Woolf, S. H., & Schoomaker, H. (2019). Life expectancy and mortality rates in the United States, 1959–2017. *JAMA, 322*(20), 1996–2016.

World Inequality Database. (2019). *Top 1. World inequality lab.* https://wid.world/country/usa/.

Wright, H. K. (1998). Dare we de-centre Birmingham? Troubling the "origins" and trajectories of cultural studies. *European Journal of Cultural Studies, 1*(33), 33–56.

Wright, H. K. (2003). Cultural studies: (Making) an autobiographical case. *Cultural Studies, 17*(6), 807–822.

Wright, H. K., & Maton, K. (2004). Cultural studies and education: From Birmingham origin to local presence. *The Review of Education, Pedagogy, and Cultural Studies, 26*, 73–89.

Zembylas, M. (2020). The affective modes of right-wing populism: Trump pedagogy and lessons for democratic education. *Studies in Philosophy and Education, 39*(2), 151–166.

Index

About the Author

Scott Ellison is an associate professor of Social Foundations of Education at the University of Northern Iowa and is a visiting scholar at the University of Iowa. His work employs tools from cultural studies, political economy, and critical policy sociology to study contemporary trends in education policy and practice.